Financial Crises and Recession in the Global Economy

Second Edition

This book is dedicated to the students of St. Mary's College of California

Financial Crises and Recession in the Global Economy

Second Edition

Roy E. Allen

Professor of Economics
St. Mary's College of California, USA

Edward Elgar
Cheltenham, UK • Northampton, MA, USA

Published by
Edward Elgar Publishing Limited
Glensanda House
Montpellier Parade
Cheltenham
Glos GL50 1UA
UK

Edward Elgar Publishing, Inc.
136 West Street
Suite 202
Northampton
Massachusetts 01060
USA

First published 1994
Second edition 1999
Second edition reprinted 2000
Paperback edition 2000

A catalogue record for this book
is available from the British Library

Library of Congress Cataloguing in Publication Data
Allen, Roy E., 1957-
    Financial crises and recession in the global economy /
    Roy E. Allen.– 2nd ed.
    Includes index.
    1. Financial crises. 2. Recessions. 3. Economic history–1990-
    4. International finance. I. Title.
    HB3722.A36 1999
    338.5'42—dc21   99–21908
                                                              CIP

ISBN 1 84064 087 1 2nd edition (cased)
     1 84064 632 2 (paperback)
     (1 85278 997 2 1st edition)

Printed and bound in Great Britain by MPG Books Ltd, Bodmin, Cornwall

Contents

Figures

Tables

Preface to the Second Edition

The first edition of *Financial Crises and Recession in the Global Economy* was published in 1994. In the five years since then, additional economic crises have occurred. This *Second Edition* adds a detailed account of the Mexican crisis of 1994–95, the Japanese crisis which began in 1989 but worsened in the late 1990s, and the Asian crisis which hit in 1997.

Academic and journalistic literature and policymakers themselves increasingly acknowledge the risk and severity of these types of episodes. More systemic and thorough explanations are sought, which increasingly identify the importance of financial globalization processes. When the first edition was published, a member of the US Federal Reserve Board concluded (in *Choice* magazine, January 1995) that the author 'grossly overstates [that financial globalization] is the principle cause and explanation of various events that Allen exaggeratedly refers to as crises'. Yet now, in light of recurring and persistent episodes, more policymakers and others admit economic 'crisis' into their thinking and lexicon. For example, the International Monetary Fund now concludes that approximately three-quarters of its more than 180 member countries had encountered 'significant' banking sector problems between 1980 and 1995, one-third of which warrant the definition 'crisis' (Lindgren et al., 1995).

The nature and causes of recent economic crises are increasingly debated, but there is very little consensus. To help in this regard, this *Second Edition* provides a more thorough taxonomy of the 'common patterns'. Also, it formalizes 'a new political economy of money' which, in the author's view, helps to explain the common patterns better than conventional literature.

This *Second Edition* also updates the statistical and institutional analysis of how money is used across the global economy, and it provides new data and analysis on various aspects of economic globalization. In this regard, a section on 'offshore financial markets' has been added.

Special thanks go to Philip Cerny for his encouragement and editing of the first edition of this book and his writing of its preface, all of which located this work within the various disciplines. Private correspondence and a review of the first edition by G. Carchedi (Carchedi, 1996) helped the author address long-standing debates over economic value and wealth creation in this *Second Edition*. Robert Laurent at the US Federal Reserve is to be thanked for his encouragement and helpful correspondence regarding the econometric analysis of Chapter 3. Various colleagues at St. Mary's College of California are to be thanked for their support over the years, especially Wilber Chaffee of the Politics Department and Asbjorn Moseidjord of the Economics Department.

Excellent editing and camera-ready preparation support has been provided by Eric Delore and Nicole Forst. Research help has been provided by Marc Pollard and Hayden McKee.

Finally, the author would like to thank the many students at St. Mary's College of California who have helped the author develop and clarify this material.

Roy E. Allen
May, 1999
Moraga, California

Introduction

The author originally decided to write this book because of his dissatisfaction with the typical textbooks in international economics, macroeconomics, and the related subjects that he teaches. These textbooks do not present the major structural changes and recent events in the global economy to his satisfaction; insufficient attention is typically given to financial market globalization, new trade patterns, new forms and uses of money, monetary-wealth processes, recent changes in the velocity of circulation of money, and recent financial crises and recession. Chapters 1–4 cover these topics.

Chapters 1–3 are organized in a manner which provides background material for Chapter 4's discussions of economic crises. The detailed case studies include the global recession of the early 1980s, the world stock market crash of 1987, the 1980s and continuing world debt crisis, the slumps of the early 1990s, Mexico's crisis of 1994–95, Japan's crisis after 1989, and Asia's crisis after 1997. Less detailed mention is made of the Great Depression of the 1930s, the US savings and loan crisis of the 1980s, the Russian crisis of 1998, and various other slumps.

The concluding Chapter 5, International Adjustments and Political Responses, summarizes what the book might contribute to the fields of international economics, macroeconomics, and related subjects such as international political economy. In addition, Chapter 5 provides suggestions for policymakers – especially how they might minimize the risk of economic crises. The role of the G7, the World Bank, and the IMF are developed, and policy proposals are provided. Chapter 5 also directs attention to the ways that nations might find domestic advantage within the evolving structure of the global economy with domestically driven monetary, fiscal, and trade policies. The conclusions of previous chapters are contrasted with current thinking on the processes of international economic adjustment.

This book is rooted more in the international economics, macroeconomics, and international political economy literature than in other disciplines, but the author hopes that it can be useful to a wide range of social scientists, practitioners, and policymakers. The case studies are not tailored to a particular discipline; instead the author has tried to make them accessible to a wide audience. If the reader has some practical experience in the international economy or some academic training in economics and related fields, then most of his discussions should be readily accessible. Unlike most scholarly books, there are many citations from periodicals such as *The Wall Street Journal* and *The Economist* in addition to academic references.

Occasionally, as per the more theoretical interest rate parity discussions of Chapter 1, foreign exchange market discussions of Chapter 2, and monetary velocity discussions of Chapter 3, the less academic reader or non-economist reader may want to skip forward. Unfortunately, the more profound and insightful conclusions require these difficult sections, and the reader is encouraged to devote extra time fighting through them. At least to the author sorting out this theoretical material has been well worth the effort – it has gained him many new insights into the globalizing economic system, and it has resolved much of his dissatisfaction with the typical textbooks.

One source of the author's dissatisfaction with the textbooks in international economics, macroeconomics, and related fields is that they typically explain change as an out-of-equilibrium situation which will eventually adjust back to equilibrium based upon traditional, static models. Instead, in the new global economy, economists and others should think of change as something more evolutionary, and even revolutionary. A whole series of related structural changes that are presented in this book have no historical precedent, and they continue to provoke other structural changes.

In the author's view, it is within this context of an evolving global economy that one must attempt to understand recent financial crises and recession. He does not see recent economic crises as stages of typical Keynesian business cycles. Nor does he believe that recent crises are fully explained by the well-researched excesses within free-market capitalist systems or other systems. If these crises could be so rooted in traditional thinking, then typical textbook coverage of them would suffice.

This book elaborates a whole series of related structural changes in the globalizing economy that then might allow the reader a more realistic understanding of recent economic crises.

Chapter 1 presents a structural change which shadows most other recent developments in the international economy: the rapid expansion and globalization of financial markets. This chapter documents and defines financial globalization and discusses what caused it: developments in information-processing technologies; government deregulation; and the more global nature of all economic activity. International interest rate parities and financial strategy parities within 'one-world financial markets' are discussed, including the recent convergence of international debt/equity and price/earnings ratios.

In contrast to traditional economic thinking, Chapter 2 argues that the financial market globalization, interest rate parity, and financial strategy parity processes as discussed in Chapter 1 have caused, rather than accommodated, large trade imbalances since the 1980s. Proper consideration of these structural changes leads to new conclusions about the international adjustment mechanisms and key variables that affect trade and investment flows. Increasingly, the nation should not be seen as a self-sufficient or 'balanced' economic region. Identifying exactly what is meant by 'trade' versus 'investment' in the new global economy also leads to some interesting conclusions.

In Chapter 2 typical trade protectionism is shown to be increasingly impractical because: trade deficits are now required by countries which, due to interest rate and financial strategy parity conditions, receive a net capital inflow; rising imports as a share of national purchases are increasing the national welfare cost of using trade protectionism; increases in international joint business venture activity and overseas production are making it less likely that trade protectionism will achieve the desired income transfers; and the increase in international ownership of once national corporations is also making it less likely that trade protectionism will achieve the desired income transfers.

Chapter 3 argues that the expansion and globalization of financial markets as discussed in Chapter 1 has in turn altered the use of money in the international economy. Proportionally more money has been used to accommodate the fast growth of financial markets and proportionally less money has been available for non-financial or GDP purposes. Stated in terms of the famous quantity equation, the income velocity of money has declined from its historic trend. Explosions of financial activity lead to increased demands for money balances for financial market participation and less of the available money supply facilitates the production and sale of GDP. This recent absorption of money for financial market purposes is not generally accepted by the economics profession, but it is demonstrated in Chapter 3. If central bankers do not accommodate this extra demand for money for financial market participation by increasing money supplies, then a 'money-liquidity crisis' can result and increase the risk of economic crises.

The author quantifies the profitability of financial versus non-financial market activity in Chapter 3 by introducing 'financial market turnover' as a significant new variable into monetary policy research. His builds upon his previous research (Allen, 1989), and his regression analysis appears in the Appendix to Chapter 3. International flows of capital also prove to be helpful in identifying which regions of the global economy are experiencing lower relative profitability, and therefore which regions are more likely to experience financial crises and recession.

Also in Chapter 3, 'the recent history of money and wealth' is presented, which includes case studies of the Great Depression, the recent rise of 'offshore financial markets', and an assessment of how monetary wealth is currently being created and transferred across the global economy. In contrast to mainstream economic thinking, the author demonstrates that new money forms, new payment systems, and the labor of financial operators in 'one-world financial markets' can create, destroy and transfer wealth independently of the real economic activity that is occurring in non-financial markets. Changing perceptions and expectations of underlying wealth or value in 'real' economic activity has always provoked chaotic and unpredictable repackaging of this value in financial markets, but value has none the less been thought to flow from the real economic activity. However, the author argues that wealth can be created, destroyed, and transferred independently of what is even perceived to be happening in non-financial markets.

Chapter 4 presents the case studies of recent financial crises and recession, and finds common patterns. Typically a country or region initially experiences a financial liberalization phase. The financial sector expands as it captures profit from new efficiencies and opportunities allowed by globalization. The country or region, for a time, may be favored by international investors; thus the banking system, including government, is well-capitalized and able to expand money-liquidity. Assets increase in monetary value and interest rates are low, and consumption, borrowing, business investment, and government spending are encouraged. Productive resources are more fully utilized and economic growth is well supported. There is a 'boom', as measured by increased (a) monetary wealth held by private and public sectors of an economy, such as the value of stocks, real estate, currency reserves, etc., and/or (b) the current production of merchandise and services (GDP). In this financial liberalization phase, excessive, risky speculation and investment is sometimes encouraged by the notion that 'if I fail, a lender of last resort or government institution will bail me out', i.e. the 'moral hazard problem'.

Then, typically, the supply of base money (m) times its rate of circulation or velocity for GDP purposes (v) contracts, and therefore so does the equivalent nominal GDP. The decline in nominal GDP is usually split between its two components, real GDP which is the volume of current production measured in constant prices (q), and the GDP price level (p). By definition, the quantity equation requires (m x v = p x q). When (q) declines for a sustained period (typically at least six months) we call it a recession, and when (p) declines we call it deflation. After this process starts, monetary policymakers may react by rapidly expanding (m), but this action may be too little too late – individuals and institutions may have unpayable debts, banks may even be failing, and international confidence in the country or region may already be damaged. A weak financial system may be unable to maintain the circulation rate of secure currencies for productive activities, especially if people are hoarding money. An unsecured domestic currency may lose much of its value in undesirable episodes of inflation and depreciation.

The initial contraction in 'effective money' (m x v) may be caused by monetary authorities or national and international investors draining money (m) from the country or region, or there may be a decline in (v) for reasons having to do with the inability of the financial system to direct money toward productive activities. A contraction in effective money supplies or withdrawal of international investment may undermine equity markets, debt markets, bank capital, or government reserves, and monetary wealth is then revalued downwards. General economic or political uncertainty worsens the situation – the resulting austerity mentality causes a contraction of spending and credit, and an increased 'risk premium' attached to business activity scares away investment. Interest rates rise, the demand for quasi-money and credit – i.e. the desire to hold and use the insecure 'monetary float' – declines and people try to convert the monetary float into more secure base money such as cash. No reserve-currency banking system is able to cover all of its monetary float with secure bank reserves if customers try to redeem all of the float at once, and thus 'runs' on banks can destroy the banks. A deteriorated banking sector may be unable to honor its deposits, bad loan problems surface and a 'lender of last resort' such as the International Monetary Fund (IMF) may need to be found.

The author would call these types of episodes (a) a 'financial crisis' if there is a significant decline in monetary wealth held by private and public sectors, and/or (b) a 'recession' if there is a significant decline in real GDP.

Based upon these processes and the discussions of Chapters 1–4, in this *Second Edition* the author outlines 'a new political economy of money' (Chapter 5). Essentially, he finds that financial markets can redistribute wealth and redirect production and consumption intensities somewhat independently of what is initially happening, or even perceived to be happening, in the 'real' economy. This finding, not accepted by either mainstream or Marxist economics, can nevertheless account for what the mainstream has understood as 'business cycles' or 'debt-deflation' and what Marxists have understood as crises of 'underconsumption', 'overproduction', and 'disproportionality'.

Following up on some recent developments in the international political economy literature, the author's new political economy of money treats money, stocks, and other pecuniary assets as 'wealth' in the sense that they give the holder a claim on the social product. Monetary wealth is understood not only as consumption power and production power, but also as the power to direct and control large social processes. The accumulation of monetary assets, or what Marxists would call the accumulation of finance capital, represents a social-power-claim that becomes a key driver in the evolution of the world system. Reversing Marx's causality, it is sometimes true that autonomous (even transcendental) financial processes drive the physical (empirical) relations of production. Once monetary capital is understood as ownership claims over the entire social product, then its growth is limited only by the degree to which 'differential power' can be gained in the world system.

As part of this process, Chapter 3 documents the fact that central banks and other financial market participants can (usually haphazardly) increase or reduce not only nominal but also real monetary wealth, and therefore real social power, independently of any initial changes in the production of GDP, perceived rates of return on investment, or other 'real' economic prospects. These types of wealth revaluations and transfers have occurred especially across the wide spaces of the global economy.

Also playing a role in this process, as confirmed by the author's econometric work in Chapter 3 (updated since the first edition), is the ability of financial markets to 'absorb' money so that the money is not contemporaneously available to support the 'real economy'. Perhaps this absorbed money-power is used at a later date to command production, consumption, or other social processes, or perhaps it is destroyed in an economic crisis before its title-holders can exert the differential power which it represents. Thus, claims on the social product can be revalued and transferred over time as well as space. Depending on the magnitudes of the revaluations and transfers of monetary wealth over (how much) time and space, serious real effects can be produced over time and space, i.e. monetary wealth is not neutral.

Based on these processes, and as demonstrated in case studies, this *Second Edition* shows that the US and the rest of the 'hard-currency-core' of the global economy benefit from what the author would call 'money-mercantilism' at the expense of the 'soft-currency-periphery'. Because of the way that the international monetary system currently works with the US dollar as the dominant reserve currency, over time various monetary-wealth transfers from the periphery to the core have occurred independently of any other inherent instabilities in the global economy.

In present-day money-mercantilist US, economic growth might thus be significantly driven by a 'thickening' and 'commodification' of domestic markets as social agreements and institutions allow foreign and newly-created domestic monetary wealth to be spent domestically. Following this pattern, in the 1990s the US economy boomed ahead with unexpectedly great work-force participation and 'stressed-out' industriousness despite no obvious initiating increase in the inherent per-hour productivity of the average worker.

1. The Expansion and Globalization of Financial Markets

The rapid expansion and globalization of financial markets shadows most other recent developments in international economics. This chapter documents and defines financial globalization and discusses what caused it: developments in information-processing technologies; government deregulation; and the more global nature of all economic activity. International interest rate parities and financial strategy parities are presented as new, dominant, dynamic equilibria in the global economy.

An understanding of these structural changes and new equilibria provides a necessary introduction to subsequent chapters, where it will be argued that the financial globalization processes have increased the risk of economic crises. In later chapters it will also be argued that financial market globalization has been a driving force behind the large US trade deficits and other controversial new trade patterns. In addition, the self-adjustment mechanisms within the global economy have been irreversibly changed by financial globalization.

I. THE RAPID EXPANSION OF INTERNATIONAL FINANCE

Clearly, the last two decades has seen an explosion of international financial activity. The London Eurodollar market, now the major market for the world's largest financial institutions, was in its infancy several decades ago – turnover in the entire year of 1970 was $59 billion. But by the mid-1980s it was turning over $300 billion of financial capital on an average working day. This volume was many times the total reserves of the world's central banks and at least 25 times the value of world trade in merchandise and services. The Euro-market for all currencies (in which securities issuers avoid home country regulations) grew to several trillion dollars of outstanding securities in 1997.[1]

From 1980 to 1985, global foreign exchange trading volume doubled to a level of $150 billion per average working day, which was at least 12 times the value of world trade in merchandise and services. By 1990, the average volume of foreign exchange trading had reached $600 billion per day[2] and during the European currency crisis in late 1992, $1 trillion per day. Since 1992, daily trading has averaged over $1 trillion.[3] Because each foreign exchange transaction involves two or more payments, it may be that $3.2 trillion moves through the foreign exchange settlement systems each day.[4]

Virtually every type of international financial asset experienced a similar increase in trading, and the list of such assets seems endless. Notably, the cross-border trading of corporate stock, which had increased from $100 billion in 1980 to $800 billion in 1986, recovered from the world stock market crash of 1987 to reach $1.6 trillion by 1990.[5] Short-term commercial paper (CP) borrowing by corporations, often with bank guarantees, grew from $40 billion in issues in 1970 to $700 billion in 1997.[6]

The US government securities market, with $3 trillion of securities outstanding by the end of the 1980s and a daily turnover of more than $100 billion, became the largest single-asset capital market in the world. The US government debt limit was raised in early 1996 to $5.5 trillion so that the government could pay its bills, and the annual deficit had been adding more than $200 billion per year to that total. Not until 1998 was the deficit reduced to a surplus, thus peaking the debt limit. The certification of foreign firms as primary dealers gave this market a boost in the 1980s. Primary dealers, the first-round traders with the Federal Reserve Bank, have an advantage because large institutional investors prefer doing business with primary dealers. Because the buying and selling of government bonds by the Federal Reserve Bank is the main instrument of US monetary policy, foreign firms and their foreign clients now play an active role in US monetary affairs. Up to 30 percent of new US government borrowings were supplied by foreign, especially Japanese, firms by the mid-1980s. To downplay the significance of this, the Japanese securities firms have been quick to point out that more than half of the clients for whom they trade US government securities are US citizens.[7]

International financial transactions denominated in US dollars increased, until by the late 1980s dollar holdings by foreign investors reached $1 trillion, over 60 percent of which were in Japanese banks. To put this number in perspective, $1 trillion was the annual amount being spent by the US Federal Government in the late 1980s, and equal to 20 percent of US annual gross domestic product (GDP).

The growth of 'offshore financial markets' (Chapter 3) makes this type of data increasingly difficult to measure. But, it is likely that non-US-owned savings in dollars of almost $300 billion were made available for new uses in the global economy in 1996 compared to less than $150 billion in 1992. Sixty percent of the world's money supply in recent years has been provided by the US dollar, and more dollars circulate outside the US than inside.

By the end of the 1980s, global financial markets were generating a *net* international flow of funds of more than $3 trillion each month, that is, the flow of funds between countries which reconciles end of the month balance of payments data. The *gross* monthly flow is several orders of magnitude higher than this net flow, and it is increasingly impossible to measure given the often unregulated use of electronic funds transfers. Of the $3 trillion net monthly flow, $2 trillion is so-called stateless money, which is virtually exempt from the control of any government or official institution, but available for use by all countries.[8]

Derivatives and other new exotic 'off-balance-sheet' contracts, which are based on underlying balance sheet assets such as stocks, bonds, and commodities, have also added to international finance. The Bank for International Settlements estimates that over-the-counter trading in derivatives, worldwide, was $1 trillion in 1995, based upon outstanding contracts worth $40.7 trillion. Outstanding contracts increased to $55 trillion in 1997, and regulatory authorities had not yet found a way to get companies to account for derivatives on their balance sheets.[9] Also, daily turnover of exchange-listed (as opposed to over-the-counter) interest rate and futures derivatives contracts was even higher, based upon outstanding contracts worth $16.6 trillion.[10]

This recent explosion of international financial activity has several root causes: perhaps most importantly global advances in information technology and governmental deregulation of financial markets. Both developments enhanced the potential profitability of international finance, as discussed next.

II. THE GLOBAL INFORMATION REVOLUTION AND GLOBAL FINANCE

A financial transaction can loosely be defined as any business arrangement where money changes hands but the only other thing that changes hands is documentation. Both money and documentation are moved by information technologies; therefore financial market activity is enhanced by advances in those technologies. Expanding use and performance of electronic and regular mail service, telephones, computers, fax machines, image processing devices, communication satellites, fiber optics, the World Wide Web and so on creates better opportunities in finance.

The explosion of information technologies in recent decades does parallel the explosion of international finance. For example, in 1946 the world had only one widely recognized computer, the ENIAC, built at the University of Pennsylvania, weighing 30 tons, utilizing 18,000 vacuum tubes, standing two stories high, covering 15,000 square feet, and costing several million dollars. In 1956, there were 600 computers in the US, in 1968, 30,000, in 1976, half a million, in 1988, several million, and by the end of the century it is estimated that half of all the households in the US will have a free-standing computer (Blumenthal, 1988, p. 529).

Transistors were invented at Bell Laboratories in 1947 and integrated circuits – the ability to put large numbers of transistors on one silicon chip – were developed in the late 1950s. But by the late 1980s one memory chip could hold as many as one million bits of information. Computer technology benefited from the convergence of three recent breakthroughs: artificial intelligence, whereby computers solve problems by manipulating symbols and decision rules, making inferences and other probability decisions, and generally simulating human methods of intelligence; silicon compilers, which allow the complete design of integrated computer circuits on a computer by any computer-literate person with a $50,000 work station; and massively parallel processing, whereby many computer operations occur simultaneously. Carver Mead of the California Institute of Technology, one of the industry experts and the inventor of the silicon compiler, predicted that these and other developments will result in a 10,000-fold increase in the cost-effectiveness of information-based computer technology over the last two decades of the century.[11]

Other major scientific developments which are fueling the information revolution are: the development of fiber optic cables, a few pounds of which can now carry as much information as a ton of copper cables; and continuing development and deployment of communication satellites, which bounce information around the world at nearly the speed of light. A single communication satellite now displaces many tons of copper wire, and this displacement factor is increasing. By the mid-1980s approximately 60 percent of the trans-Pacific foreign currency trading and 50 percent of the trans-Atlantic foreign currency trading was done via satellite transmissions,[12] which allowed for a greatly increased global flow of funds. Satellite transmissions facilities are collectively owned and operated by national governments through Intelsat in proportion to national use.

In the late 1980s, the telecommunications industry became the largest source of new jobs in the US and perhaps the world. Although the jobs are so scattered among equipment manufacturers, installers, and users that they are hard to keep track of, it was estimated in 1986 that more than 2 million were employed in this industry in the US, and the number was growing by 200,000 each year.[13] In the US fewer letters were written in the 1980s, but there were more telephone calls – an average of four calls per day per person. More calls were made through computer modems to retrieve information from databases. In 1980, very few US homes had modems, but by the late 1980s close to one million homes had them.[14] This technology and others, including the facsimile (fax) machine, enhance the efficiency of legal and business documentation. First-generation fax machines from the 1970s took six minutes to send one page of documentation, but by the late 1980s the transmission time was down to three seconds and the popularity boomed. In

1987, 460,000 facsimile machines were installed in the US, compared to 190,000 in 1986.[15] By the early 1990s, there were over one million installations per year. In the late 1980s, more than $100 million worth of video teleconferencing services and equipment were sold in the US each year, and prices were declining by an average of 15 percent per year. Many corporations began using full-motion images, such as those of a sporting event, in their teleconferences. To handle all of this growth in the late 1980s, the capacity of international data circuits had to rise by 40 percent per year.[16]

Today, private bank telecommunications networks include Manufacturers Hanover Trust's T1 (high-speed) backbone network between its US locations which links with its global X.25 packet-switching network based on Telnet (now Sprint hardware and software) that connects 52 cities in 27 foreign countries. In the 1980s, Citibank developed 100 separate private networks covering 92 countries, which were combined into an integrated global information network (GIN) in 1992. Chase has a similar network provided by Tymnet, which is owned by British Telecom, and Bank of America has a similar network to support its World Banking Division. Bankers Trust (purchased by Deutsche Bank in 1998) is noted for preferring earth-based to satellite links in its system in order to avoid several-second delays. In Europe, the Belgian-based Society for Worldwide Interbank Financial Telecommunications (SWIFT) handles message volumes that have risen from 3.2 million in 1977 to 604 million in 1995.

Changes in communications have always affected the structure of finance, but these developments of the last few decades are responsible for the truly global nature of today's financial markets. As participants use these new technologies and networks, linkages are formed between various national and international sub-economy financial markets. New international opportunities have occurred for centuries, but only recently has interdependence become so pervasive to merit the word 'global'. The transatlantic cable was completed way back in 1867, and the price of the dollar in London could then be found out in two minutes rather than two weeks. Even further back in the history of information finance, the Rothschilds used carrier pigeons to gain advance (and therefore profitable) news of the Napoleonic wars. Perhaps no single example of new international financial technology in the last few decades is more important than these, but thousands of lesser examples have been collectively more important in the globalization process.

The switching of financial markets from paper-driven trading floors to computer screens as with America's NASDAQ and its hookups with London's 'off-(the London Stock) exchange market' is one example of how a new computer-based technology has encouraged global trading. It is estimated that between $200 million and $300 million of foreign stock shares changed hands daily in London's off-exchange market in the 'Big Bang' deregulation year of 1986, roughly double the levels of 1981, with half of that volume in US stocks.[17] That level equaled as much as half the volume on the London Stock Exchange, which also trades many non-British securities.

Networks which now handle staggering amounts of money include the Clearing House Interbank Payments System (CHIPS) which is run by private banks out of New York. CHIPS mostly handles foreign exchange and other large-value, wholesale-level international transactions, and the net settlement of its transactions is in dollar reserves through the Federal Reserve Bank of New York. Transfers through CHIPS increased from $16 trillion in 1977 to more than $310 trillion in 1997. The Federal Reserve's Fedwire is its electronic facility, which transfers reserve balances among private banks through dedicated wire and is the favored system for large domestic transfers. Transfers through Fedwire increased from $2.6 trillion in 1977 to more than $225 trillion in 1997. On a daily basis, CHIPS and Fedwire now move more than $2 trillion. Retail systems such as credit and debit cards transfer an additional several hundred billion dollars per day. These daily recorded flows amount to half the entire broad money (M3) stock of the US, and more than one-third of the US gross domestic product for the whole year.[18] Compared to the US, Europe uses even more electronic transfers: for example, its GIRO credit transfer system sends money directly from the buyer's account to the seller's and accounts for 19 percent of transactions, whereas indirect and debit-based checks account for only 2 percent.

Countless other new technologies which enhance the opportunities in boundary-less electronic finance include automatic transfer machines (ATMs), electronic points of sale, telephone banking, interactive screen communications between financial intermediaries and their wholesale and retail customers, ever more innovative debit and credit and smart cards, and even electronic wallets. Computer, telecommunications, and other 'non-bank' firms have begun to enter these markets. The Discover card was originally offered by the retailer Sears in the 1980s, and then sold to the brokerage firm Dean Witter. Shortly after, AT&T's Universal credit card began offering Visa or MasterCard through Universal Bank. Globalization of plastic payment cards is now being realized. Worldwide spending at merchant locations on general-purpose cards totaled $1.47 trillion in 1995, and is projected to increase to $3.26 trillion in 2000 and $6.43 trillion in 2005. Of the 1995 total, the US had a 47.5 percent share, Europe 25.8 percent, and Asia/Pacific 18.0 percent.[19] Perhaps globalization of payment systems will move from plastic to the Internet with alliances between companies like Microsoft and banks. Bill Gates, Chairman of Microsoft, envisions a future of 'frictionless capitalism' on the Internet.[20]

Electronic banking programs have been used for as long as the Internet – more than two decades. The phrase which has stuck is 'electronic funds transfer' (EFT), and EFT systems have allowed 'fast money' or 'hot money' flows, and now 'virtual money'. Virtual money is a catch phrase for a host of innovative payment forms such as electronic (e-) cash and digital money. As with internet communications, virtual money deliveries can be non-centralized and 'non-physical' beyond the 0-1 on-off digital switching of computer systems.

Virtual money systems are not always subject to banking regulations. For example, in Hong Kong as of August 1998, the Octopus card system had created HK$4 billion ($516 million) of electronic money in an economy with approximately HK$100 billion of currency and coins circulating. E-money transactions in the Octopus system amounted to $HK17 billion per day. Octopus cards, owned by two-thirds of the local population, are easily read by sensors without waiting. The Octopus system is run as a joint venture by various transport companies, and is not technically a bank (yet), but the companies are free to 'reuse' and invest most of the HK$4 billion in customer deposits. Whether risk management and funds on hand are sufficient to cover reliably customer-redemptions of the float is continually under review by the Hong Kong Monetary Authority.

What remains to be seen is the degree to which new virtual money systems create new money stock, versus the degree to which these systems merely move around 'real money' which already exists in bank accounts in deposit form. Chapter 3 develops this issue further, by relating the money stock and its velocity of circulation to the 'real' growth of financial and non-financial markets. Increasingly, it is difficult to know whether economy-wide growth in total transactions is being accommodated by increased money stock or increased velocity of circulation of money. Perhaps the distinction between money 'stock' and 'circulation of the stock' will become less useful as the monetary system co-evolves with new information-processing technologies.

More of the money stock moves as electromagnetic waves or photon particles. The average retail user of money still depends mostly on paper money and plastic cards, but the multinational corporation or financial institution or trader relies mostly on satellite and fiber-optic routing. The large wholesale amounts are transferred electronically. For 1995 the US Federal Reserve estimated the *value* of US electronic transactions at $544 trillion, check transactions at $73 trillion, and currency and coin transactions at $2.2 trillion. However, the physical number or *volume* of currency and coin transactions was estimated at 550 billion, check transactions at 62 billion, and electronic transactions at 19 billion.

III. GOVERNMENTAL DEREGULATION AND INTERNATIONAL FINANCE

The globalization of financial markets has also been encouraged by government deregulation. Governments have been abandoning financial-market protectionism, deciding instead that the benefits provided to their citizens by the new international opportunities will outweigh any losses to previously protected groups.

Linked together with new information-processing technologies, borrowers and lenders are completing transactions in new international markets which are more profitable than any opportunities within the old domestic markets. Governments have recognized the value of giving their citizens access to the new international markets, especially before other countries extend the same opportunities to their citizens. As with any profitable new markets, those who are able to participate first are often the most successful. Eventually, as competition increases, the profitability is reduced to more normal levels.

A threshold was reached by the early 1980s: governments began rushing toward financial market deregulation and internationalization in order to capture a large share of the new profitability for their own money centers, and in order to attract new international funds into their own economies. Policymakers removed ceilings on interest rates, reduced taxes and brokerage commissions on financial transactions, gave foreign financial firms greater access to the home financial markets, allowed increased privatization and securitization of assets, and took other steps which allowed money to move more freely and profitably between international and national markets.

Much of the global deregulation movement came from the Reagan/Thatcher supply-side movement of the early 1980s in which the private markets were encouraged to take the lead – often without a clear understanding of what 'free markets' mean in international finance. Speaking to the author's class years later, the early 1980s US Comptroller of the Currency stated that he, Reagan, Federal Reserve Chairman Volker and others 'believed in the principle of free market finance, but we could not have possibly imagined the long run consequences'. In 1996, the US Comptroller of the Currency issued a rule permitting national banks, in principle, to own subsidiaries in any financial services business, but debate continues regarding what this rule means in practice.

Deregulation was advanced under the consensus that financial market protectionism had failed. For example, The US Interest Equalization Tax of the 1960s was a form of protectionism; various US lenders were taxed for lending overseas, and immediately reduced their foreign activities and increased their domestic business. A long-run problem with protectionism, however, especially in financial markets, is that businesspeople usually find a way around the protectionism. The Interest Equalization Tax reduced taxable capital outflows from the US to negligible amounts in 1964, but non-taxable outflows rose to fill the gap by 1966. The tax encouraged the development of international financial markets, especially in Europe, that US banks could lend from, but which US policymakers could not regulate. New 'non-European' bond issues in Europe increased from less than $200 million in

1962 to nearly \$1.5 billion in 1966.[21] The Interest Equalization Tax was finally removed in 1974.

Other regulations that had shifted US bank activity to the Euromarkets were Regulation Q on interest rate ceilings, the Foreign Credit Restraint Program and rules of the Office for Foreign Direct Investment. These types of regulations were dismantled in the 1980s.

On 1 April 1986, the US government ended the 5.5 percent interest rate ceiling on passbook accounts as the last stage in its deregulation of consumer interest rates paid by banks and savings and loan institutions. Especially important in this process had been the creation of automatic transfer services (ATS) in 1978, negotiable order of withdrawal (NOW) accounts in 1981, and Super NOW accounts in 1983. These are checkable 'money' accounts which, for the first time, offered interest rates high enough to attract funds which otherwise would be spent on merchandise and services or put into 'non-money' financial assets such as stocks, bonds, and money market funds (MMF). By 1984, 8 percent of all checking accounts at US banks and 30 percent of all checking accounts at US thrifts were Super NOW accounts,[22] which were able to pay interest rates almost as high as MMFs.

Also in 1986, three of Japan's biggest securities firms were allowed to become primary dealers in US government securities. Nomura and Daiwa Securities Companies were then able to trade directly with the New York Federal Reserve Bank as part of their battle for global markets. Additionally, the Industrial Bank of Japan gained this privilege via its purchase of primary dealer Aubrey G. Lanston & Co. On that date five other foreign firms – one Canadian, one Australian, one from Hong Kong and two British institutions – already owned primary dealers.[23]

The US Glass-Steagall laws of the 1930s which separate commercial and investment banking are also being slowly dismantled despite some attempts at re-regulation during each financial crisis. US banks can now trade stocks for their customers, but non-bank commercial enterprises cannot generally own banks.

UK financial deregulation in the 1980s paralleled that in the US, and due to the international dominance of New York and London as financial centers, these two countries influenced financial developments elsewhere. In October 1979 the UK removed all inward and outward barriers to capital flows. Consequently, Britain experienced an annual portfolio investment outflow for the 1980–83 period that was 1800 times higher than in the 1975–78 period (Taylor and Tonks, 1989).

Finally, on 26 October 1986 London's 'Big Bang' financial market deregulation scrapped 85 years of fixed commissions for brokers as well as separation of powers between brokers. As stated by John M. Hennessy, chairman of Credit Suisse First Boston Ltd., a leading international investment bank based in London, 'Big Bang is an attempt to generate a few global competitors among the British institutions'.[24] Competition increased immediately. Forty-nine firms, including American, European and Far East financial giants had signed up before 26 October to market British stocks and government bonds; only 19 companies had been doing this trading previously.[25] In addition, after 26 October commissions charged by financial intermediaries dropped as much as 50 percent.

Recognizing the more integrated and global nature of their financial system, the European Community Commission began moving toward a unified financial-services market for the twelve Common Market countries (by 1992), including uniform lending restrictions and reporting of large loans.[26] Also, as of 1992 all international banks subject to the auspices of the Bank for International Settlements (most developed countries and in the future some LDCs) must meet common capital adequacy targets – the first real attempt at a global standard for banking.

Anxious not to lose business to New York and London, other countries embraced the international financial markets in the 1980s. On 4 December 1986, the Ontario, Canada, government announced that it would open the highly restricted Canadian securities industry to unrestricted access by foreigners and Canadian financial institutions. Previous law prohibited foreigners and Canadians outside the securities industry from owning more than 10 percent of a securities dealer. Under the new regulations, foreigners could own 50 percent of a Canadian securities dealer after 30 June 1987 and 100 percent after 30 June 1988.[27]

By 1984, Japan had given US banks virtually free access to many of the Tokyo financial markets including the underwriting of Japanese government bonds. The Japanese government had decontrolled most national interest rates by the late 1980s, thus finishing a process started in 1979, when increased competition was created between Japanese banks, securities firms and insurance companies. Notably, Japanese reform of the Foreign Exchange and Foreign Trade Control law in December 1980 allowed these companies greater ability to issue bonds, buy and sell securities, and hold foreign currency deposits. While the holding of foreign securities by Japanese insurance companies has been restricted, statutory limits have not been binding (Davis, 1990). And, by the mid-1980s, US securities firms had become active players in the Tokyo market. Paine Webber opened a large Tokyo branch office in April, 1986, Morgan Stanley & Co. at that time had built a Tokyo staff of 160, Goldman, Sachs & Co. had 60 people, Salomon Brothers had 80, and Merrill Lynch had 260. And, what has been called Japan's 'Big Bang' occurred in April 1998 when the Foreign Exchange Law abolished the remaining restrictions on international financial transactions.

Mr. Yusuke Kashiwagi, chairman of the Bank of Tokyo, prophesied during an important lecture to the International Monetary Fund in Washington in September, 1986, that Tokyo will eventually be linked with New York and London, to form a 'three-part axis of global finance'.[28] Tokyo sits in a time zone between New York and London and it makes a natural bridge for 24-

hour-a-day trading. Mr. Kashiwagi estimated that the American financial market had an annual volume of $7.1 trillion in 1986, Japan was second in the world with $2.2 trillion and Great Britain was third at $1.6 trillion. Between 1970 and 1985, Japan's financial markets grew at the rate of 18.3 percent per year, Great Britain's at 14.5 percent and the US at 8.8 percent. Integration between these markets has more recently made it difficult to estimate separate statistics. The US Federal Reserve has extended the opening time of Fedwire to 12:30 A.M. (Eastern time) from 8:30 A.M., so that the system can receive and process foreign exchange transactions while both European and Asian markets are also open. A related initiative by banks from 20 large industrial countries is currently in progress to create a limited-purpose bank to clear foreign exchange transactions and thus remove payment delays in CHIPS.

Germany's major deregulation was its liberalization of foreign exchange controls in March 1981. International capital movements were also encouraged when Germany abolished its withholding tax on interest payments to foreigners in August 1984 – one month after the US had removed its withholding tax, and during the same several months that Japan reciprocated.

The process of financial globalization was further encouraged where there was a need to reduce budget deficits, because governments now had a ready source of funds in the international privatization of their assets. For example, after Mitterrand's socialist revolution lost support in France and Chirac was elected Prime Minister in 1986, the center-right coalition embarked on an ambitious denationalization program to privatize ownership of many large companies. An unexpectedly popular $40 billion sell-off of government corporations to the private sector seemed to mark the end of the socialist revolution. The denationalization program allowed foreign investors to buy up to 20 percent of the newly privatized firms. In October 1986, the British broker Morgan Grenfell Securities International placed a $100 million package of French securities with US and British institutional investors, the biggest transaction of its kind in French history.[29] By January 1990, France had completed its piecemeal liberalization of foreign capital flow regulations.

Even the historically-closed China and USSR began developing links with global financial markets in the explosive mid-1980s. In November 1986, a group of top Wall Street executives met with high Chinese political and financial officials in Peking for talks on how securities markets should be run and on how financial capital can be raised. Stock trading in China began on 26 September 1986 for the first time since the Communists took power in 1949: The Jingan-district branch of Shanghai Trust & Investment Co., China's main venue for stock trading, eventually had to move in December 1986 from a branch office measuring only 430 square feet to a new location five times as large.[30]

Besides beginning to trade local issues in securities markets, China also sold more than $2.5 billion of debt securities on international markets in 1985 and 1986 and began developing a modern banking system.[31]   China's five-year plan for 1986–90 resulted in approximately $30 billion in new foreign loans, which increased China's foreign debt from $14 billion to $40 billion over that period. China issued its first Eurodollar bonds in August 1987, two months after settling a 38-year dispute with the British government over defaulted bonds and British assets that were seized during the Communist uprising in 1949.[32]

Perhaps the most significant economic change in the USSR during the Gorbachev period was the increased access to Western financial markets. In 1987 the USSR settled czarist debts with Britain and Switzerland in order to gain access to the European bond markets. In 1988, the USSR had its first public bond offering on the international capital markets and owed $25.9 billion to western commercial banks compared to $11.3 billion in 1985.[33]

IV. FINANCIAL MARKET GLOBALIZATION AND INTEREST RATE PARITY

Richard O'Brien provides some helpful definitions of globalization processes:

> *International* means activities taking place between nations...*multinational* describes activities taking place in more than one nation...*global* should refer to operations within an integral whole, if it is to have a separate meaning from the foregoing terms. Global combines the elements of international and multinational with a strong degree of integration between the different national parts...A truly global service knows no internal boundaries, can be offered throughout the globe, and pays scant attention to national aspects. The nation becomes irrelevant, even though it will still exist. The closer we get to a global, integral whole, the closer we get to the end of geography (O'Brien, 1992, p. 5).

For the purposes of this book O'Brien's definition of globalism is useful – operations taking place within an integrated whole whereby geographic boundaries are not important. Given the increasing financial openness of even China and the Commonwealth of Independent States the 'integrated whole' now includes most developing as well as developed countries.

The globalization of financial markets has meant that borrowers, lenders and other investors have increased ability to make inexpensive international contracts through financial intermediaries. Globalization is encouraged by the information revolution, which makes businesspeople and financial intermediaries more aware of, and networked to, all the international opportunities, so that the financial markets become more dynamic and competitive. Dynamic means that the reactions of market participants are quickly provoked and accommodated. Competitive means that no businessperson or financial intermediary has a strong advantage over others for a significant period of time. For example, each must accept the interest rate for certain types of transactions that the global market produces.

Some efficiencies result from the dynamic, competitive nature of the globalized financial market. Financial intermediaries must adopt the cheapest information-based technologies that can reliably perform the necessary services if they are to profitably survive. Embracing the information revolution is crucial to them. Also, financial intermediaries must be well informed about the needs of their customers. If they do not supply the mix of financial services which their customers are most willing to pay for, then they will also be competed out of the global market.

With fewer restrictions on international financial transactions, interest rates – or more precisely the total expected return including foreign currency risk – for similar types of loans are more uniform around the globe, and these new global interest rates are lower than the average of all the old national interest rates. The new global interest rates are lower, because countries or individuals that can offer lower interest rates have expanded loans, high interest rate loans have contracted. There has been a net expansion of the volume of loans because more people have borrowed at the lower global interest rates. The issuers of the low interest rate loans have profitably expanded to accommodate these new borrowers. In other words, low interest rate lenders have taken customers away from high interest rate lenders and have furthermore encouraged some new borrowers to get into the market.

For example, the high interest rates in international markets in the early 1980s were in US dollars, and the low interest rates were in Japanese yen and German marks. Then, as financial markets were rapidly deregulated and integrated between 1983 and 1988, the dollar's share of international lending fell from 72 percent to 53 percent as US banks and thrifts were outcompeted, the yen's share increased from 3 percent to 10 percent, and the mark's share increased from 5 percent to 10 percent.[34] In addition, the volume of international lending increased faster than at any time in modern history, as average interest rates in the global economy were cut in half. Also, interest rates in the major currencies moved closer together during this period. Long-term dollar interest rates adjusted for inflation had reached a peak of 10 percent in the middle of 1984, but then declined steadily to 3.5 percent at the end of 1986. But the comparable yen and mark interest rates rose slightly over this period.

An important equilibrium position of globalized financial markets is called 'interest rate parity' (IRP). First, IRP requires that national and international interest rates for the same types of loans in the same currency have to be equal. Otherwise, arbitragers would simultaneously borrow in one market and lend in another and make tremendous profits, profits much greater than could ever be attained from merchandise and services trade. Since the early 1980s, financial market arbitrage has become much more profitable on the margin than merchandise and services trade. Therefore, as elaborated in Chapter 2, the fully-arbitraged IRP equilibrium position of financial markets is likely to be the driving force that merchandise and services trade must conform to. This dominance of IRP differs from most traditional thinking whereby financial transactions are instead believed to accommodate merchandise and services trade.

Using the equality of national and international interest rates in the same currency as a measure of the globalization of national financial markets, it is clear that many types of financial transactions between the major industrial countries were fully globalized by the early 1980s. For example, between October 1983 and May 1984 the average differential between three-month Eurodollar interest rates and the corresponding rates in New York was an insignificant 0.1 percentage points. The same test comparing D-mark interest rates in the Euromarket and German markets showed a differential of 0.04 percentage points.[35]

Frankel (1989) has shown that domestic versus international own-currency interest rate differentials for Germany collapsed in 1974 when most capital inflow restrictions were removed. The differential for Italy and France collapsed in about mid-1986 when capital outflow restrictions were removed in those two countries and the European Monetary System was realigned. Also, Artis and Taylor (1989) have shown that this differential tended toward zero in the United Kingdom after inward and outward capital controls were removed in October 1979.

Japan's case study also shows the relationship between financial market deregulation and globalization in the early 1980s. Between 1975 and 1979, before Japanese deregulation, the differential between three-month yen interest rates in the Eurocurrency and Japanese markets averaged a large 2.06 percentage points. The Japanese government began removing the restrictions on its financial markets in the early 1980s, and in 1984 this interest rate differential had been reduced to 0.31 percentage points. Finally, in 1985, Japan's financial markets, with respect to these statistics, had become as globalized as those in the US, UK, and Germany – this yen interest rate differential had dropped to 0.05 percentage points (Artis and Taylor, 1989).

Secondly, IRP requires that the same types of loans, which have been insured against foreign currency risk, produce the same total return for the investor even though they are denominated in different currencies. Currency risk can be covered or hedged away via transactions in the forward-looking markets.

For example, suppose that Eurodollar interest rates were currently 8 percent, Euromark interest rates were 13 percent, and the current spot market exchange rate was $1 for 1.5DM. Suppose also that one could agree today to swap $1 for 1.57DM one year from now. If an investor had his savings in dollars today but wanted his savings converted into marks one year from now, should he: (a) convert on the spot market today at $1/1.5DM and begin earning 13 percent on his newly acquired marks; or (b) agree today to convert one year from now at the $1/1.57DM future rate and continue earning 8 percent on his dollars until that time; or (c) continue earning 8 percent on his dollars and convert them into marks one year from now at whatever the spot market exchange rate happened to be then?

Ignoring commissions and any other transactions costs, options (a) and (b) would produce the same DM savings one year from now with certainty. For example, savings of $100 under option (a) would be converted into 150DM today and earn (150DM x 0.13) = (19.5DM) in interest for a total of 169.5DM one year from now, and under option (b) savings of $100 would earn interest of ($100 x 0.08) = ($8) for a total of $108 one year from now which would then be converted with the futures contract at $1/1.57DM. The $108 would thus be converted into (108 x 1.57) = 169.5DM one year from now. (Note: these calculations are approximate, and exact equations are developed in textbooks.)

The risk-free equivalence of options (a) and (b) demonstrates the IRP equilibrium for different currencies, and it is summarized as follows: the current interest rate differential between currencies (in this case a 5 percent differential in favor of the mark) must be eliminated by the difference in the spot versus forward exchange rate (in this case the dollar carries a forward premium against the mark of approximately 5 percent from 1.5 to 1.57), to yield the same total return for options (a) and (b).

For the major currencies with well-developed, forward-looking market opportunities, such as those that are actively traded in the Eurocurrency markets, 100 percent of the deviations from (a) and (b) equivalence can be accounted for by commissions and other normal transactions costs (Taylor, 1988), a result called 'covered interest parity'. When arbitrage eliminates differences in national versus Eurocurrency interest rates on the same currency, it also eliminates differences in the risk-free total return on different currencies. In the above example, money would be moved between dollar and mark loans until interest rates and/or forward versus spot exchange rate differentials adjusted to produce the equivalence. Non-equivalence could not be sustained because of the tremendous profit-seeking flows of capital that would exploit the inefficiency until equivalence was produced.

Option (c) in the above example would expose the investor to currency risk, unlike options (a) and (b), and therefore may or may not be used given his risk tolerance. If used, option (c) would result in a superior return to options (a) and (b) if the spot exchange rate for $1 appreciates above 1.57DM at year-end, and option (c) would produce a lower return if the dollar ended the year lower than 1.57DM. In other words, whether or not the spot rate ends the forward-looking time period above or below today's risk-free forward rate will determine the desirability of speculating as per option (c) versus hedging as per options (a) and (b). Therefore, beliefs about future spot rates may also lead to tremendous profit-seeking flows of capital and realignment of interest rates and exchange rates until investors believe option (c) to be equally desirable to options (a) and (b).

If option (c) produces the same return as (a) and (b) the result is called uncovered interest parity. However, most research indicates that substantial errors in predicting future spot rates does not allow for uncovered interest parity (Frankel and Froot, 1989). In other words, the risk-free forward rate is not a good predictor of the future spot rate, and speculators must assume substantial risk when accepting option (c).

As currency exchange rates adjust as part of the process whereby interest rate parity is achieved, international currency-adjusted prices for merchandise can be pushed substantially out of alignment. Therefore, trade balances can fluctuate wildly as driven by these financial processes. As elaborated in Chapter 2, historic relationships between currency exchange rates and trade balances no longer prevail. Purchasing power parity (PPP), the theory that currency exchange rates move up or down to equate national and international prices of merchandise and services (and thus trade is always rebalanced), has become unreliable for forecasting purposes. For example, no longer does a country's currency necessarily increase in value if it has an export price advantage and is selling more merchandise and services to the rest of the world than vice versa. If an export-driven country is able to lower the interest rates on its currency, its currency could even depreciate due to a substantial outflow of investment funds to higher interest rate currencies.

Table 1.1 shows just how much the exchange rate of the US dollar has deviated in the 1990s from its PPP levels relative to the Japanese yen and the German mark. These PPP exchange rate levels equate the average prices of tradable merchandise and services between the US, Japan and Germany. There has been no stability or convergence of exchange rates to PPP levels. The yen and mark remained persistently overvalued against the dollar in the 1990s, yet the US current account balance first improved and then worsened (see Figure 2.2).

Table 1.1 Purchasing power parity exchange rate levels of one US dollar (versus actual exchange rates)

	1990	1993	1995	1997
Japan (yen)	195 (134)	184 (112)	169 (103)	163 (130)
Germany (mark)	2.09 (1.49)	2.10 (1.73)	2.02 (1.43)	2.00 (1.79)

Source: Organization for Economic Cooperation and Development.

V. FINANCIAL STRATEGY PARITIES

The IRP equilibrium discussed above equates the total expected return on different sources of international borrowing and lending. Money moves between the globalized countries and currencies until, on the margin, the market for borrowing and lending is efficient. Arbitragers are then indifferent between countries and currencies for their next transaction.

Borrowing and lending is associated with debtors and creditors – those who exchange bonds, commercial paper, certificates of deposit, and other fixed-income IOUs. It is for these types of financial transactions that IRP has been statistically verified. Total expected returns on these 'pure debt' instruments have indeed converged. However, IRP can be more generally understood as financial-strategy-parity (FSP). For those globalized countries and currencies now subject to IRP, a more general convergence of financial strategies has been occurring as participants are presented with more similar opportunities in other, non-pure-debt markets. Specifically, corporations are choosing more similar debt vs. equity financing strategies. Also, the price to earnings ratios of international stock markets are converging. As arbitragers and other participants compare returns and risks on a more global spectrum of financial assets, the best common strategies are chosen.

A.   International Debt to Equity Ratios Converge

The recent increase in US corporate debt can be seen as a convergence toward desirable international debt to equity ratios. Before financial markets became rapidly globalized, that is between 1972 and 1982, the percentage of total debt in the capital stock (machines, factories, etc.) of Japanese and German manufacturers averaged 66 percent and 64 percent, respectively, more than twice the 30 percent of US manufacturers.[36] These figures indicate that, in effect, 30 percent of the machines and factories etc. used by a typical US manufacturing company during 1972–1982 were not owned by the company, but by the bank which loaned money to the company. Although popular sentiment disagrees, it is likely that this lower debt-position of US corporations disadvantaged them relative to their Japanese and German competitors before 1982; and, it is likely that the well-publicized increase in US corporate debt after 1982 has been a move in the right direction.

An argument defending the increase in US corporate debt after 1982 proceeds as follows: US managers, especially in the post-1982 period of 'nuclear finance', impatient owners, and hostile leveraged buyouts of companies, must insure high short-run returns on machines, factories, land, etc. which are owned outright (i.e. the equity or stock of the firm) in order to maintain high stock prices. High stock prices, prices that fully reflect the replacement value of the machines, factories, land, etc., please the current owners and discourage hostile corporate 'raiders' from buying stock and gaining control of company assets. In other words, during the boom years for financial markets in the early and mid-1980s, it became popular to radically reorganize the ownership of business assets, and those assets had to be well-presented for marketability – high short-run returns and prices.

However, managers have not needed to insure such high short-run returns on debt capital, because it is not the equity of the firm, but of the lending institution. Debt-capital need only produce enough revenues over the long-run to justify the loan which financed it. Debt-capital is not so marketable or so subject to new ownership as equity-capital, and thus debt-capital has been more insulated from disruptive reorganization by nuclear finance and corporate raiders. From 1972 through 1982, the average before-tax, gross return on capital for equity-biased US manufacturers was 21.1 percent, compared with 14.2 percent and 15.7 percent in debt-biased Japan and West Germany, respectively.[37]

Gross returns on capital should not be confused with corporate profitability for four reasons: (1) they are before-tax returns, and tax systems vary; (2) other non-capital expenses such as wages affect profitability; (3) the gross return on capital becomes institutionalized as a cost of capital, for example to the newer firms who must buy or rent it away from competing uses. In 1981 the cost of raising capital in the US was 16.6 percent, which compared unfavorably with 9 percent in Japan and West Germany;[38] (4) the profitability or net return on a firm's capital operations should be measured as the difference between the gross returns and the costs of raising capital. This calculation indicates that profit rates on capital in Japan and West Germany were one to two percentage points higher than in the US before the rapid globalization period beginning in the early 1980s.

The capital cost disadvantage of US industry may have worsened in the early 1980s. Economists at Georgetown University concluded that in 1985 US industry spent 19 percent more than Japan to service its capital, i.e. raise it, depreciate it and pay taxes on it.[39] Taxes were identified as the key reason, because Japan was found to tax its capital formation at a 37 percent lower rate than the US. 'If the Japanese system [including higher debt; non-existent taxes before 1986 on the dividends and capital gains of individuals; etc.] were adopted in the US, the cost of US capital...would fall by 16 percent. This is the equivalent to an increase in profit margins on output of 5 percentage points [about double our present rate] and is an amount larger than total US corporate income tax receipts'.

The lower US profit rates on machines and factories compared to Japan and Germany in the 1970s and early 1980s, due to higher taxes and less debt, meant that fewer corporate investment projects could be justified in the US compared to Japan and Germany. Especially hard hit in the US were investments in product innovation and the opening of new industries and markets. These endeavors are risky and expensive at first, but are very important to the long-run competitiveness of industries in an increasingly international marketplace.

Due to the lower profitability, 'gross fixed capital formation' as a percentage of gross domestic product was lower in the US than in most other large industrial nations in the 1970s and 1980s – the US ratio averaged 18 percent compared to 23 percent in West Germany and 32 percent in Japan.[40] Also, less economy-wide capital formation in the US during this time period allowed less improvement in industry competitiveness, as measured by output per worker (productivity).

Despite popular sentiment, therefore, the recent increase in US corporate debt seems desirable, because US capital costs can be lowered at least as much as the gross return on capital. Increased profitability on capital occurs, more investment in US industry can be justified, and worker productivity improves. There is less chance that US corporations have the liquidity problems and low stock market values which invite hostile takeovers and disrupt long-run strategies. Instead, the corporations' bankers have more control over the corporation, and a greater self-interest in seeing that the corporation is successful in the long run. As acknowledged by Benjamin Friedman (in Feldstein, 1991, p. 20):

> Some observers have argued that most of the [US] substitution of debt for equity in recent years has occurred in the context of reorganizations that are likely to promote business efficiency and hence provide the higher earnings with which to service the added debt; also, that these transactions are explicitly designed to minimize conventional bankruptcy problems in the event that the anticipated higher earnings do not materialize. Others have pointed out that even after the refinancings of the 1980s, US corporations on average remain much less highly levered than their counterparts abroad.

Also, the globalization of financial markets in the 1980s provided the greatest benefits to the borrowers who had historically paid the highest interest rates. In the 1970s and early 1980s, before the globalization of financial markets, it was the US interest rates which were the highest. Therefore, it was US borrowers, especially those who creatively took advantage of the new international opportunities, who found the greatest savings with globalization. American corporations realized the benefits of increased borrowing, especially from the new international markets: Eurobonds issued by American corporations grew from $7 billion in all of 1983 to $35.1 billion in only the first ten months of 1986.[41]

By 1990, the globalization of debt and equity markets had already led to similar debt/equity ratios between the US, Japan, Germany and others. Within the more commonly-shared financial environment, corporations were choosing more similar financial strategies. For example, in 1990 the average debt/equity ratio of companies listed on the Tokyo Stock exchange was approximately equal to the average debt-equity ratio of all US companies.[42]

Computing this ratio is extremely problematic because many new financial instruments have both debt and equity characteristics, but it is likely that average US and Japanese corporations had approximately equal debt to equity ratios of 50 percent in 1990.

With reference to the 1972–1982 statistics presented above, Japanese companies thus reduced their debt levels in the 1982–90 period just as significantly as US companies increased their debt levels until corporate debt burdens were approximately equal in the two countries. Rather than seeing increased US corporate debt in the 1980s as a worrisome development originating in the US, therefore, it seems better to view this increased debt as a natural and healthy process of convergence or globalization. US, Japanese and other corporations settled upon similar financial strategies in their new commonly-shared financial markets.[43] Initially, more attractive takeover targets were found in the equity-biased US capital stock, that is, until the late 1980s when globalization had brought international debt-equity ratios closer together, and when financial markets became more similarly regulated and accessible.

B.   International Price-Earnings Ratios Converge

A natural process of convergence or globalization has also occurred recently with international price-earnings ratios of corporate stock.

Different investors are willing to pay different stock prices for the ownership of corporate assets, depending upon: expectations about the size and riskiness of future dividends and other cash pay-outs; preferences for having more cash in the present versus the future; availability of cash; and the availability of alternative investments. For example, in the Japanese stock market in the 1980s, investors were willing to pay an average of $50 dollars for corporate stock for every one dollar of current annual earnings generated by the stock, i.e. a price-earnings ratio of 50.   For Nippon Telephone and Telegraph, which had a total stock market value of $320 billion on 31 March 1987 (more than the entire West German stock market), investors paid a remarkably high price-earnings ratio of 261.7.[44]

In the US stock market, investors in the 1980s were willing to purchase stock at an average price-earnings ratio of 15, less than one-third of the Japanese stock market ratio, indicating a combination of the following structural conditions, labeled (1)–(5):

1.   Future earnings and therefore cash pay-outs were not expected to be as high on US corporate stock compared to Japanese corporate stock;
2.   Investors as a group felt that the dollar was likely to lose some of its exchange value relative to the yen, and they had not fully hedged away this currency risk;

3. In Japan investors were willing to pay a higher price and commit more savings for the expectation of future income compared to the more consumer-oriented US. Also, savings has been given more favorable tax treatment in Japan than in the US;
4. The Japanese tendency to retain earnings within the corporation rather than pay it out as dividends, and other institutional differences meant that a significant amount of Japanese earnings was hidden from the statistics;
5. There was more cash 'bottled-up' in the less deregulated Japanese financial markets, and there were fewer attractive alternatives to stock ownership compared to the US, such as home ownership.

In the 1980s, structural conditions (1)–(5) maintained the average prices of Japanese corporate assets at levels more than three times higher than US corporate assets, relative to the current income generated by those assets. These structural impediments, which maintained separate institutional and behavioral identities for the world's two largest stock markets, have become less significant in the new global economy, however. Consequently, there is a trend toward more similarly priced corporate assets in the US and Japan.

Structural condition (1) has become less significant with the increased participation in joint ventures and overseas production by US and Japanese firms, the dual-listing of corporate stock in both exchanges, the recovery of US companies, such as those in automobiles, from exceptional Japanese competition of the early 1980s, the maturation of the Japanese economic miracle, the increased use of debt-financing in the US, and the massive net inflow of foreign funds into the US beginning in the 1980s which has lowered US interest rates and the cost of capital while increasing them in capital-exporting Japan.

Condition (2) has become less significant with the widely-perceived bottoming-out in the decline in foreign exchange value of the dollar, and with the rapid development of futures markets where foreign exchange risk can be hedged as per covered interest rate parity discussed earlier. Condition (3) has become less significant with the removal of various tax incentives to save within Japan since 1986, and as the Japanese economy becomes more consumer and leisure-driven. Condition (4), which is more a statistical oddity rather than an economic condition, has become less significant with the more standardized accounting techniques used by more internationalized (especially Japanese) corporations. And, condition (5) has become less significant with the rapid deregulation and integration of the US and Japanese financial markets and increased learning, especially by Japanese investors, about foreign opportunities.

As these structural differences between the world's two largest stock markets began to lose their importance in the 1980s, perhaps especially as (5) became less significant, it was inevitable that Japanese investors began to purchase a lot of US stocks. In effect, the reasons for maintaining higher prices for corporate assets in Japan relative to current corporate earnings began to lose their importance, and the lower US price-earnings ratios became quite attractive to Japanese investors.

Thus, the reduced importance of structural conditions (1)–(5) explains the well-publicized Japanese 'buying of America' in the 1980s. However, the removal of structural differences and impediments between financial markets everywhere has encouraged a less-publicized, more general foreign buying of America. For example, German purchases of US business assets in the 1980s rivaled purchases by the Japanese, but neither country maintained as large a historic claim on US assets as Britain or the Netherlands. The International Monetary Fund (IMF, 1989) has estimated that about half of both Japanese and German direct investment and other long-term capital outflows in recent years have been to the US. However, 'the channels from Japan to the United States are more direct than those from Germany to the United States,' which might explain some of the greater attention paid to the Japanese purchases.

Structural integration of stock markets began to encourage the rapid foreign buying of American business assets in the mid-1980s. For example, foreign investors purchased $5 billion of publicly-owned US corporate stock in 1985, $25 billion in 1986, and $30 billion in 1987. The world stock market crash of 1987 slowed this upward trend only temporarily. By 1989, 11.1 percent or $500 billion of America's $4,550 total business assets were foreign-owned.

As structural impediments between the major equity markets continue to erode, and as portfolios are appropriately reallocated, price–earnings ratios seem to be converging toward something like twenty to one. Adjusting for differences in institutions and accounting rules which remain, a 1992 study found that 'true' P/E ratios for Japan, the US, Britain, France, and Germany were, respectively, 22.1, 26.5, 19.6, 14.5, and 19.1.[45] Compared to stock market levels of the late 1980s, and assuming reasonably constant growth rates of corporate earnings in the US and Japan, this convergence required a doubling of US stock market prices and a 50 percent decline in Japanese stock market prices from the late 1980s to 1992 – which is exactly what happened.

NOTES

1. Federal Reserve Bank of Kansas City (1997), p. 300.
2. 'Capital Markets Survey', p. 7, *The Economist*, 21 July 1990.
3. Federal Reserve Bank of New York, *April 1995 Central Bank Survey of Foreign Exchange Market Activity*, 19 September 1995.
4. Sesit, Michael R., 'Central Banks Issue Warning on Trading', *New York Times*, 28 March 1996, C1.
5. Ibid.

6. Federal Reserve Bank of Kansas City (1997), p. 263–4.
7. 'Japanese Firms Make Controversial Bid In the US Government Securities Market', *The Wall Street Journal*, 7 January 1986, p. 32.
8. 'The Globalization of the Industrialized Economies', *Barron's*, 4 May 1987, p. 45.
9. 'New Guidelines For Derivatives Are Delayed', *The Wall Street Journal*, 9 May 1997, p. A4.
10. Bank for International Settlements, *Central Bank Survey of Derivatives Market Activity*, Basle: Bank for International Settlements, 18 December 1995.
11. 'The New American Challenge', *The Wall Street Journal*, 3 November 1986.
12. 'The Global Money Market', *The New York Times*, 4 May 1986, p. 10 F.
13. 'Your Future in Telecommunications', *Business Week Careers*, November 1986, p. 59.
14. Ibid.
15. 'Business Bulletin', *The Wall Street Journal*, 10 March 1988, p. 1.
16. 'Business Goes Body Shopping', *Newsweek*, 10 July 1989, p. 46–7.
17. 'Foreign Issues Flood London OTC Trade', *The Wall Street Journal*, 18 April 1986, p. 22.
18. Solomon (1997), p. 7.
19. Data from Spencer Nilson and *The Nilson Report* (Oxnard, California, mid-1996).
20. Gates et al. (1995).
21. This case study, as it affected the US Balance of Payments, is analyzed in: Cooper, Richard E., 'The Interest Equalization Tax: An Experiment in the Separation of Capital Markets', *Finanzarchiv*, Vol. 24, Fasc. 3, 1965, p. 447–71.
22. 'Bank and Thrift Performance since DIDMCA', *Economic Perspectives*, Federal Reserve Bank of Chicago, September/October, 1985, p. 58.
23. 'Three Big Japanese Firms Enter Ranks Of Primary Dealers Despite Opposition', *The Wall Street Journal*, 12 December 1986, p. D-1.
24. 'Stakes High for Britain's Financial Firms in Freer Markets', *The New York Times*, 6 October 1986, p. 34.
25. 'London's Exchange Braces for Big Bang Set to Occur Monday', *The Wall Street Journal*, 24 October 24 1986, p. 1.
26. 'Common Market Seeks New Rules on Limiting Exposure of Lenders', *The Wall Street Journal*, 1 December 1986.
27. 'Ontario Will Open Securities Industry to Foreigners, Domestic Finance Firms', *The Wall Street Journal*, 5 December 1986, p. 38.
28. 'Global Finance: Tale of 3 Cities', *The New York Times*, 31 October 1986.
29. 'French Denationalization Lures US Firms', *The Wall Street Journal*, 24 October 1986, p. 28.
30. 'China's Embryonic Stock Market Expands', *The Wall Street Journal*, 12 November 1986, p. 38.
31. 'School at China's People's Bank Trains New Generation of Financial Whiz Kids', *The Wall Street Journal*, 18 November 1986, p. 39.
32. 'China's Initial Offering Of Eurodollar Bonds is Set', *The Wall Street Journal*, 21 August 1987, p. 21.

33. 'Confronting the Soviet Financial Offensive', *The Wall Street Journal*, 22 March 1988, p. 34.
34. Source: Bank for International Settlements (BIS), based on information from banks in the BIS reporting area, comprising 18 industrialized countries and seven off-shore banking centers.
35. 'Capital Unchecked', *The Economist*, 19 October 1985.
36. 'US Business Should Take On More Debt', *The Wall Street Journal*, 1 December 1986.
37. Ibid.
38 Ibid.
39. 'Japan's Tax Policy – A System that Works', *San Francisco Chronicle*, 21 November 1985.
40. Source: International Monetary Fund.
41. 'Finance Officers' Wider Role', *The New York Times*, 20 October 1986.
42. 'Escape From Debt', *The Economist*, 21 July 1990, p. 84.
43. The replacement of equity with healthy debt-financing in the US does seem to be minimizing the disruptive, uninsured, junk-bond financing techniques of corporate raiders. In 1990, shortly after the indictment of its junk-bond-king Michael Milken, Drexel Burnham Lambert declared bankruptcy. Drexel Burnham Lambert had accounted for 40 percent ($10 billion) of junk-bond trading in 1989, and in the late 1990s this market has yet to recover to its levels of the late 1980s.
44. 'Soaring Shares Of Japan's NTT Worry Analysts, Delight Holders', *The Wall Street Journal*, 24 April 1987, p.17.
45. 'All the World's a Ratio', *The Economist*, 22 February 1992, p. 72.

2. Financial Market Globalization and New Trade Patterns

Unexpectedly large trade and investment imbalances developed between the US, Japan and others during the 1980s, which have continued through the 1990s. Since 1984, the US has had a trade deficit of more than $100 billion per year, and has received a net inflow of foreign investment of more than $100 billion per year – both of which are now increasing in the wake of the 1997– Asian crisis to approximately $200 billion. Early explanations of these imbalances are found in the proceedings from a conference organized by the Institute for International Economics in late 1990 (Bergsten, ed., 1991), and in the proceedings of the 1990 conference of The International Economics Study Group (Milner and Snowden, 1992).

Despite intense focus on this topic by the economics profession, there is still disagreement over the international adjustment mechanisms and key variables that link trade and investment flows. For example, Paul Krugman and many others argue that imbalances in US trade and finance can be appropriately reduced by movements in currency exchange rates and government policy responses such as protectionism:

> The need to reassess became especially acute in the late 1980s as widespread disappointment emerged over the continuation of sizable imbalances despite large changes in exchange rates and other policy measures aimed at reducing the imbalances...[however] once we clean up the data, it seems possible to argue that trade flows have responded to exchange rates in just about the way that an economist who had avoided listening to any new ideas [since 1970]...would have expected (in Bergsten, ed., 1991, p. xi, 11).

Yet Robert Mundell among others has argued that currency realignments and trade barriers play no useful role in improving trade balances and may even be harmful in the US case:

> The claim that [favorable consequences] will follow from depreciation is sheer quackery. It is closer to the truth to say that a policy of appreciating the yen and the European currencies relative to the dollar will cause deflation abroad, inflation at home, a larger dollar deficit, and vast equity sales to foreign investors. Ownership of factories, technology, and real assets will be exported to finance an even larger trade deficit without there being much, if any, real expansion in exports or

reduction in the dollar value of imports. US assets will be sold abroad at bargain-basement prices. If the American dog gets fed better, it will be by eating its own tail (Mundell, 1987).

The Mundell side has been taken by those, especially from the Japanese perspective, who argue that only the US can improve its trade deficit, when it saves and invests more and improves its productivity:

The fundamental causes of the dollar's depreciation [over 1985–95] are the US budget deficit and an unfavorable balance of payments which shows no sign of improving. Only the US itself can recover the dollar's status as an international key currency. Therefore, in the long run, decreasing the budget deficit and enhancing productivity are vital steps.[1]

Taking issue with each of these quotes, this chapter argues that the financial market globalization, interest rate parity, and financial strategy parity processes as discussed in Chapter 1 are new driving forces responsible for the large trade and investment imbalances of the 1980s and 1990s. *More autonomous and controlling international financial flows are often causing changes in trade and economic growth, rather than vice versa.* Proper consideration of the structural changes from Chapter 1 leads to some new conclusions about the international adjustment mechanisms and key variables that affect trade and investment flows. Increasingly, the nation should not be seen as a self-sufficient or 'balanced' economic region. Identifying exactly what is meant by 'trade' versus 'investment' in the new global economy also leads to some interesting conclusions. In this new environment, typical trade protectionism is shown to be increasingly impractical.

I. SAVER AND DISSAVER COUNTRIES

As discussed in Chapter 1, more lenders have been put in contact with more borrowers by financial market deregulation and the information revolution. Larger sums of money have been moving more quickly and profitably around the world. Those who tend to spend more than their current income, dissavers, have been more quickly accommodated with an appropriate interest rate by those who tend to spend less than their current income, savers. Inherent tendencies, whether toward dissaving or saving, have thus been encouraged for individuals, firms and countries.

The establishment of saver and dissaver countries was especially noticeable during the 'boom years' for international financial markets in the early and mid-1980s. The biggest new saver country was Japan, where individuals were saving more than 15 percent of their disposable personal income. In addition to accommodating the borrowing needs of its business and government sectors, personal savings allowed Japan to increase its net long-term lending to the global financial markets from less than $20 billion in 1983 to $50 billion in 1984 to $62 billion in 1985.[2]

The biggest new dissaver country has been the US, where individuals reduced their personal savings rates from 9 percent in the early 1980s to an average of only 4 to 5 percent after the mid-1980s. In late 1998, US savings rates actually reached zero. European personal savings rates have been midway between the Japanese and US rates in the 7–13 percent range.

No matter how US personal savings is measured, beginning in the early 1980s it has not been nearly enough to meet the borrowing needs of the US business and government sectors. For example, without the benefit of foreign lending and investment in 1985, US personal savings would have provided only $58 billion for the business sector after financing the $200 billion federal budget deficit – not enough to keep the economy running at its 1985 output rate of $4 trillion.

It was the increase in the net inflow of foreign lending and investment into the US from $9 billion in 1982 to $118 billion in 1985 which allowed the US business sector to maintain a high level of output and employment in the mid-1980s, while at the same time the US government was running record deficits. Since the mid-1980s, the US economy has continued to dissave or 'absorb' an average of more than $100 billion per year, net, of the rest of the world's savings. As discussed throughout the remainder of the book, this continuing absorption and use of world savings in the US economy is one of the most significant structural changes associated with the new global economy, and it affects just about everything including economic growth, government budgets, trade patterns and various financial crises and recession. For example, as discussed in Chapter 4, the 1997– Asian financial crisis and the 1997– unexpectedly strong US economy were (not coincidentally) associated with a sudden jump in this net financial inflow into the US to levels exceeding $200 billion per year.

Why is the US personal savings rate exceptionally low compared to, for instance, Japan? The generally accepted reasons are:

1. Earnings on US savings (interest and dividends) are taxed, whereas interest expense on borrowing (for home ownership and business-related purposes) is tax deductible. The incentive is therefore to borrow and spend, not to save. In Japan, most savings have been completely exempt from taxes, that is, until 1 April 1988, when many of 'the world's largest tax loopholes' were closed.[3]
2. The US baby boom, that is, people born from 1946 to 1958, have been in their key spending years for housing, cars, etc. The savings years and the earnings power are just arriving as the baby boomers enter their fifties.

3. The US social security system covers a broader base of people than does Japan's system, which reduces the anxiety to save. A more developed corporate pension plan in the US also reduces concern for the future. The Japanese must generally save as individuals for their retirement. Social security contributions in the US, the largest income security program,[4] are not measured as personal savings; thus the commonly reported US personal savings rate understates the true level of savings.

4. Americans are home owners compared to the Japanese. By spending money on home ownership, Americans are building up equity and financial security for their future, but this 'residential investment' reduces rather than adds to the supply of loanable funds. The Japanese must save more money for future rental of housing, including furniture and appliances because they do not as commonly own these things. Also, when the Japanese buy a home they must save for a more substantial down-payment.

5. Many credit accounts in Japan still work like the US system of decades ago – little black books at the corner store or post office. The credit card revolution in the US has encouraged borrowing by making it easier and more socially acceptable. In 1980, the average unpaid balance per American cardholder was $375, in 1986, approximately $940 and by 1990 it exceeded $2000.

6. A larger share of farm income has historically been saved in the US compared to other sources of income, and farm income has declined from 4 percent of all personal income in 1973 to less than 1 percent of all personal income after 1990.

7. An additional, rarely mentioned explanation of the low US savings rate, which has applied especially since the 1980s, is that the new global economy has provided the US with new, low-interest rate borrowing opportunities. The US savings rate declined from over 8 percent in the early 1980s to 4 percent in the mid-1980s, which was the same period of time during which the US financial markets were integrated with the financial markets of Japan and other lower-interest-rate, saver countries. US interest rates declined by approximately 4 percentage points from the early 1980s to the mid-1980s, largely due to the inflow of newly deregulated profit-seeking foreign funds. Consequently, the US incentive to save was reduced, and the incentive to borrow and spend was increased, both of which reduced the US personal savings rate.

Most likely, it was (7) the globalization of financial markets which reduced the US personal savings rate to post-World War II lows by the mid-1980s. Most of the other (1–6) commonly accepted reasons for the low US savings rate were in place in the 1970s as well as the 1980s, and it is unlikely that they caused the dramatic drop in the US savings rate right after 1981. But many of the financial market deregulations mentioned in Chapter 1 occurred right at the beginning of the 1980s, including UK and Japanese liberalization of foreign capital controls. Profit-seeking foreign capital, which allowed for lower US interest rates and lower US savings, was also attracted to the US by the big Reagan tax cuts of 1981–83 which enhanced returns on US investment. The Reagan tax cuts also led to the large federal budget deficits and government dissaving and attractive returns on Treasury securities (see Chapter 4).

Removal of the US withholding tax on interest payments to foreigners in 1984 further encouraged foreign purchases of US Treasuries in 1984–85. There was no increase in foreign purchases of US corporate bonds in 1984–85 due to removal of the withholding tax, because corporate bonds had been available in the Eurodollar market for some time without being subject to withholding.

Lower US interest rates and lower US savings after 1981 were also allowed when US banks reduced their exposure to less developed country (LDC) debt and repatriated funds back to the US. Virtually all new private loans to the LDCs stopped when the world debt crisis hit in 1982.

The low US personal savings rate together with record federal government budget deficits caused the US to become a 'debtor' country in 1985; the first time since 1914. In just four years, from 1982 to 1986, the US reversed its position as the world's biggest 'creditor' nation and became the world's biggest debtor nation. Japan became the biggest creditor nation. By the mid-1990s, Japan had accumulated $800 billion net ownership of foreign assets, and the US found that foreign ownership of US-based assets exceeded US ownership of foreign-based assets by more than $1 trillion.

Since 1984, the 'net international investment position' of the US has declined by an average of more than $100 billion a year. Commonly reported as the annual increase in US 'debt' to foreign countries, actually much of this $100 billion per year is not debt in the normal sense. Rather, much of it indicates that foreigners are purchasing more US real estate, business assets and other property compared to US claims on foreign property. The Commerce Department estimates that more than 10 percent of the $4.5 trillion in US business assets were foreign-owned by 1988, 1.3 percent of the $7.5 trillion in US real estate, and 5 percent of the $8.4 trillion in debt owed by all US sources – the foreign ownership portion of these assets has thus been increasing by an average of more than $100 billion per year.

The $100 billion per year figure simply indicates that, on balance, $100 billion per year of foreign savings is converted into dollars and injected into the US economy (over and above the amount of US savings sent abroad). The US is increasing its net liabilities to the rest of the world, i.e. the amount of money that it will eventually have to pay back, but not by $100 billion per year. Instead, much of the $100 billion reflects 'the buying of America' by foreigners.

Although this net foreign disinvestment of the US had accumulated to more than $1 trillion by the mid-1990s, this disinvestment is based upon historic purchase prices of business assets, real estate, and true debt-instruments, rather than current market prices. Because America's investments abroad are older than foreign investment in the US and have thus appreciated more, America's investments abroad are relatively more undervalued by the official statistics. A more appropriate measure of the international investment position of the US would be the 'net foreign investment income', i.e. the current flow of income generated by US investment abroad minus the current flow of income generated by foreign investment in the US. This alternative statistic shows the US moving from creditor status of $25 billion inflow in 1985 to zero net inflow in 1990. Based upon the ability of foreign investment to generate income, the US would thus not be a 'debtor' country until the early 1990s.

Determining how much of the $100 billion/year net foreign investment inflow into the US reflects increasing US liabilities to foreigners, and how much of it reflects sales of real property is impossible to measure accurately. Sixteen US government agencies collect data on foreign investment in the US, different methodologies are used, and there is a lot of confusion when the data is aggregated. Also, the complicated channels whereby money is now routed through multinationals, and various privacy acts which protect the identity of investors complicates the problem. The US Congress itself admits that the data is extremely unreliable.

Whether or not it is bad for the US to be a dissaver relative to Japan and other countries is becoming analogous to whether or not it is bad for one US state to dissave relative to the other states. This analogy makes sense now that the US economy is losing its national character and becoming part of the global economy, especially with regard to finance as documented in Chapter 1. Very few analysts make this analogy, however, even though it seems easy to argue that it is natural and good for a state or region with high borrowing needs and a shortage of investment funds to borrow money from another state which has a surplus of liquidity.

One fear is that US interest and dividend payments to the rest of the world will eventually drain away much US wealth at a time when this money is critically needed for investment in the economy, especially in faltering industries. A popular sentiment seems to be that the US government and these industries should not have expanded so much in the first place, and what financing was required should have been supplied domestically so that the large interest and dividend payments would be received by US citizens. That is, a popular sentiment seems to be in favor of financial market protectionism.

The worry of protectionists that the inflow of foreign capital will drain wealth out of the US economy seems strange at a time when more than $100 billion of foreign savings, net, has been sent to the US economy year after year – some as debt, and some as purchases of US business assets and real estate. Protectionists are thus worrying about the financial soundness of the US at a time when a record amount of foreign savings is being freely placed into the US – more international funds than have ever before been transferred to any country. In addition, as argued in Chapter 1, the foreign buying of US business assets and real estate, and the increased US corporate borrowing, is an inevitable globalization process whereby interest rate parity is achieved and international debt/equity and price/earnings ratios converge. It was also argued in Chapter 1 that US businesses have improved their profitability by increasing their debt to normal international levels.

As elaborated later in this chapter, US sales or 'exports' of business assets and real estate beginning in the mid-1980s, if combined with US final-product exports, make US 'trade' approximately balanced since the mid-1980s. In this sense, the 'playing field' is much more level than as characterized by many US protectionists. Yet US protectionists commonly believe that sales of real property to foreign interests is not as beneficial to US economic interests as sales of final products made from the property. Many protectionists even say that it is always best to maintain ownership of the property, as long as the owner receives a normal rate of earnings.

But what is the normal rate of earnings that justifies continued property ownership? In the US during the 1980s, the answer would be 6.7 percent, as determined by the average US price-earnings ratio of 15, i.e. $(1/15)x(100) = 6.7$. If the average US investor in the 1980s expected a certain US corporate stock to yield a return of significantly less than 6.7 percent, then he could not justify purchasing that stock or maintaining his ownership of that stock. He was better off putting his money elsewhere in the stock market where he expected the return on equity, from the sales of products produced by that equity, to be at least 6.7 percent. Money naturally moves in this manner out of bad stocks into good stocks, until the price of bad stocks has declined and/or the price of good stocks has increased enough for the average investor to find them equally attractive.

Of course money also moves between the US stock market and the rest of the economy. Investors were continually deciding in the 1980s whether the average return on US corporate equity of 6.7 percent was the most attractive savings opportunity, and, given all of the ways to save, whether they were saving enough money as opposed to purchasing enough final products.

Based upon these arguments, it was beneficial to the US economy when Japanese or other foreign investors bought US stocks in the 1980s, as long as the sales prices reflected average price-earnings ratios of more than 15, or, equivalently, average returns on equity of significantly less than 6.7 percent. In these cases the US sellers benefited from windfall capital gains, i.e. the premiums paid by the foreign investors over and above normal prices. These windfalls could be used by US citizens to increase consumption of final products. Alternatively, windfalls could be reinvested in the financial markets, in effect postponing a now higher level of consumption to some future date.

Clearly, the evidence indicates that Japanese and other foreign investors have paid prices for US property and business assets far in excess of what the US sellers could receive from US buyers. For example, in 1986 and the first six months of 1987, Tokyo-based Shuwa Corp. purchased $2 billion worth of US real estate, including the twin Arco Plaza towers in Los Angeles, the PaineWebber building in Boston, and the American Broadcasting Co. headquarters building in New York. The prices paid for each, according to *The Wall Street Journal*, were 'much more than competing offers', and the price paid for the Arco towers was higher than for any property sale in Los Angeles history.[5]

The US stock market would not have increased ten times in value since 1980 unless the foreign investors were willing to pay price–earnings ratios significantly in excess of the levels which would otherwise have been determined by US investors. The dramatic drop in the US household savings rate from 7 percent of disposable income in the early 1980s to post-WWII lows of 3 to 4 percent in the late 1980s and zero in 1998, despite only modest gains in US wages and salaries since 1980, indicates that US earned income was not sufficiently available to account for much of the US stock market's dramatic rise over this period. Instead, foreign cash was largely responsible. As documented in Chapter 1, the inflow of foreign investment has brought the price–earnings ratio on US real property up to 20/1 in the 1990s from 15/1 in the 1980s, which is a capital gain of 33 percent to long-term holders of US real property – thanks to globalization and convergence of world equity markets.

US citizens were able to justify lower savings rates since 1980 partly because of the sizable capital gains which they were realizing from the foreign capital inflow. The value of US household wealth 'locked into' the US stock market increased more than $1 trillion in the 1980s, and more than $7 trillion in the 1990s. Based upon these arguments, US policymakers should welcome the foreign buying of America.

Logic, as opposed to protectionist sentiment, suggests that sales of US real property to Japan and other foreign investors since the 1980s have been more beneficial to the US than US exports of final products made from US real property. To summarize:

1. Sales of US real property to Japan and other foreign investors since the 1980s resulted in sizable capital gains for US citizens.
2. The US capital inflow from the rest of the world improved the profitability of US industry by reducing borrowing costs and increasing owned-equity values.
3. US citizens have had the ability to enjoy more final products, without having to incur any additional liabilities or reduce the value of their

savings, because they sold real property to foreign investors, rather than maintaining ownership of that real property and instead selling the final products made from that real property.

In the US case, fear of increased foreign debt should be seen either as a somewhat naive form of nationalism, or as a fear of 'bad debt'. There has been a bad-debt concern about US banks, but it is a concern that they loaned too much money overseas, for example to the less developed countries in Latin America in the 1980s, or now to Asian countries in the 1990s. In this case popular sentiment would have argued in favor of an *increase* in US net foreign debt. *Fewer* US loans to foreigners, i.e. more net US foreign debt, would have improved the profitability of US banks and avoided some of the excessive debt-indulgence in the rest of the world. As discussed below in the case study of US trade, the large increase in the US net foreign debt during the 1980s actually began when US banks began withdrawing monies from the rest of the world, not when foreigners began lending money to the US.

A general fear of bad debt is based upon concern that the borrower will be unable to achieve a net benefit from the loan, or worse, that he will be unable to pay back the loan and have to forfeit business or personal collateral. The borrower is seen as too much of a risk-taker or too naive to assume so much debt. If the borrower is the US government, one might also worry that too much debt would be assumed because of the short-sighted, 'pork-barrel' nature of political decision-making. Why worry about a debt that can be hidden within a massive federal bureaucracy and will soon be the responsibility of other officials?

However, it should be pointed out that the $100 billion per year, net, of foreign savings that was being sent to the US after 1984 pushed US interest rates down dramatically. Instead of having to borrow money at long-term interest rates of 12–14 percent as in the early 1980s, this increased foreign debt allowed the federal government to borrow at long-term interest rates of 7–9 percent in the late 1980s and less than 6 percent in the mid-1990s. The Asian financial crisis resulted in massive capital flight from Asia to the US, and 30-year US Treasury Bonds were paying interest rates of less than 5 percent in the fall of 1998. Certainly policymakers should be able to justify increased borrowing and spending on certain types of public goods at the lower interest rates. To the extent that more public goods can be justified, increased government borrowing, especially from foreign sources, can also be justified.

The author's position is that US federal budgets with deficits over $150 billion would not have been passed between the mid-1980s and the mid-1990s without the ready availability of foreign savings. A (hypothetically) financially self-sufficient US economy in this period with $100–$150 billion of household savings 'left over' for the business sector assuming a $150 billion federal deficit would have been severely recessionary.

National policymakers, whose electiveness and careers frequently require them to maintain economic growth, thus began encouraging the inflow of foreign funds in the 1980s. In a surprising turnaround from previous speeches, President Reagan argued on 11 January 1987 that 'inflows of foreign capital are not necessarily a sign of an economy's weakness'.[6] Comparing the national debt to California's external debt to other states, Reagan said 'does this augur bad days ahead for California? On the contrary, one might argue it's a sign of strength'.

With current international savings trends continuing, with further governmental deregulation of financial markets, and with the profit motive continuing to drive the information revolution, national economies are becoming more dependent upon each other through saver–dissaver relationships. As discussed further in the 'Case Study of US–Foreign Trade 1981–' below, these financial relationships are the driving force behind many new trade patterns.

II.   CASE STUDY OF US–FOREIGN TRADE, 1981–

The US, a country especially exposed to the globalization of financial markets since the 1980s, was, consequently, especially exposed to new patterns of merchandise and services trade. The US economy, therefore, provides a good case study for the arguments of this chapter. For example, it is argued next that the continuing large US trade deficit is a result of the continuing large net inflow of foreign savings into the US. Contrary to conventional wisdom, the inflow of foreign savings is argued to be the more initiating, autonomous development, and the US trade deficit is argued to be the more accommodating development.

Before the 1980s, the major purpose of most international financial transactions was to accommodate merchandise and services trade. Growth in trade produced a nearly equal growth in international financial markets, especially the amount of foreign currency that was swapped. In contrast, by the early 1980s the expansion of international financial markets had taken on a profit-seeking life of its own. As discussed in Chapter 1, the deregulation of financial markets and the global information revolution made international borrowing and lending and other investment very efficient and profitable by the mid-1980s. Consequently, most of the money which was moving between countries by the mid-1980s had little to do with merchandise and services trade, but instead was accommodating 'pure' financial transactions – those which involve only the exchange of money and documentation. For example, between 1980 and 1986 the volume of foreign currency trading doubled, so that by 1986 this volume was roughly 12 times the volume of worldwide trade in merchandise and services.

Whether the international businessperson is engaged in financial or non-financial transactions, often the currency exchange rate is the key determinant of his profit rate. No other production or sales condition is likely to have such a large impact on the gap between costs and revenues from one year to the next. For example, from January, 1981 to January, 1985 the trade-weighted exchange value of the US dollar increased 65 percent, meaning that the side of a US–foreign transaction which made the currency conversion could have lost or gained a similar change in revenue depending upon when they chose to make the conversion. Also, between January 1985 and January 1987, the trade weighted exchange value of the dollar reversed its upward trend and fell 50 percent (Figure 2.1).

Figure 2.1   The trade-weighted exchange value of the US dollar, 1978–97 (March 1973=100)

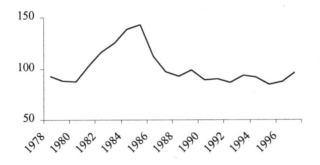
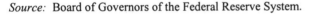

Source: Board of Governors of the Federal Reserve System.

Due to the increased volatility of exchange rates, and the increased importance of international commerce to the US economy, by the late 1980s one out of four US companies surveyed were trading foreign currencies as a hedge against foreign exchange losses.[7]

As discussed in Chapter 1, interest rate parity became the dominant equilibrium in international commerce during the 1970s and 1980s, and participants were paying increasing attention to interest rate differentials. Increasingly, any shock to the system which pushed interest rates up in one country encouraged the international community to lend money there, and discouraged the international community from borrowing money there.

Two such shocks were occurring in the US in 1981 that eventually pushed US interest rates up to record highs: the administration of newly-elected President Reagan began pursuing policies which increased the size of the Federal budget deficit; and the US Federal Reserve Board was restricting the growth of the US money supply. The increased Federal budget deficit increased the borrowing needs of the US government and the slower growth of the US money supply reduced the ability of US financial institutions to make money available for lending. In order to ration the scarce funds of lenders among competing borrowers, interest rates were raised to very high levels compared with what the economy would otherwise have produced.

For example, the US prime interest rate moved in 1981 to 5 or 6 percentage points above the rate of inflation as measured by the US consumer price index, and stayed there until 1984. In contrast, through the mid and late 1970s, the US prime interest rate had stayed within 2 percentage points (above and below) the rate of consumer price inflation.

If the US financial markets had been closed to foreign investors in the early 1980s, then the extra US government borrowing and reduced US money growth might or might not have increased the total loan volume in the US – despite more government borrowing, some borrowing by US businesses and individuals would have been 'crowded out' by the higher interest rates.

However, given the rapid deregulation and globalization of financial markets that was occurring, high US interest rates in the early 1980s created a strong incentive for the worlds' lenders: find a way in the new global markets to gain access to these rates! For example, Japanese lenders saw US money market interest rates jump up 9 percentage points higher than Japanese money market interest rates in 1981, compared to an average US advantage of only 0.2 percentage points from 1971–1980. Many US lenders also suddenly found themselves with money tied up abroad at equally disadvantageous interest rates; their portfolios were thus overexposed to foreign borrowers in the early 1980s even without considering the new risks of default that began to surface on US loans to developing countries.

Accordingly, in the early 1980s, US and foreign lenders began to favor the US market. As shown in Table 2.1, which is a summary of US international financial transactions from 1980–1985, US lenders were able to direct their funds into the US faster than foreign lenders, certainly because US lenders already had more unregulated connections to US borrowers. The 'capital outflow' from the US made its significant drop from 1982 to 1983, a drop of $71 billion dollars. However, it took foreign lenders some time in the rapidly globalizing financial markets to take advantage of the high US interest rates. The 'capital inflow' to the US actually declined from 1982–83 before increasing $20 billion from 1983–84 and $24 billion from 1984–85.

The statistical discrepancy account in Table 2.1 is used to reconcile measured flows of commerce and payments for those flows. This account became very large in the late 1970s and 1980s – it assumed a debit balance averaging less than $1 billion from 1960–77, then a credit balance averaging $21 billion during 1978–86, then large debit and credit balances since 1987 including a credit of $64 billion in 1990 and a debit of $53 billion in 1996.

The statistical discrepancy is generally considered part of the capital account balance, i.e. its large credit position shown in Table 2.1 is assumed to reflect an unmeasured part of the international flow of funds coming into the US. However, there is no way to verify exactly how much of the statistical discrepancy reflects actual flows of capital.

Table 2.1 The turnaround in the US Capital Account, 1980–85 ($billion)

	1980	1981	1982	1983	1984	1985
Capital inflow to US	58	83	94	83	103	127
Less capital outflow	86	111	121	50	24	32
Equals net identified inflow	-23	-28	-27	35	79	95
Plus statistical discrepancy	26	21	36	11	27	23
Equals net capital inflow	-2	-6	9	47	107	118

Note: Components may not add due to rounding.
Source: US Commerce Department.

For example, what if much of the $64 billion credit position of the statistical discrepancy account in 1990, its largest imbalance ever, did not reflect an actual inflow of capital to the US? Then one could more easily conclude, as the author does in Chapter 4, that the US recession of 1990–91 has its explanation. Without some of this inflow, especially given the simultaneous drop in the net identified inflow, US investment and consumption growth could not be sustained. In the author's case study of the early 1990s US recession in Chapter 4, he documents that the economics profession is unable to explain the recession, and also that the profession ignores this possibility. Similarly, the author argues in 'The Asian Crisis, 1997–' in Chapter 4 that unmeasured as well as measured capital flows coming into the US from Asian and elsewhere made for an unexpectedly strong US economy.

The bottom line in Table 2.1 sums up yearly changes in the international financial position of the US over the 1980–85 period. This bottom line is called the net balance on the US capital account, which went from a deficit (or debit) to a surplus (or credit) in 1982. After sending more investment funds to other countries than were received from other countries by $2 billion in 1980 and $6 billion in 1981, the net flow reversed direction and the US began receiving foreign investment on balance. In 1982, 1983, 1984 and 1985 the US received more funds from the rest of the world than it sent to the rest of the world by $9 billion, $47 billion, $107 billion and $118 billion, respectively.

What was happening in the foreign exchange market to the value of the dollar as approximately $157 billion, net, of international investment flowed into the US in the important reversal period 1981–84? Because US investment is conducted in dollars, and because foreign investors have other currencies to invest with, the demand for dollars from the foreign exchange market increased by $157 billion, and the supply of other currencies to the foreign exchange market increased by an equivalent amount. In other words, $157 billion dollars moved out of the inventories of foreign exchange traders into the US economy and an equivalent amount of other currencies moved out of the global economy into the inventories of foreign exchange traders.

However, merchandise and services trade as well as international investment requires currency swaps and therefore also exerts pressure on exchange rates. From 1981 to 1984, the US bought $155 billion more worth of merchandise and services from the rest of the world than the US sold to rest of the world. This excess of US imports over exports (including government grants and private remittances abroad) is called a $155 billion deficit or debit in the current account of the US.[8] The current account summarizes all non-financial transactions between the US and the rest of the world, just as the capital account summarizes all financial transactions.

The $155 billion deficit in the US current account from 1981–84 affected the foreign exchange market as follows: foreign exporters to the US generally want to receive their own currency as payment and US importers generally have dollars to spend, therefore one side of a US importing transaction must buy the foreign currency from the foreign exchange market with the unwanted dollars. The opposite happens in a US exporting transaction. Therefore, because US importing exceeded US exporting by $155 billion in 1981–84, $155 billion dollars, net, were sold to the foreign exchange market from the rest of the global economy and an equivalent amount of other currencies were bought from the foreign exchange market. To accommodate the US current account deficit global foreign exchange trading thus exerted downward pressure on the value of the dollar from 1981 to 1984.

At first glance the downward pressure on the exchange value of the dollar exerted by the deficit in the US current account seems to be approximately equal in magnitude to the upward pressure exerted by the surplus in the US capital account, i.e. $155 billion of downward pressure compared to $157 billion of upward pressure. One might naively conclude that the value of the dollar probably stayed constant between 1981 and 1984.

Nothing could be farther from the truth, however, as the trade-weighted exchange value of the dollar increased 50 percent from 1981 to 1984. A less naive understanding is necessary, which results in the following scenario:

1. Deregulation and globalization of financial markets in the 1980s led to:
2. a large net flow of international funds into the US (US capital account surplus), a dissaver country due to its high interest rates and productive, safe-haven environment, which led to:

3. a higher valued foreign exchange price for the dollar as international investors on balance demanded more dollars from the foreign exchange markets to gain access to the new investment opportunities and high interest rates in the US, which inevitably led to:

4. more US imports and a less US exports, because the higher valued dollar made US products less competitive in international trade, and the net inflow of international investment into the US increased US economic growth and imports relative to other countries; and:

5. this US trade deficit (US current account deficit) had to widen until it was large enough to supply foreign exchange traders with the amount of dollars that they needed to accommodate the increased flow of international funds into the US.

Figure 2.2 illustrates this scenario. The current accounts of the US, Japan and (West) Germany were balanced in 1980–82. Then, the deregulation and globalization of financial markets resulted in substantial flows of investment funds from West Germany and Japan into the US, which in turn resulted in the high-valued dollar, US current account deficit, and the Japanese and German current account surpluses. These changes in the direction of merchandise and services trade between the world's three largest economies, largely caused by the deregulation and globalization of financial markets, are the most significant directional changes in world trade since World War II.

Figure 2.2   Changes in the direction of merchandise and services trade between the world's three largest economies, 1980–97 (current account balances, $billion)

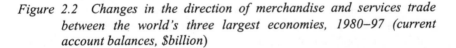

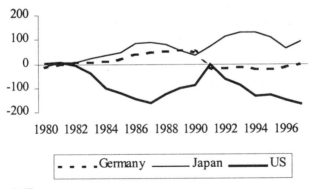

Source: IMF.

As elaborated in Chapter 4, these trade imbalances shrank during the early 1990s due to unique circumstances, such as the Persian Gulf crisis, German reunification, and a money-liquidity crisis in Japan, but they soon returned to historically high levels because of the continuing flow of investment funds into the US.

Why couldn't the deficit in US merchandise and services trade have happened first in 1981-84, thus forcing changes in the US international investment position until the currency inventories of financial intermediaries were maintained? Maybe foreign firms in Japan, West Germany, and elsewhere were producing superior products more efficiently than US firms, and foreign firms were making so much money taking business away from the US that they had a lot of funds to lend, and the US needed to borrow a lot of funds to maintain its output and develop new industries?

In the 1981–84 important reversal period for international trade and investment, changes in investment must have been the driving force, while merchandise and services trade followed, for one simple reason: the dollar dramatically increased in value to balance the dollar supplies of financial intermediaries in this period, rather than decreasing in value. The US current and capital accounts were each in approximate balance at the beginning of this period. Therefore, if the current account had started moving first toward its large deficit position, then the value of the dollar would have started decreasing rather than increasing. Financial intermediaries would have been gaining dollars on balance from the rest of the global economy, rather than losing them as was actually the case.

In turn, the dollar would have had to continue falling until it brought the US current account back into balance, which was certainly not the result seen, i.e. the dollar increased in value approximately 50 percent during 1981–84 as the US continued to have record current account deficits. Also, the US Capital Account would not have been likely to move so quickly toward such a large surplus position if the current account had deteriorated first, because not so many foreign investors would have wanted to buy dollars for US investment purposes if the dollar was (expected to be) declining in value.

So, a cause–effect scenario as headlined by many analysts, including *BusinessWeek* on September 23, 1985, that: 'the soaring [US] trade deficit... is destroying US manufacturing jobs...and turning the US into a debtor nation'[9] is quite inconsistent with the facts. The old-fashioned understanding of initiating and autonomous merchandise and services trade forcing the major changes in accommodating financial flows must yield in this case study to a new understanding that initiating financial flows forced the most significant changes in merchandise and services trade since World War II. In Chapters 3 and 4, the author also supports this thesis with statistical analysis which identifies the time-lags between each phenomenon.

Since the early 1980s, when a US exporter finishes the year with lower sales, it is likely to be because foreign buyers of US products have found something better to do with some of their dollar funds: invest them, especially in US-dollar-denominated assets. Such a scenario has become more and more likely with the globalization of dollar-denominated financial markets. US exporters (who sell their products to get dollars) are no longer in competition only with other international suppliers of the same merchandise and services, but also with every international borrower of dollars. And in the early 1980s the latter form of competition became more difficult to overcome than the former – it pushed the weighted average foreign exchange value of the dollar up by 65 percent, and thus reduced the international price competitiveness of US exporters more than any other factor.

When there was a net flow of international investment into the US in this period, the dollar increased in value until enough foreign currency products, such as Japanese cars, were bought in place of US-dollar-denominated products, such as American cars, that foreign exchange traders maintained their dollar inventories. In this period the foreign countries' share of the market for all US industrial goods climbed from 14 percent to 20 percent.[10]

The US automobile workers who became unemployed in this period and the holders of US automobile company stocks were unlucky because they lived in a country that received a lot of funds for borrowing and investment. Unless, for example, they happened to become successful borrowers in the expanded US credit markets – the loan to Chrysler Corp. from the US government (which in turn was expanding its foreign borrowing) was successfully used to maintain the company through this difficult period. On the other hand, people associated with the Japanese auto industry were lucky in this period because they lived in a country which was sending a lot of money into the international markets. However, the Japanese capital outflow meant that there was less money available for borrowers in the Japanese credit markets.

Was the US, overall, better off after receiving the net flow of international funds in 1981–84? It depends on the balancing-out of two effects: the successful new US borrowers and other beneficiaries of this investment created jobs, economic growth, and other social benefits; but, costs were imposed on various US industries and consequently the US economy due to the stiffer competition from imports. Was the rest of the world better off when it sent more of its money on balance to the US? The new-found successes of foreign export industries compared to their American competition, combined with the new-found successes of foreign investors in the US markets created various benefits for foreign economies; but, there was less successful borrowing and investing within the foreign economies.

These questions are difficult to answer statistically, because the benefits of household and government spending cannot be adequately quantified beyond their dollar magnitude (unlike the profit measure of net benefit used in the business sector). Certainly, however, the new international flows of interest-rate and financial-strategy parity-seeking funds was an inevitable consequence of the deregulation and globalization of financial markets.

Also, these structural changes resulted in more profitable international borrowing and lending, and therefore more spending and economic growth for the global economy as a whole.

Assessing the benefits and costs of these structural changes, and allocating the benefits and costs to various country groups is the task of Chapters 3 and 4. Generally speaking, the case studies show that the US has benefited greatly from financial globalization, and many other parts of the world have suffered losses.

III.   NEW DEFINITIONS OF TRADE AND THE FOLLY OF PROTECTIONISM

Using the traditional definition of trade as the flow of products across national boundaries, trade protectionism is then the use of tariffs, quotas, and other customs barriers to restrict the flow of foreign products into the domestic market. The historical justifications used by governments to restrict imports are well known: to maintain stable employment and profit levels in the protected domestic industries; to preserve domestic production of certain products which are important to national security; to protect an 'infant-industry' while it develops; to retaliate against the unfair trading practices of another country; to reduce the country's trade deficit, etc.

Protectionism is primarily used as a means of redistributing income. When imports are taxed with a tariff, the government of the importing country attains the tariff revenue at the expense of: the consumers of the imported product, who now pay a higher price; the foreign exporters of the product, who are left with a lower after-tariff price. The protected industry is able to achieve higher consumer prices and/or more output of its product when the price of the competing import product is increased by the tariff.

The income transfers are the same with a restrictive import quota, except that the government of the importing country may not receive revenues from sales of the restricted import. If the domestic importers or foreign exporters are given the exclusive right to sell the now-scarce, imported product, then they are often able to get higher windfall prices.

Historically, whichever form of protectionism is used, whether consumer prices are increased directly by tariffs or indirectly by import quotas, the major effect is to transfer income within the importing country from its domestic consumers to its protected domestic firms.[11]   Politicians, for obvious reasons, emphasize the benefits that are provided for domestic firms rather than the costs that are imposed upon domestic consumers. Yet one group usually gains only at the other group's expense – a net increase in domestic welfare is seldom created when governments restrict international trade.

In the new global economy, restricting foreign imports with tariffs and quotas is becoming less practical as a way to transfer income from domestic consumers to politically-favored domestic firms. It is harder to redistribute significant amounts of income with these devices, and the income that is redistributed is more likely to reach other less politically-favored groups.

The increasing folly of trade protectionism is due to four structural changes associated with the new global economy: (A) as discussed in the previous section, trade deficits are now required by countries which, due to interest rate and financial strategy parity conditions, receive a net capital inflow; (B) rising imports as a share of national purchases are increasing the national welfare cost of using trade protectionism; (C) the increase in international joint ventures and overseas production is making it less likely that trade protectionism will achieve the desired income transfers; and (D) the increase in international ownership of once national corporations is making it less likely that trade protectionism will achieve the desired income transfers.

This section elaborates the importance of (A)–(D) to trade policy-making in the global economy. As part of the discussion, the author expands the historical definition of trade to include the integration of production processes and ownership between nations. Appropriate trade policy-making should of course be coordinated with appropriate monetary and fiscal policy strategies in order to avoid financial crises and recession, and this discussion is therefore important for the purposes of this book. Appropriate policy alternatives to trade protectionism are presented in Chapter 5 in the context of 'National Strategies in the Global Economy'.

A. The Folly of Protectionism Now That Trade Deficits are Required by Interest Rate Parity (IRP) and Financial Strategy Parity (FSP)

As discussed in Chapter 1, IRP and FSP explain the initiating, profit-seeking flows of finance between countries, and, as elaborated in the previous section, it is the IRP and FSP-influenced equilibrium position of globalized financial markets that merchandise and services trade must conform to. Otherwise, financial arbitragers would exploit inefficiencies in IRP and FSP and make tremendous profits, much greater profits than could ever be achieved from merchandise and services trade.

The exchange rates which are produced by the IRP and FSP processes could in one period give a country's exporters a tremendous price advantage in international trade, and in another period a tremendous price disadvantage. In addition, the subsequent changes in that country's merchandise and services trade balance may be large by historical standards, but small relative to the flows of international investment funds between that country's currency and other currencies.

In the future, policy-makers who do not want their national trade balances to accommodate IRP and FSP will increasingly have very little choice but to accept the linkage. For example, if policy-makers were somehow able to reduce the net flow of international funds into their country to a level that would depreciate their currency enough to improve prospects for their export industries, adopting such a policy would prove to be unwise. The costs of losing foreign investment in the global economy might outweigh the trade benefits, as was argued earlier in the US case. Also, there is no guarantee that policymakers would know how strategically to manipulate the international financial flows so that the desired effects on merchandise and services trade would be produced at the correct time.

Using some form of trade protectionism to limit imports or exports in some industries will only encourage further movements in exchange rates until the necessary trade balance effects are derived from other unprotected industries. Protectionism that covers all imports or exports is doomed to failure in the long run because of the currency shortages that would occur in the foreign exchange markets. For example, when the US receives $100 billion of net foreign investment in one year, then $100 billion dollars moves out of the inventories in the foreign exchange market and into the US economy. Foreign exchange traders keep the value of the dollar high enough so that their dollar inventories are replaced via a US Current Account deficit of approximately $100 billion. No other mechanism for maintaining foreign exchange inventories is practical in the new global economy, not even intervention by central banks.

Official attempts to stabilize international monetary flows based on different currency reserve cushions and national money supplies are often not possible. Private financial flows can push exchange rates too fast, and inflation/economic growth considerations limit the ability of central banks to control exchange rates to this degree. The growth of international financial transactions will continue to outpace the growth of the currency reserves held by national central banks. Therefore, in Chapter 5 the author proposes a reduction in the number of currencies and various other measures in order to bring greater stability to the international monetary system.

Thus, it is quite inconsistent with the structure of the new global economy to advocate trade protectionism as a means of reducing trade deficits. But even financial leaders who presumably are well aware of IRP, FSP, and how the foreign exchange markets work continue to propose such policy-making. For example, Willard Butcher, chairman and chief executive officer of the Chase Manhattan Corporation, argued in 1990 that trade certificates should be required in order to sell foreign products to the US.[12] How to obtain these certificates? Only by buying an equivalent dollar amount of US exports.

B. The Folly of Protectionism as Imports Capture a Larger Share of National Purchases

Countries are increasingly purchasing merchandise and services from each other, both in absolute terms and as a percentage of their total purchases. From 1962 to 1982, the two decades before the rapid globalization of financial markets, imports as a share of total world purchases increased at an average annual rate of approximately 3 percent. Imports accounted for 17 percent of total world purchases in 1982.

After 1982, the growth of international trade accelerated. In 1986, the value of world commerce among the 92 trading nations ascribing to the General Agreement on Tariffs and Trade (GATT) topped $2 trillion, and in 1989 this figure exceeded $3 trillion.[13] Annual increases in the actual dollar value of world trade were 17 percent in 1987, 14 percent in 1988, and 7.5 percent in 1989, which far outpaced the 2–4 percent dollar inflation in those years. In some countries, such as Germany, Canada, and South Korea, imports plus exports now account for approximately half of all economic activity.

When countries buy more foreign products in place of domestically produced ones, then labor, capital, land, and other productive resources are diverted from the declining import-competing industries into the new export industries. In situations where resources, especially labor, have been forced out of declining industries too quickly, protectionism is common in order that adjustments can be made more slowly and less painfully. Businesses need time to retool and develop new products so that wasteful bankruptcies are avoided, and workers need time to retrain and relocate themselves so that difficult periods of unemployment are avoided. However, in the new global economy this reallocation of productive resources is inevitably occurring.

The US automobile industry provides an excellent example of how protectionism has been used when productive resources are forced out of an import-competing industry too quickly, yet how in the long run the inevitable increase in import share makes protectionism impractical. This last point is developed after a discussion of the income transfers that occurred when US automobile imports were restricted in the 1980s.

In the US, competition from smaller, more fuel-efficient imported cars became particularly intense during the OPEC oil price increases of the 1970s. The import share of the US market jumped from less than 10 percent in 1970 to 30 percent in 1980.[14] Eventually the US firms were unable to meet the remarkable competition, especially from Japan, whose share of the US market increased from 14.5 percent in 1978 to 16 percent in 1979 to 21 percent in 1980.[15] The US industry lost combined profits of $4 billion in 1980[16] and the number of laid-off workers reached 220,000.[17]

The US government, in order to provide a reasonable profit and employment outlook for this industry which directly or indirectly employed one out of every seven US workers, began arranging for Japanese imports to be restricted. Japan agreed to 'voluntarily' restrict the number of cars its automobile manufacturers would ship to the US to 1.68 million per year beginning on April 1, 1981. The restriction was intended to last for a few years until the US industry was able to develop more competitive, fuel-efficient cars. In fact, the 1.68 million limit was used for three years, then from April 1, 1984 to March 31, 1985 the ceiling was raised to 1.85 million. Since March 31, 1985 the ceiling has not been set so formally, but some restraints have remained.

By the beginning of 1985 the average price of US-made cars was estimated to be anywhere from $300 to $1000 higher than it would otherwise have been in the absence of the four years of voluntary export restraints. Price increases on the imported Japanese cars were estimated at $500 to $2000. Clearly, policy-makers felt that severe import restrictions were necessary so that US buyers would turn toward the US industry in sufficient numbers to restore its profitability.

Although this protectionism did give the US automobile industry enough time and money to profitably adapt to increased international competition, it came at a great cost to US car buyers. Of the total US industry profits of $9.8 billion in 1984,[18] $3.1 billion or 31 percent of the total can be attributed solely to the protectionism – to the higher prices that US car buyers paid for US cars due to the import restrictions (Babcock et al., 1985). Also, US car buyers paid an average of $500–$2000 more for imported cars (Japanese cars accounted for more than 80 percent of imports) depending on whose estimate is used. This $500–$2000 per imported car is a rough estimate of the net cost to the US economy of protecting its automobile industry, i.e. the net amount of income that is transferred from US citizens to foreign citizens rather than between US citizens.

So, in addition to transferring money from US car buyers to US car makers, US automobile protectionism effectively created a foreign export cartel which, just like OPEC, attained monopoly profits by restricting their exports and driving up prices. The voluntary export restraint agreements gave the Japanese Ministry of International Trade and Industry (MITI) in conjunction with Japanese car makers the authority to form a cartel arrangement, and the weak bargaining position of the competitive US importers allowed the Japanese (and other foreign) firms to capture all of the price windfalls on US imports.

Although the Japanese companies would have sold anywhere from 15 percent to 40 percent more cars to the US by 1984 without the restrictions,[19] the price windfall from US car buyers more than compensated them for this decline in volume. The Japanese auto-makers realized 80 percent of their total profits from the US in 1984, a record one trillion yen (more than $4 billion at 1984 exchange rates).[20] This continuing windfall encouraged MITI to retain the quota, a 2.3 million limit on passenger car sales to the US in

1989, under the auspices that a political favor is being provided to the US. The US industry position in 1989, eight years after the quota was first put into place, was that 'the quota is a necessary evil until the serious imbalance in US–Japan trade is corrected'.[21]

As this case study of US automobile trade demonstrates, with voluntary export restraints or with any other trade quotas which allow foreign exporters to receive higher prices, there is an immediate net welfare loss to the protectionist importing country. The size of this welfare loss depends upon how significantly trade is restricted (enough to increase imported car prices by $500–$2000 in this case) and how important imports are to the economy (30 percent of all cars purchased in this case). As per the title of this section of the book, if imports are a larger share of national purchases, then the size of the national welfare loss due to protectionism increases.

Voluntary export restraints are now the most common form of protectionism used by the US, negotiated recently to protect its automobile, sugar, beef, steel, textile and other industries. Despite the net welfare loss to the US economy, these types of restrictions are popular because they give domestic producers the desired level of protection without sufficiently hurting the foreign trading partner, who may in fact benefit as in the US automobile case.

Also, US policy-makers probably like the power that they have to change the share of the voluntary export quota which is allocated to particular foreign exporting countries, as in the case of steel. In recent years, 20 percent of the US steel market has been divided up and given to foreign countries. Because of changing economic and political circumstances, Mexico's share of the US market for 1990 was almost doubled from 0.48 percent to 0.95 percent, while Japan's share was reduced from 5.9 percent to 5 percent.

Trade quotas which, alternatively, give the monopoly cartel-like power to restrict trade to the domestic importers are seldom used because the foreign trading partners would be too severely hurt. Not only would the foreign exporters be selling less volume, but they might also have to make some price concessions to the more powerful importers. Currently, the US is not administering any trade quotas in this manner.

Similarly, tariffs are rarely used as a significant form of protectionism.[22] Transferring significant amounts of income to politically-favored domestic firms or industries with these devices would also hurt foreign exporters more than is politically desirable. Since the Kennedy Round of international trade negotiations in the 1960s, which resulted in the US cutting tariffs an average of 35 percent on $40 billion worth of imports, the international community has consistently reduced tariff barriers. Under the international General Agreements on Tariffs and Trade (GATT), which has now been replaced by the World Trade Organization, high tariffs are acceptable only to counteract unfair practices by one's trading partner, such as the 'dumping' of products at prices below production costs.

For example, the 100 percent US tariffs on various Japanese semiconductor products which caused considerable controversy in March and April, 1987 were passed more to punish Japan for violating previous semiconductor agreements than to transfer significant amounts of income from US consumers to US producers. Many of the restricted products are also available from Taiwanese, South Korean and other foreign suppliers, meaning that 'US consumers should not be greatly hurt',[23] meaning that US semiconductor firms should not be greatly benefited. These restrictions covered only $300 million-worth of Japanese imports, and therefore could make only a small dent in the US electronics trade deficit with Japan, which was $20.4 billion in 1986.[24]

These US semiconductor tariffs were worrisome to many US trade officials because of the possibility that they might ignite a mutually destructive trade war between the US and Japan. This concern was widely felt even though the tariffs were designed to be punitive rather than protectionist, and therefore within the guidelines of GATT. If instead the US government had wanted to transfer a significant amount of income to US semiconductor firms, tariffs would not have been the chosen policy instrument. The GATT guidelines would have been violated, and the US would have jeopardized its trading relationship with Japan more than was politically acceptable.

As the semiconductor case and other recent cases have shown, if protectionism restricts imports enough to greatly benefit domestic producers, policy-makers prefer that the protectionism does not impose significant costs on the restricted foreign exporters, even when it is likely that they have violated international trade agreements. National economies have become too integrated, and therefore too dependent upon the good will of foreign policymakers. Japanese investors were supplying 30–40 percent of the new money borrowed by the US government during the semiconductor controversy, and the threat of a Japanese investment 'pull-out' in response to the tariffs sent a confidence scare through US financial markets and may have contributed to the conditions which led to the 1987 stock market crash. Not only might a pull-out have been initiated by Japanese policymakers, but also by the Japanese investors themselves who were faced with the increased risk of exchange rate losses. When the tariffs were announced, the US dollar immediately sank against the yen due to the confidence scare and the threat of a costly trade war, and US interest rates jumped up and increased the US government interest expense.

Japanese voluntary export restraints immediately began to be substituted for the US semiconductor tariffs as the preferred way of resolving this trade conflict: on 23 March 1987, MITI ordered Japanese microchip makers to cut back production 11 percent in the April–June period; failure by MITI to issue export licenses further reduced exports in this period; and meanwhile the US government began reducing the number of imported products that would be subject to the 100 percent tariffs.[25] As in the automobile case, the voluntary export restraints have not provoked worries of a trade war.

Clearly, the immediate net welfare loss to the domestic economy of foreign voluntary export restraints has not prevented them from being the dominant form of protectionism. Such protectionism persists, apparently because the long-term benefits of allowing businesses the time to adapt to increased import competition are felt to be greater than the immediate welfare loss to consumers in the protectionist country.

However, increased import competition will have to be adapted to. As elaborated previously, imports as a share of national purchases are inevitably increasing at the average annual rate of more than 3 percent. Governments are unable to buck this trend. Despite US protectionism in the 1980s, GM, Ford and Chrysler saw their market share in the US decline substantially.

As firms adapt to the new, more competitive global economy, protectionism will become less practical. Government policy-makers and corporate executives will increasingly have to accept the inevitability of increased trade. Consequently, firms might be less able to claim the need for special protection, and less able to claim that they had too little time to adapt to the structural changes. Also, the immediate cost to national economies of current protectionist policies, which increases in proportion to the increased import share, will soon outweigh the long-term benefits to the protected industries in most cases.

C.   The Folly of Protectionism as International Joint Ventures and Overseas Production Become More Common

The need to adapt to new international competition in the global economy has in turn provoked an important structural change in the marketplace: firms are participating in more international joint ventures and shifting more of their production overseas. This structural change also makes the use of tariffs, import quotas and other trade barriers less practical as a way to transfer income to politically-favored firms. For example, merchandise manufactured by an American-owned company in Japan and shipped back to the US is counted as a Japanese export and a US import, and would be subject to tariffs just as a 'pure' Japanese export. US tariffs would hurt rather than help such a 'US' company, much like shooting oneself in the foot.

Firms have increasingly gone global since the 1980s through joint ventures and overseas production arrangements, first, because selling to foreign customers in the more dynamic and competitive international marketplace requires a better understanding of and access to those foreign customers. For example, US semiconductor firms did an 'about-face' in 1986 when they decided that it is easier to crack the Japanese market from within through friendly associations than from the outside in an adversarial posture. Intel, one of the firms which brought a suit against Japanese firms for illegally dumping their products in the mid-1980s, contracted with a Japanese firm in 1987 to produce various Intel chips in Japan. Advanced Micro Devices, also a defendant in the dumping lawsuit, began courting Japanese buyers with large banquets in 1987. For similar reasons, Honda Motors of Japan shifted responsibility for its North American operations from Tokyo to the US in January 1987. This move followed IBM's relocation of its Asia–Pacific Group headquarters to Tokyo.[26]

Secondly, firms have gone global to assure themselves legal access to a profitable share of foreign markets. The protectionism which the increased competition from imports has provoked can be avoided this way. Overseas production is a way around the trade barriers. For example, in 1987, Honda became the first Japanese auto-maker to build all the major parts for its cars in the US. The combined production of Toyota, Nissan and Honda in the US reached 7 percent of all US-based automobile production in the late 1980s.

Thirdly, firms have gone global to take advantage of cheap foreign labor and other special production opportunities. For example, the Mexican *maquiladoras* program, whereby foreign firms are given favored tax status to manufacture products in Mexico for export, boomed in the 1980s due to the rapid devaluation of the Mexican peso and other conditions which made Mexican labor extremely inexpensive to foreign producers. The *maquiladoras* program now generates more trade-related revenue within Mexico than the tourism industry, and is the second source of trade-related revenue next to oil production.

Fourthly, firms have gone global in the 1980s to adapt to the increased volatility of foreign exchange rates, which in turn has been caused by the deregulation and expansion of international financial markets. These wild swings in exchange rates can be the most important factor in the international competitiveness of firms. For example, the 50 percent drop in the value of the US dollar relative to the D-mark from 1985 to 1988 meant that German firms would have needed to double the dollar prices of their exports to the US in order to continue receiving the same D-mark prices. Alternatively, if the German exporters had charged the same dollar prices for their exports, they would have received half as many marks for each unit sold. Typically the dollar price was raised somewhat, but not doubled, as German exporters attempted to maintain their sales volume as well as a reasonable profit margin per unit sold.

In order to avoid some of these large currency-related losses on sales volume or profit margins, a German exporter might have been able to buy more of its production inputs from the US, which would decrease in D-mark price with the strengthening of the D-mark. However, despite the export successes achieved by Japan and a few other nations which import most of their productive resources except labor, it is generally more efficient to locate production overseas where the inexpensive resources are. Transportation costs can be avoided with this strategy, and so can much of the currency-related risk.

As another example, Japanese exports captured 18.3 percent of the US light truck market by 1986, but the 30 percent fall in the dollar in the next two years reduced this share to 11.6 percent. So, in 1988, instead of competing directly with Ford's popular Bronco II sports utility vehicle, Mazda agreed to sell these Fords through its own US dealerships – the first such marketing agreement by a Japanese auto-maker.

Increasingly, firms should participate in international joint ventures and overseas production so that marginal production levels can be immediately shifted to the low-cost country when exchange rates change. For example, the big losers from the high-valued dollar of the mid-1980s were those US exporting industries without foreign affiliates. The American machine tool industry had world leadership in the 1970s, but it operated almost entirely out of the US. The high-valued dollar cut its exports, made it defenseless against imports, and deprived it of the profits which are critically necessary to maintain effective research and development projects. On the other hand, what saved Ford Motor Co. in the mid-1980s was its leadership position through foreign partners in the European market. The high-valued dollar allowed Ford to develop its new models in Europe, which made Ford highly profitable again in the US. Ford's profits in the first quarter of 1988 were a record for the US industry, 'as unexpectedly strong overseas results overcame lower earnings in the US'.[27] GM, though twice Ford's size, operated more essentially out of the US in the late 1980s, and continued to have financial difficulties.

As another example, the 30 percent fall in the foreign exchange value of the dollar from 1986–8 encouraged Honda to ship cars produced from its US plants across the Pacific for sale in Japan. Honda's first such shipment arrived in Japan on 8 April 1988, the same day that its one-millionth US-produced car rolled off its assembly line in Ohio.

Corporations have rapidly globalized their operations in the last two decades because of the above reasons, so rapidly that economic policymakers have often seemed ignorant of how extensively the global strategies are used. So, for the record, a few statistics are in order:

By the late 1980s, more than five million US jobs depended directly on international trade, and approximately half of US corporate profits came from abroad.[28] In contrast, US businesses reported that only 13 percent of their revenue came from outside North America in the late 1980s.[29] Overseas business was more profitable than domestic business, and it grew more quickly – US corporations earned more than 25 percent of their revenue from outside the US in the 1990s.

More global than US corporations, more than 30 percent of European corporate revenue comes from outside Europe. And, more than 15 percent of Japanese corporate revenue comes from outside Japan.

The European Community announcement that most internal barriers would be dismantled by 1992 led to a rapid increase in foreign investment there. Majority-owned foreign affiliates of US companies increased capital spending in Europe from $15.4 billion in 1987 to $18.8 billion in 1988 to $21.1 billion in 1989. Total foreign capital spending by majority-owned foreign affiliates of US companies increased by 12 percent from 1988 to 1989, the third consecutive yearly increase after a declining trend from 1982 to 1986 (Quijano, 1989, p. 20–22). By 1989, 411 Japanese manufacturers had opened or made plans to begin production in the European Community, which was nearly triple the number since 1983. Japan's offshore manufacturing (everywhere) more than doubled from 3.5 percent of total Japanese output in the mid-1980s to 8.7 percent of total output in 1990.[30]

From 1983 to 1988, US and Canadian companies made only 9 percent of their investments outside North America. From 1989 to 1993, that figure rose to 16 percent.[31]

Noteworthy statistics such as these regarding the growing presence of multinational companies are typically ignored in trade data. For example, merchandise manufactured by an American-owned company in another country and then shipped to the US is counted as a US import. Merchandise manufactured by an American-owned company in another country and then sold in that country does not directly affect trade data. However, firms are frequently protected on the basis of export and import statistics for their industry. If the statistics show greater import penetration, the importing country is more likely to resort to protectionism. If the statistics show reduced export penetration, then the exporting country is more likely to resort to protectionism to retaliate against possible unfair restrictions on its exports.

In some cases economic policymakers should be more careful to investigate what it is they are protecting with tariffs and quotas – reasonable sounding trade statistics, or national economic interests? For example, US politicians were quick to call the American trade deficit with Japan unacceptable and intolerable when it jumped to $31.2 billion in 1984, meaning that the US imported $31.2 billion more-worth of merchandise and services from Japan than it exported to Japan. It was commonly felt that this trade deficit indicated not only a poor performance by US firms relative to Japanese firms, but also that Japan must be unfairly biased against US products. Loud calls to restore the 'level playing field' were heard.

However, in that same year, Japan purchased $43.9 billion-worth of products made in Japan by American-owned firms, whereas the US only purchased $12.8 billion-worth of products made in the US by Japanese firms[32] – a US advantage of $31.1 billion due to the activity of multinationals. Therefore, including the activities of multinationals, US–Japanese trade was balanced in 1984. Furthermore, because the US has twice the population, US firms actually sold twice as much to the typical

Japanese buyer compared to the level of Japanese sales to the typical US buyer in 1984.

Far from indicating a poor performance by US firms or that Japan must be unfairly biased against American products, statistics which are revised to reflect the increasing number of international joint ventures and overseas production activities can show just the opposite results. Peter Drucker, the US management expert who helped design Japan's economy in the 1950s, characterized the US–Japanese trade situation in 1990 by stating:

> I don't know a single Japanese in a responsible governmental or academic position who believes in the (Japanese) export surplus...It is a mirage...It is not the result of Japan's industrial prowess.

In the 1980s, of the world's 100 largest, publicly-owned multinationals, 50 were American, 33 were Japanese, and 17 were European. The biggest US earner abroad was IBM, with foreign earnings of $7 billion per year from a physical presence in 83 countries.[33] The US Commerce Department data for the late 1980s showed that overseas affiliates of American companies were generating $800 billion in annual revenues. That was three times the value of US merchandise 'exports'.

Ultimately, analysts will view much of international commerce not as 'trade' but as the integration of production processes across national borders. According to George Gilder, an expert on the growing high-technology 'trade':

> Some two-thirds of the US trade deficit with Asia consists of critical components and subassemblies for US manufacturers; devices designed in the US and assembled or packaged abroad; unique capital equipment vital to US productivity; and crucial items in American product lines.[34]

And as estimated by the US Department of Commerce in 1997,

> Cross-border transactions between affiliated units of multinational companies account for a major share of US international trade in goods. In 1994, these transactions – commonly referred to as 'intrafirm trade' – accounted for more than one-third of US exports of goods and for more than two-fifths of US imports of goods (Department of Commerce, 1997, p. 23).

In this environment, typical trade protectionism, i.e. restricting the flow of products across national boundaries, is increasingly impractical as per the common analogy of shooting oneself in the foot.

D. The Folly of Protectionism as the International Ownership of Once National Corporations Becomes More Common

The increased international ownership of once national corporations has been dramatic, especially since the boom years for international financial markets in the early and mid-1980s. The deregulation of financial markets and the development of information-based technologies have given investors greater access to profitable international opportunities. Also, firms have had access to low-cost funds for mergers and acquisitions.

For example, between 1983 and mid-1987, British companies spent at least $25 billion on acquiring American businesses – 'the most massive British thrust into the world economy since Victorian times'.[35] Total acquisitions of US corporations by foreign companies grew from $5.9 billion in 1983 to $41.9 billion in 1987.[36]

Venture capitalists and other financial intermediaries were often the buyers, such as the firm Kohlberg Kravis Roberts & Co., which acquired more than forty companies between 1976 and 1992, including RJR Nabisco for $31 billion in 1988. Similar to the years 1897–1904, when 4,277 American companies consolidated into 257 corporations, there was a rebirth of financial capitalism, but this time *The New Financial Capitalists* (Baker and Smith, 1998), were more global.

The 1987 world stock market crash interrupted only briefly the dramatic increase in international mergers and acquisitions and cross-border trading of corporate stock. By 1990, trading of equities between nations had reached $1.6 trillion per year, up from $800 billion in 1986.[37] 1996 was a record year for US and international mergers and acquisitions, but as this book is written in 1998 it appears that both records will be beaten. In 1998, Daimler Benz acquired Chrysler to become the world's biggest auto-maker, Deutsche Bank acquired Banker's Trust for $10 billion to become the world's biggest bank, and in the biggest merger of all time, Citicorp (worth $82 billion as the deal was announced in April) and Traveler's Group (worth $84 billion) joined.

Governments which take months to pass trade legislation cannot expect the legislation to benefit only their citizens. The world information network quickly evaluates national economic policies, and millions of computer screens and other information technologies transmit how investors expect these policies to affect stock prices. The large stockbrokers, such as Merrill Lynch and Nomura, now have trading offices in almost all of the large industrial cities, and can buy and sell securities 24 hours a day for their international clients in whichever markets happen to be open.

Many small stockholders have not yet learned how to diversify their savings internationally. Also, managers and employees of some corporations may own sizable portions of their company's equity. Protectionism can benefit these two national economic interests if policymakers are able to transfer income to them effectively with tariffs and quotas.

Yet only a small and rapidly decreasing share of stock market capitalization around the world is owned by individuals, especially individuals who remain internationally undiversified. The majority of stock is now owned by large institutional investors who immediately exploit new international opportunities including changes in protectionism. In Tokyo, where accurate statistics are kept, the ownership by individuals declined from 50 percent in 1960 to 20 percent in 1989.[38]

Historically, the major economic effect of trade protectionism was to transfer money within a country, from domestic consumers of a product to the owners of domestic corporations which supply the product. But recently, as international ownership of domestic corporations increases, more of this money ends up in the hands of international investors. At some point, as individual investors increasingly take advantage of the international opportunities through mutual funds and retirement funds, and relinquish their stock ownership to institutions, trade protectionism of national economic interests will be too costly to be practical. Policy-makers might no longer be able to justify the increasingly large transfers of income from their consumers to international investors.

NOTES

1. Wakasugi, R. (1987), 'Attack the Problem at its Source', *Look Japan*, July, p. 3.
2. 'Japan's Foreign Fundings', *The New York Times*, 13 April 1986.
3. 'Japan to End One of the World's Largest Tax Loopholes', *The Wall Street Journal*, 23 March 1988, p. 22.
4. In 1986, according to the US Census Bureau, the value of US poverty programs was equal to $48.2 billion, while Social Security benefits amounted to $196.1 billion ('Benefits Beat Taxes as Income Equalizer', *The Wall Street Journal*, 28 December 1988, p. A2.).
5. 'Maverick Tokyo Firm Acquires Office Towers In US at a Fast Pace', *The Wall Street Journal*, 23 September 1987, p. 1.
6. 'Reagan Says October Crash Resulted From Markets, Not Deficits and Dollar', *The Wall Street Journal*, 12 January 1988, p. 3.
7. 'Business Bulletin', *The Wall Street Journal*, 14 January 1988, p. 1.
8. Without including government grants and private remittances abroad, the value of exports minus imports would equal the more commonly mentioned 'Trade Balance'.
9. 'Bushwacked by the Trade Issue', *Business Week*, 23 September 1985, p. 32.
10. 'America's War on Imports', *Fortune*, 19 August 1985, p. 26.
11. Costs imposed upon foreign exporters by protectionism, while frequently mentioned to highlight the political favor being done for domestic firms, are generally small compared to the costs imposed upon domestic consumers. Foreign exporters may even gain from cartel-like price increases, as in the automobile case discussed in this chapter.
12. 'Trading Away the Trade Deficit', *The New York Times*, 8 April 1990, p. 13.

13. 'The Globalization of the Industrialized Economies', *Barron's*, 4 May 1987, p. 45.
14. *Automotive News*, 27 October 1980, p. 50.
15. 'Congressmen Call For Japan Auto Curbs', *Los Angeles Times*, 19 November 1980, Part IV, p. 2.
16. 'Senate Panel Wants to Curb Auto Imports', *San Francisco Chronicle*, 4 February 1981, p. 27.
17. 'Toyota to Limit Exports to the US', *Chicago Tribune*, 19 February 1980, Section 1, p. 10.
18. 'Talks With Japan Near the Flash Point', *Business Week*, 11 March 1985, p. 34.
19. Ibid.
20. 'Nearly 80 Percent of Their Profits Come From the US', *Automotive News*, 22 October 1984, p. E16.
21. 'What is Too High For Some, But Too Low for Others?', *Autoweek*, 30 January 1989.
22. One notable exception is the US's 42 percent tariff on imported wool fabric – tariff as of January, 1987.
23. This quote reflects the Reagan administration's widely publicized position. The quote is from: 'Mixed Reaction to New Tariffs', *San Francisco Chronicle*, 28 March 1987, p. 48.
24. 'Chips Fight: Reagan Plan to Raise Tariffs May Be Watershed in US–Japanese Ties', *The Wall Street Journal*, 30 March 1987, p. 1.
25. 'Japan Urges Chipmakers to Cut Production', *Oakland Tribune*, 19 February 1987, p. B1.
26. 'Japan's Trade Failure', *The Wall Street Journal*, 1 April 1987, p. 28.
27. 'Ford's Profit Jumped by 9 percent In 1st Quarter', *The Wall Street Journal*, 29 April 1988, p. 3.
28. 'The Globalization of the Industrialized Economies', *Barron's*, 4 May 1987, p. 45.
29. 'Going Global: Vision Vs. Reality', *The Wall Street Journal*, 22 September 1989, p. R20.
30. 'Tokyo's End Run Around its "Trade Problem",' *Business Week*, 13 July 1987, p. 54.
31. 'Going Global: Vision Vs. Reality', *The Wall Street Journal*, 22 September 1989, p. R20.
32. 'Japan's Trade Failure', *The Wall Street Journal*, 1 April 1987, p. 28.
33. 'The Globalization of the Industrialized Economies', *Barron's*, 4 May 1987, p. 45.
34. 'Trade Gap Is Inevitable – and Good', *The Wall Street Journal*, 15 January 1988, p. 22.
35. 'The Transnational Economy', *The Wall Street Journal*, 25 August 1987, p. 8.
36. 'Accounting Rules favor Foreign Bidders', *The Wall Street Journal*, 24 March 1987, p. 26.
37. 'Capital Markets Survey', p. 7, *The Economist*, 21 July 1990.
38. Ibid. p. 26.

3. New Uses and Forms of Money, Monetary Velocity, and Wealth Transfers

Structural changes in the global economy provoke other structural changes, as is true of most evolving systems. In Chapter 1 it was argued that advances in information technology and government deregulation provoked the rapid expansion and globalization of financial markets. Because of their 'marriage' with the communications revolution, financial markets have more quickly expanded and became globalized than markets for merchandise and non-financial services. Analysts including Peter Drucker were emphasizing as early as the mid-1980s that the evolving financial markets had taken on a profit-seeking life of their own, quite independently of the markets for merchandise and services (Drucker, 1985-6). For example, by the mid-1980s the value of trading on the London Eurodollar market was 25 times the value of world trade in merchandise and services. Eurodollar deposits and trading were non-existent two decades earlier.

The expansion and globalization of finance allowed Eurocurrency, which is currency used outside its home country, to become a dominant new money form in the 1980s. Continuing advances in technology and international payment systems are now allowing even more exotic new money forms. Chapter 1 documents the rise of e-money, virtual money, and other 'quasi-moneys' that are now being swapped with more traditional 'real money' as electronic payment systems expand. The creation and use of these new money forms has allowed an explosion of financial transactions. In the US payments systems alone, the Federal Reserve estimated electronic transactions value at $544 trillion for 1995, and globally this number might be an order of magnitude higher – nobody knows for sure because of the speed with which money can recycle between accounting measurements.

Revolutionary changes require us to rethink how the system works. In Schumpeter's terms, clusters of new innovations can destroy the old ways of doing things, and create new ways – a process of 'creative destruction'. This chapter identifies two such phenomena which are not consistent with traditional economic thinking.

First, Sections I–IV demonstrate that more of the money supply is being used to accommodate the fast growth of financial markets, and proportionally less of the money supply is available for non-financial or GDP purposes. In terms of the famous quantity equation, this phenomenon shows up as a decline in the income velocity of money. Explosions of financial activity lead to increased demands for money balances for financial market participation; and less of the available money supply facilitates the production and sale of GDP. The recent absorption of money for financial market purposes, so that the money is not simultaneously available for 'real' economic activity, is not generally accepted by the economics profession, but is demonstrated in Sections I–IV.

Secondly, Section V demonstrates that new money forms, new payment systems, and the labor of financial operators in 'one-world financial markets' can create, destroy and transfer 'wealth' independently of the real economic activity that is occurring in non-financial markets. Changing perceptions and expectations of underlying wealth or 'value' in 'real' economic activity has always provoked chaotic and unpredictable repackaging of this value in financial markets, but value has none the less been thought to flow from the real economic activity. However, Section V shows that wealth can be created, destroyed, and transferred independently of what is even perceived to be happening in non-financial markets. In the author's view, as elaborated further in Chapter 5's 'A New Political Economy of Money', appropriate definitions of wealth and value include considerations of 'social consensus' and 'differential power'. The labor of financial operators, including central bankers and other monetary officials, is an important 'driver' in this process. The autonomous expansion or contraction of money and credit can have real and lasting effects in this regard.

The explanations of recent financial crises and recessions in Chapter 4 rely upon these two phenomena as well as upon conventional economic thinking. An understanding of money demand theory, monetary velocity, and economic value-creation is thus crucial for the purposes of this book.

I. TRANSACTIONS AND ASSET DEMANDS FOR MONEY, AND MONETARY VELOCITY

In the US, from 1960–80, the income velocity of money (v), measured as the ratio of nominal GDP to a narrow measure of the money supply (m1), grew predictably at 2 to 4 percent per year (Figure 3.1). (m1) includes coins, currency, and checkable demand deposits in the banking system. This predictability allowed for the use of (m1) money supply targets by central banks to guide movements in income and inflation, as specified by the 'quantity equation':

$$(m1) \times (v) = (p) \times (q) \qquad\qquad (3.1)$$

where (p) is the GDP price level, (q) is real GDP and (p x q) is nominal GDP.

Figure 3.1   Worldwide instability and weakness in the growth of the income velocity of money after 1980

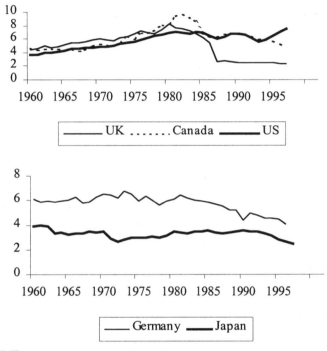

Source: IMF.

Before 1980, US monetary policy could therefore be based upon the following cause-and-effect relationships: due to the relative stability of (v), an increase in real money balances (m1/p) will increase (q) by a predictable amount; the increase in (q) occurs because the increase in (m1/p) causes interest rates to decline, which in turn stimulates borrowing and purchasing across the economy. Thus, aggregate demand for GDP rises, and producers respond to meet that demand. Because central banks can directly control (m1) but not (m1/p), they may stress the importance of interest rate targets rather than money supply targets.

The expansion of narrow money supplies (m1) is usually successful in increasing economic growth (q), because (m1) usually rises faster than inflation (p), and because nominal interest rates usually fall relative to inflation, i.e. real interest rates fall. However, if there is not much capacity in the system to expand production, or if there is not much incentive or ability to expand loans and purchases, then the expansion of (m1) may be ineffective – inflation rather than economic growth may be the result. Also, excessive inflation may hurt growth and lead to other undesirable instabilities in the system.

Typically, a successful expansion of (m1), which lowers real interest rates and stimulates borrowing and spending and economic growth, will be associated with a proportionate expansion of broader monetary aggregates, such as (m2) and (m3). In the US, (m2) equals (m1) plus retail money-market-fund balances, savings deposits, and small time deposits. (m3) equals (m2) plus large time deposits, and various institutional accounts such as repurchase agreements, Eurodollars, and institution-only money-market-fund balances. When the central bank expands (m1) and generates a borrowing and lending expansion and lower real interest rates on these narrow money accounts, then the expansion will usually 'spill over' into broad money accounts.   Growth of broad money accounts also encourages economic growth, because some of the accounts which are included in (m2) and (m3) are held for GDP-participation purposes, although they may not be so 'liquid' as (m1) accounts. The complicated relationships between (m1), (m2), and (m3), for example when they do not change together, is elaborated in Chapter 4 as part of 'Japan's Crisis, 1989–' and 'Asia's Crisis, 1997–'. For the purposes of this chapter, and its case studies, it is sufficient to frame the analysis in terms of (m1) and assume that the various monetary aggregates move together, except where indicated otherwise.

Since 1980, the (m1) income velocity of money has become quite unstable, and has declined (or broken downwards) from its historic trend in many of the money centers (Figure 3.1). In Japan's case, a significant decline began in 1993. Hence, the historic cause-and-effect linkage from (m1/p), to interest rates, to real GDP has become unpredictable, and monetary policies now seem to react haphazardly to economic conditions instead of finding a sound base in economic theory. The use of monetary aggregates which are broader than (m1) has been less than satisfactory, leading *The Wall Street Journal* to comment in 1988 with regard to the US situation:

> Money-supply growth targets have been dethroned, and Fed officials are desperately seeking a substitute. Chairman Alan Greenspan dissects the monthly employment data; Vice Chairman Manuel Johnson eyes the credit markets, Governor Wayne Angell watches gold and soybean prices. And the financial markets look on in confusion. The Fed, they fear, is adrift.[1]

And, as echoed in the economics literature:

> Including data from the 1980's sharply weakens the postwar time-series evidence indicating significant relationships between money (however defined) and nominal income or between money and either real income or prices separately. Focusing on

data from 1970 onward destroys this evidence altogether (Friedman and Kuttner, 1992, p. 472).

This section argues that the structural changes in globalizing financial markets as discussed in Chapter 1 are the root cause of the instabilities and declines in income velocity since 1980. A careful consideration of these structural changes in the context of monetary theory helps regain the relationship between narrow monetary aggregates and GDP. A more optimistic outlook for the rationalization of monetary policies is thus possible. Justifications are provided for the following two hypotheses:

1. The increased profitability and value of financial transactions compared to non-financial transactions are important missing variables in most monetary policy research. Their consideration allows for better predictions of the income velocity of money. In globalizing money centers, the money supply has been used less frequently for GDP transactions, because more of it has been used instead to accommodate the fast growth of financial markets.
2. During a dramatic financial upheaval or structural change as per the UK's Big Bang deregulation in 1986 or Germany's reunification in 1990 or Japan's financial crisis in the 1990s, income velocity also declines as the new opportunities are figured out and reacted to. Temporarily, there is not sufficient information for investors to pursue rational strategies, and the price of money-liquidity rises sharply. An increase in money demand occurs to reduce the risk of loss and in order to regain an optimal investment portfolio quickly once the information environment improves. In the author's view, this options demand for money can divert money-liquidity away from GDP and other markets during chaotic times, however it is not generally recognized in monetary theory.

Neither the economics profession nor monetary policymakers have fully considered these structural changes, as indicated by a recurring bias in macroeconomic forecasts, and the recurring use of overly restrictive monetary policies. Incorporating these structural changes into more conventional monetary theory is the objective at hand.

The quantity equation (3.1) is frequently rearranged as:

$$(m1) = (1/v) \text{ x } (p \text{ x } q) \tag{3.2}$$

Here, the equation better represents the income version of the quantity theory of money, which originally assumed that people want to hold a constant fraction $(1/v)$ of nominal GDP $(p \text{ x } q)$ in the form of money. More recent research predicts that the fraction $(1/v)$ will decrease (increase) when there is: an increase (decrease) in the interest rate (Goldfeld, 1973,1976); an increase (decrease) in real GDP (Goldfeld, 1973,1976); an increase (decrease) in the expected rate of inflation (Judd, 1983); and an increase (decrease) in the state of financial market innovations (Dotsey, 1985). The empirical evidence for these theories and others are contained in Judd and Scadding (1982), Laidler (1985), Stone and Thornton (1987), and Friedman (1988).

Historically, changes in interest rates have been found to be the most important reason why (1/v) changes. If interest rates increase, then the asset demand for money declines relative to the asset demand for high-interest-rate financial securities, money is used more efficiently to accommodate GDP transactions (as people take advantage of the high interest rates in non-money accounts), and (1/v) declines. The asset demand for money might also decline with higher inflation, because money is more quickly spent rather than held as people try to maximize purchasing power over time. Also, at higher levels of real GDP and with improved financial market innovations, there are economies in the use of money for transactions purposes, and (1/v) declines due to a proportionate decline in the transactions demand for money.

In the 1960s and 1970s, the income version of the quantity theory of money was generally preferred instead of the transactions version. The transactions version replaces nominal GDP in equation (3.2) with the value of all transactions in the economy, including not only GDP transactions, but also transactions involving second-hand and intermediate sales of merchandise and services, and transactions involving non-money financial assets. The transactions version implies that people want to hold money in proportion to all of the transactions which they make, rather than just the GDP transactions. A discussion of the quantity theory of money, and the limitations of the transactions version are contained in Friedman (1970).

The transactions version drew increased attention in the 1980s, however, because of widespread failure to predict (1/v) as it is defined in the income version. For example, between 1973 and 1980, US households and businesses were holding much less money than predicted by Goldfeld's equations, which were based upon the income version. As estimated by Porter et al. (1979), this shortfall amounted to approximately $30 billion in mid-1976 and $55 billion in early 1979. Then, after 1981, the 'case of the missing money' was replaced by the 'case of the reappearing money' as more money was held than predicted.

The unexpected rise in (1/v), i.e. decline in (v), beginning in the early 1980s, as it is defined by the income version, has been especially troublesome. For example, as per Equations 3.1 and 3.2, it meant that the 1982 US recession was not foreseen. From 1981:Q3 to 1982:Q4, the growth rate of US nominal GDP declined by 9.7 percentage points. But, forecasters missed the collapse of velocity and predicted a decline of only 3.3 percentage points (Chapter 4).

Spindt (1985) attempted to explain this collapse of velocity by identifying the uses of money directly, from data on the debits to various money accounts. However, his direct measurement of (v), when used in the quantity equation has not 'demonstrated any apparent gain over (m1) for policy purposes [of predicting nominal GDP], and is more difficult to calculate' (Batten and Thorton, 1985, p. 29).

The direct measurement of (v) has not proved to be practical because, for each type of money account, one must decide how much of the turnover is for the purchase of a final product (GDP) instead of for: check cashing or other movements of money between money accounts; non-final product purchasing, including raw materials purchases, wholesale purchases by a retailer, second-hand sales; and the purchasing of non-money financial assets. However, the alternatives to direct measurement are also not practical because, in Spindt's words, they are not 'equipped to deal with a changing payments mechanism or menu of financial assets'.

II. FINANCIAL GLOBALIZATION AND MONETARY VELOCITY

The author's research (Allen, 1989) indicates that the structural changes in financial markets discussed in Chapter 1 – advances in information technology, deregulation, and internationalization – are of crucial importance in understanding the recent decline and increased variability of the income velocity of money.

1. Advances in information technology: technological advances continue to reduce the costs of transferring money and paper documentation and therefore the costs of financial transactions. In this regard important advances have been made in electronic and regular mail service, telephones, computers, modems and fax machines, image processing devices, communication satellites, fiber optics, automatic transfer machines (ATMs), electronic points of sale, telephone banking, interactive screen communications between financial intermediaries and their wholesale and retail customers, debit and credit and smart cards, electronic money and transfer systems, the World Wide Web, etc.

2. Deregulation: policymakers have removed ceilings on interest rates, reduced taxes and brokerage commissions on financial transactions, given foreign financial firms greater access to the home financial markets, allowed increased privatization and securitization of assets, and allowed increased competition between banks, securities firms, insurance firms and other financial institutions. These deregulations and many others have increased the profitability of domestic finance and blurred

the differences between money and non-money financial assets. For example, the US created negotiable order of withdrawal (NOW) accounts after 1981, which allowed interest to be earned on checkable, (m1) accounts for the first time. NOW accounts thus accumulated funds that would otherwise be put into non-money financial assets such as money market funds (MMF).

3. Internationalization: advances in information technology and government deregulation have in turn allowed funds to move more freely and profitably between international and national markets. As documented in Chapter 1, virtually every type of international financial asset has experienced a dramatic increase in trading since the early 1980s. Financial globalization is supported by increased globalization of all economic activity.

In the new global economy these structural changes allowed financial transactions to become comparatively more profitable than merchandise and services transactions. Consequently, the demand for money for financial market participation increased. Deregulation as per new interest-earning NOW accounts increased the asset demand for money, as did new opportunities to shop globally for the best money-asset accounts. Improved technologies and new international opportunities increased the transactions demand for money for financial market participation – opportunities for financial speculation, hedging, and arbitrage were created as never before.

Transactions costs associated with financial market participation were lower and new opportunities for favorable interest rates and portfolio-composition were created. A threshold was reached whereby increasingly significant amounts of labor and capital services were devoted to the transfer of money and documentation. Financial market activity expanded rapidly.

Most researchers have not found defensible relationships between the expanded trading volumes of finance and the income velocity of money. Wenninger and Radecki (1986) made a noteworthy early attempt, but their approach is subject to several limitations.

They treat (m1) or (m1/p) as the variables to be predicted with a one-equation econometric model when financial market volumes are included as alternate independent variables, rather than (v) or (1/v) as the variables to be predicted. (m1) and to some extent (m1/p) have been controlled as important target variables by the central bank, and thus Wenninger and Radecki have the simultaneity problem of trying to explain money supply and money demand with the same variables. Alternatively, (v) has not been significantly controlled by the central bank, and (v) can be predicted with the one-equation approach without a significant simultaneity problem.

Changes in (v) are more directly related to changes in money demand than to changes in money supply, and it is changes in (v) and money demand which forecasters have failed to predict since 1980, not changes in money supply. Wenninger and Radecki's simultaneity problem limits their ability to contribute to previous research in this regard. For example, they conclude that when GDP and financial market volumes 'are included together in the... equation at most one performs well' because both 'are alternative proxies for total transactions in the economy... and one of the two is redundant'. However, GDP and financial market volumes might not be redundant in an equation which explains (v); if, for instance financial market volumes are a more important demand variable and GDP is a more important supply variable, i.e. central bank monetary policy reacts more to GDP trends than financial market trends. These problems should be considered more explicitly before they conclude that 'the more rapid growth of financial transactions is not having a very large effect on (m1) growth'.

And, they use data only through 1985, just when financial markets began expanding the most dramatically, and began reaching a high profitability relative to the non-financial markets. It was the last few years of their data set, especially 1985 itself in which 'it seems that financial transactions played a major role, adding roughly two percentage points to (m1) growth'. However, they dismiss the volume of financial transactions as a variable which is likely to be significant, even in the mid-1980s, because the 'rapid growth of financial transactions over the longer run (1959–1985) has not been associated with an acceleration of (m1) growth. For financial transactions to explain the rapid growth of (m1) in 1985, it would be necessary to find reasons why the historical relationship between financial transactions and (m1) might have changed'. In the author's view, the missed historical changes are advances in information-processing technology, deregulation, and internationalization.

Perhaps Milton Friedman (1988) provides the most noteworthy attempt to relate the expansion of financial markets to the income velocity of money. He puts forth the first direct 'econometric attempt to relate the level of stock prices to the demand for money' and also considers the estimates of financial and non-financial transactions debits compiled by Spindt (1985).

Friedman rationalizes an inverse relationship between stock prices and monetary velocity (or direct relation between stock prices and the level of real cash balances per unit of income) in three different ways:

(1) A rise in stock prices means an increase in nominal wealth and generally, given the wider fluctuation in stock prices than in income, also in the ratio of wealth to income. The higher wealth to income ratio can be expected to be reflected in a higher money to income ratio or a lower velocity. (2) A rise in stock prices reflects an increase in the expected return from risky assets relative to safe assets. Such a change in relative valuation need not be accompanied by a lower degree of risk aversion or a greater risk preference. The resulting increase in risk could be offset by increasing the weight of relatively safe assets in an aggregate portfolio, for example, by reducing the weight of long-term bonds and increasing the weight of short-term fixed-income securities plus money. (3) A rise in stock prices may be

taken to imply a rise in the dollar volume of financial transactions, increasing the quantity of money demanded to facilitate transactions (Friedman, 1988).

Offsetting the inverse effect of items (1–3) is the positive effect of what Friedman describes as a (4) substitution effect: 'the higher the real stock price, the more attractive are equities as a component of the portfolio'. Using quarterly data from 1961 to 1986, he concludes that items (1–3), especially the wealth effect, 'appears stronger than the substitution effect...(however) annual data for a century suggest that the apparent dominance of the wealth effect is the exception, not the rule'.

Friedman's use of Spindt's data leads him to conclude that 'the volume of [both financial and non-financial] transactions has an appreciable effect on (m1) velocity but not on (m2) velocity'.[2] In his (m1) velocity equations, he is unable to conclude whether it is non-financial transactions debits or financial transactions debits, as a ratio to GDP, which is the more significant variable. These results do not allow him to accept the hypothesis that financial transactions 'would "absorb" money, hence reducing income velocity'. Instead, Friedman seems to side with 'the received view (of Wenninger and Radecki and others) that financial transactions are so highly money-efficient that they do not absorb any appreciable quantity of media of exchange and have little if any effect on velocity'.

In other words, current literature still sides with the income version of the quantity theory of money rather than the transactions version. People are believed to hold money in proportion to the level of GDP rather than in proportion to all of the transactions which they make. However, as argued below, there is now strong evidence from case studies of the US, the UK, Germany and others that just the opposite is true.

III. THE DECLINE OF (m1) INCOME VELOCITY IN THE US

The decline from trend, and increased variability of US (m1) income velocity occurred at the end of 1981. As documented by Stone and Thorton (1987), replacing nominal GDP in the income velocity formula with any other measure of non-financial transactions does not significantly change the basic rise and fall of the velocity chart; other measures include gross domestic final demand, Spindt's broad measure of non-financial transactions debits, and permanent income. Also, replacing (m1) with most other measures of money is concluded to make very little difference with regard to this decline of velocity, including the Fed's (m2), (msi), and Spindt's (mq).

However, replacing nominal GDP in the income velocity formula with various measures of the volume of financial transactions, such as Spindt's financial transaction debits, produces a 'financial transactions monetary velocity' which does not decline in the 1980s. The annual growth rate of Spindt's financial transactions debits velocity averaged about 10 percent over the 1980s, compared to 12 percent from 1970 to 1981. From the late 1970s to the late 1980s, this financial market velocity ratio increased at a remarkably regular rate of about 20 points each year. Money was thus used more efficiently in the 1980s to accommodate financial transactions, but this increase in efficiency was fairly steady and predictable.

In the author's view, the growth in the volume of financial transactions beginning in the early 1980s was faster than the increase in the efficiency with which money was used to accommodate these transactions. These transactions thus absorbed money taken away from other markets. When data is considered that shows a rapid, geometric growth beginning in the early 1980s in the total volume of those types of financial transactions which are especially likely to absorb money away from other uses (Figure 3.2), then the following hypotheses become obvious: the rapid expansion of US financial transactions beginning in the early 1980s may be a dominant, exogenous factor which caused the simultaneous break in the US income velocity of money. Furthermore, because technological change, deregulation, and internationalization are the root causes of the increased profitability and rapid expansion of US financial transactions, this hypothesis implies that they would be the root cause of the break in the US income velocity of money.

Several types of financial transaction included in Spindt's aggregate cannot be expected to make money unavailable for alternate uses for a significant period of time; some not even as the debit itself is entered. These include, especially, the movement of funds between money accounts, such as check cashing, and the movement of funds between money and near-money accounts, such as when certificates of deposit are redeemed. The types of financial transaction which are more likely to absorb money are purchases and sales of stocks, bonds, government securities and other longer-term investments, such as when five working days were required before securities sales could be cashed.

In June 1995 the US Securities and Exchange Commission shortened the settlement time for corporate and municipal securities from five to three days, and in February 1996 the securities industry converted to a 'same-day funds settlement system'. Therefore, money-absorption in these markets was reduced, which can be seen in Figures 3.1 and 3.2 as an increase in US (m1) velocity after 1995.

International transactions may especially tie up funds in financial markets, at least until international transfers move as efficiently as national transfers, and until the same margin-holding requirements and quick settlements are applied. In most countries outside the US, funds-settlement is rarely faster than five days. Furthermore, chaotic financial globalization ties up funds in financial accounts due to an increase in the options demand for money-liquidity. The chaos prevents investors from pursuing rational strategies, and the demand for flexible and secure money-liquidity rises sharply. An increase in money demand occurs to reduce the risk of loss and in order to regain an optimal investment portfolio quickly once the information environment improves.

Figure 3.2 Expanding volumes of money-absorbing financial transactions*
in the US ($trillion/year), and the US (m1) income velocity of
money, 1975–1997

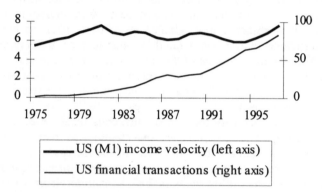

—— US (M1) income velocity (left axis)
—— US financial transactions (right axis)

* Money-absorbing financial transactions (NEWFMK in the Appendix) is the combined value of stock, bond, and government securities transactions.
Sources: US Department of Commerce, Federal Reserve Bank.

Stone and Thorton (1987) recognize that 'the financial transactions velocity measure does not show the downturn in the 1980s that characterizes the non-financial and GDP-based velocity measures'. However, they incorrectly state that the financial transactions velocity measure does not 'show substantial increases during the 1980s which would be required if the rise in financial transactions is to account for the decline in (m1) velocity' – an incorrect statement because regardless of the quantity of money which people use to facilitate a given volume of financial transactions (and how fast that quantity is changing), and regardless of how much of that money is at the same time unavailable for GDP transactions, the total volume of financial transactions could expand sufficiently to absorb money away from GDP markets, thus reducing income velocity. In fact, the ratio of Spindt's financial transactions debits to non-financial transactions debits increased from 7/1 in early 1982 to 16/1 in early 1987, suggesting that financial transactions could have absorbed enough money to significantly reduce income velocity over this period.

If the money-absorption hypothesis is rejected, how do people explain the relation between US financial market activity, GDP, (m1), interest rates and velocity over this important period? The explosion in US stock market activity and capital transactions which began in the early 1980s and accelerated in subsequent years, shown in Figure 3.2, is widely believed to be a result of declining interest rates, and an economy coming out of recession. The received scenario proceeds as follows: the reduction in real money balances of 6 percent in 1981 raised interest rates by approximately 2 percent; the high interest rates caused the growth rate of nominal GDP to decline by 9.7 percentage points from 1981:Q3 to 1982:Q4, and a majority of this decline was a decline in the inflation component; the 15 percent drop in world crude oil prices in early 1983 further broke the expectations-fed inflationary spiral; by the mid-1980s the disinflationary trend allowed expansionary monetary policy, which began in late 1982, to bring interest rates down to their levels of the early 1970s; and the expectations of and eventual realization of low interest rates, low inflation, and strong economic recovery all fueled a boom in stock and bond markets. The lower interest rates, lower inflation, and higher real GDP are seen as the cause of the decline in income velocity.

This common view, that US interest rates were determined largely by US monetary policy in this period, and that interest rates were a dominant, exogenous factor in the expansion of non-financial and financial markets, largely ignores technological change, deregulation, and internationalization. The author believes that low interest rates and a non-inflationary expansion of GDP in the US would not have been possible by the mid-1980s without these structural changes. The US savings rate began declining in 1981 until it hit a post-World War II low of 3.7 percent in 1985, and without the benefit of the new, more efficient international financial markets the US would have had a woefully inadequate $60 billion of domestic savings in 1985 after financing the $200 billion federal budget deficit to keep nominal GDP running at an annual rate of $4 trillion. As elaborated in Chapters 1 and 2, it was technological change, deregulation, and internationalization which encouraged a net capital inflow into the US of close to $100 billion per year by 1985 compared to a net capital outflow of $6 billion in 1981. The new profit-seeking US capital inflow in the mid-1980s in turn allowed for the continuing expansion of financial markets, low US interest rates and the longest post-World War II expansion of US GDP.

The author's analysis of the pre-1982 and (1982–) causality between US financial market expansion (NEWFMK), interest rates (r), income velocity (v), and other groups of variables (t,w,x,y,z), is represented by the following equations. Before 1982 financial market expansion is seen as a domestic variable which is more dependent on other domestic macro-economic variables; after 1982 – as financial globalization proceeds – it is a more exogenous, internationalized driver of domestic macro-economic variables such as interest rates and income velocity:

Pre-1982: $(r) = f_1(t)$ (3.3)

$$(NEWFMK) = f_2(w) \qquad (3.4)$$
$$(v) = f_3(r,x) \qquad (3.5)$$

(1982–):

$$(NEWFMK) = f_4(\text{tech. change,}$$
$$\text{deregulation, internationalization}) \qquad (3.6)$$
$$(r) = f_5(NEWFMK, y) \qquad (3.7)$$
$$(v) = f_6(NEWFMK, r, z) \qquad (3.8)$$

Technological change, deregulation, and internationalization in the author's view are thus the root cause of much of: (A) the rapid expansion of financial markets beginning in the early 1980s and the massive new capital flow into the US; (B) the subsequent rapid decline in US interest rates; and therefore (C) the sustained expansion of US GDP beginning in 1983. Each of (A)–(C) increases money demand, *ceteris paribus*. (A) and (C) increase the transactions demand for money, and (A) and (B) increase the asset demand for money. (A) and (B) decrease the income velocity of money; the effect of (C) upon income velocity is less certain, although some economies of scale in the use of money when GDP increases might cause it to increase velocity.

The first consequence of technological change, deregulation, and internationalization is the expansion of financial markets, and it is largely the expansion of financial markets from which the author believes that the other changes flow. Yet research, and notably the recent work of Friedman (1988), has not conclusively identified a linkage between financial market expansion and income velocity. The author believes that the econometric work of Friedman and others falls short on this score, firstly because of a failure to identify the exact time at which the structural changes began to have their strong impact; and, secondly, because recent changes within a very dynamic, evolving marketplace cannot be predicted when too much historical data is allowed to obscure the recent changes.

Friedman tests for a structural shift in his (m1) velocity equation, by running the same regressions over two sub-periods: (1970:Q1–1979:Q4) and (1980:Q1–1986:Q2). He chooses 1980:Q1 to begin the second sub-period because of 'the shift from accelerating inflation to disinflation', and 'because it so happens that total transactions accelerated sharply after 1980'.

In contrast to Friedman, the author hypothesizes that the second sub-period should begin in 1982:Q1, when the money-absorbing financial transactions accelerated and when the US began receiving the massive net inflow of foreign investment. The initial, rapid expansion of Spindt's financial transactions debits variable in 1980, as used by Friedman to date the structural shift, was due to the early deregulation-reshuffling of money between money and near-money accounts. These transactions are less likely to contemporaneously absorb money away from other uses compared to stock, bond, and government securities trading, especially when international trading is involved.

The author has used linear regression analysis to estimate Equations (3.3–3.8) for the US, and key results appear in the Appendix to this chapter.[3]

The author's regression analysis of the pre-1982 period corroborates the research of Friedman (1988) and others who, because of the date or methodology of their research, have not let the (1982–) period add significant 'noise' to their equations (3.3–3.5). Yet to the author's knowledge, no one else has estimated equations (3.6–3.8) specifically for the (1982–) period. Because (f_4), in the opinion of the author, is unquantifiable, he has taken (NEWFMK) as given, where (NEWFMK) is the combined volumes of US stock, bond, and government securities transactions. The US government 3-month T-bill yield is used for (r), and (v) is the (m1) income velocity of money.

As shown in the Appendix, regressions over the period (1982:Q1–1998:Q2) highlight the strong negative relationship that has existed between financial market expansion and both interest rates and (m1) income velocity since the beginning of 1982. (Equations A, B). These regressions thus confirm the causality of Equations (3.6–3.8) above whereby financial markets absorb money away from GDP markets. Indeed, a majority (approximately 80 percent as measured by the R^2 statistic) of the fluctuations in interest rates and income velocity (the dependent variables) can be explained simply by the fluctuations in financial market transactions (the independent variable) in a simple linear equation. In this simple equation, a 0-1 dummy variable was included (D96Q1) to account for the reduced absorption of money by financial market transactions beginning in early 1996 when, instead of a three-day settlement period for transaction funds to be released, the Securities and Exchange Commission (SEC) allowed a same-day settlement period. The regression results, as well as Figure 3.2, show a sudden increase in income velocity since 1995 due to this deregulation. Actually, the SEC moved from five-day settlement to three-day settlement in 1995, but the author's research indicates that the move from three-day to same-day was more significant for the (m1) income velocity.

When the pre-1982 and (1982–) periods are combined, then econometric equations are unable to explain changes in velocity. The author concludes that if the periods prior to and following the initial strong impact of technological change, deregulation, and internationalization upon financial market expansion are combined, then their impact upon interest rates and income velocity cannot be properly identified. Friedman's failure to identify a strong negative relationship between financial transactions and velocity can thus be attributed to his use of the period (1980:Q1–1986:Q2), which includes two years before the rapid expansion of money-absorbing financial transactions. The Appendix shows that two financial market expansion variables, NEWFMK and NYSE (New York Stock Exchange Composite Index)[4], have a statistically indefensible coefficient (as measured by the t-statistic) over Friedman's period when, as per Equation 3.5 and Friedman's equations, the interest rate is also included (Equations C,D).

The Appendix shows additional income velocity equations over the periods (1982:Q1–1995:Q3), which was a period stopping right before the SEC went from five-day to three-day and then same-day funds settlement, and (1982:Q1–1998:Q2), which includes the most recent data available. For the (1982:Q1–1995:Q3) period, when real GDP (q) is included in addition to the financial transactions variable, then a positive coefficient is estimated for real GDP (Equation F). The positive coefficient indicates that there are economies in the use of money for transaction purposes at higher levels of real GDP, *ceteris paribus*, as suggested by the literature. The author also considered the inflation rate as an additional explanatory variable in his income velocity equations. Inflation (INF) is measured by the GDP deflator, and the results of Equation F confirm that, when inflation rises, money is more quickly spent rather than held as people try to maximize purchasing power over time. The interest rate (r), as measured by the three-month Treasury bill rate, is also included in Equation F, and the results confirm that people do hold less money (velocity increases) when they are able to take advantage of increased interest rates on non-money interest-earning accounts. Of course, as documented by Equation A, most of the changes in interest rates over this period can be explained by the financial transactions variable, and including both terms as independent variables is somewhat redundant and biases the results – Equation G excludes the interest rate and is thus theoretically the best equation.

Equation H in the Appendix extends the regression period to 1998:Q2 and thus covers the recent SEC funds-settlement changes – once again the 0–1 dummy variable is included to capture the funds-settlement change. The estimated dummy variable coefficient indicates that with more efficient quick settlement the rate at which financial transactions absorb money has decreased. However, as this book is written it is too soon yet to quantify exactly how the settlement-deregulation will change the coefficients over the long run.

Regarding Friedman's (1988) suggestion of an inverse relation between income velocity and financial market expansion three-quarters earlier (the wealth effect), and a positive relation between velocity and contemporaneous financial market expansion, no such effects were found over the period (1982:Q1–1998:Q2). Lagging the financial market expansion variable reduces its level of significance in proportion to the length of the lag, and the negative coefficients are maintained.

The results shown in the Appendix thus allow the following conclusions: (1) the demand for money for financial market transactions has become an important source of money demand which absorbs money away from other uses; (2) the expansion of financial markets in the context of other variables caused the decline and increased variability in US income velocity since the end of 1981; (3) because improved technology, deregulation, and internationalization are the root causes of the expansion of financial markets, they are also the root causes of the decline and increased variability in income velocity. Aside from the author's publication (Allen, 1989) as updated in this book, these results (1)–(3) cannot be found in the economics literature.

IV. THE DECLINE OF (m1) INCOME VELOCITY IN THE UK AND GERMANY

The UK and Germany experienced recent declines and increased variability in (m1) income velocity, and for the same structural reasons as the US. Although a thorough econometric analysis for these two countries and others is beyond the scope of this book, the correlations between (m1) velocity, deregulation, internationalization, and financial market activity seem obvious enough that the reader will hopefully tolerate the author's conclusions. However, the author encourages others more familiar with the unique financial history of these and other countries to pursue a thorough econometric analysis of velocity as per his US equations. French and Italian financial deregulation and internationalization did not occur as suddenly and as forcefully as in the other G7 countries, and the author would especially rely on other researchers to test his US equations for these countries. The drop in Canadian (m1) velocity paralleled the US drop, and is especially correlated with the major Canadian financial deregulations and increased financial turnover in 1986 (Figure 3.1). The decline in (m1) velocity in Japan in the early 1990s is elaborated in the 'Policy Implications' section of this chapter and as part of 'Japan's Crisis, 1989–' in Chapter 5.

A. The UK Case

Figure 3.1 shows a decline in UK (m1) velocity beginning after 1980 and then a big drop after 1986. The collapse after 1986 is partly due to the inclusion of building society money deposits as part of the narrow money supply beginning in 1987. Beginning January 1987, as defined by the Building Societies Act of 1986, the International Monetary Fund began including these deposits in its series 34 definition of (m1) that the author uses for the purposes of this chapter. Given that building society deposits increasingly served the purpose of narrow money, the author would rely on others to figure them precisely into monetary aggregates. The UK's money definitions, unlike the IMF's, do not include the private and official sector's foreign currency deposits, and thus have this limitation – foreign currency deposits became especially important to the UK economy after 1986.

Whichever reasonable definitions are used for money in the UK, a decline in income velocity does occur contemporaneously with deregulation, internationalization and increased financial market activity. In October 1979 the UK removed all inward and outward barriers to capital flows. Consequently, Britain experienced an annual portfolio investment outflow for the 1980–83 period that was 1800 times higher than in the 1975–78 period (Taylor and Tonks, 1989), and the initial break in velocity did occur in 1980.

The even more significant deregulation, internationalization and increased financial market activity within Britain was the 26 October 1986 'Big Bang' which scrapped 85 years of fixed commissions for brokers as well as separation of powers between brokers. And, as stated by John M. Hennessy, chairman of Crédit Suisse First Boston Ltd., a leading international investment bank based in London, 'Big Bang is an attempt to generate a few global competitors among the British institutions'.[5] Competition increased immediately. Forty-nine firms, including American, European and Far Eastern financial giants had signed up before October 26 to market British stocks and government bonds; only 19 companies had been doing this trading previously.[6] After October 26, commissions charged by financial intermediaries dropped as much as 50 percent.

Figure 3.3 shows how the turnover of financial transactions in the UK, due to this new profitability and internationalization, increased after 1980 and then exploded upward during the Big Bang period. The turnover variable, which aggregates government securities, other fixed-interest securities, and equities, does mirror the (possibly exaggerated due to the building society issue) decline in (m1) velocity. The leveling off of financial turnover and (m1) velocity since 1987 in the UK suggests that the impacts of deregulation and internationalization had been mostly realized a year after Big Bang.

The author's hypothesis, that the new financial markets absorbed money taken away from non-financial markets and caused a collapse in (m1) velocity, thus appears to be confirmed for the UK. In addition to the direct absorption of (m1) as financial transactions turn over, the author would suggest that a related form of absorption occurred in the UK case due to uncertainty or of information failure experienced by holders of money, that is, during a dramatic upheaval or structural change as per Big Bang, financial portfolios must be reallocated dramatically as the new opportunities are figured out and reacted to. For a time, there is not sufficient information for investors to pursue rational strategies, and the price of money-liquidity rises sharply. An increase in money demand occurs to reduce the risk of loss and in order to regain an optimal portfolio quickly once the information environment improves.

In the author's view, this 'options demand' for money can divert money-liquidity away from GDP and other markets during chaotic times, but it is not generally recognized by the economics profession.   However, many securities market professionals swear by it. For example, Joseph Grundfest, former commissioner of the US Securities and Exchange Commission, explains the 1987 stock market crash as follows:

> Simply put, I suggest that a large component of recent market volatility is the rational result of an 'information failure' in the market for liquidity rather than the consequence of rapid and irrational changes in the market's assessment of the value of securities...The lack of information about either fundamental business prospects or about the magnitude and composition of an atypically large demand for immediate trading can be sufficient to induce substantial market volatility...[A] sharp increase in the price of liquidity is reflected in a simultaneous widening of spreads and in a general price decline in the equities and futures market alike...Once sufficient information comes to the market describing expected short-term trading flows, and once the returns to providing liquidity become high enough, the peak-load nature of the demand subsides, the risk involved in trading is reduced, the price of liquidity declines, spreads narrow, and equity prices recover a large portion of their losses (Grundfest, 1991, p. 67–8).

Figure 3.3   The relation between financial market growth (£ million) and (m1) velocity in the UK during the Big Bang deregulation period

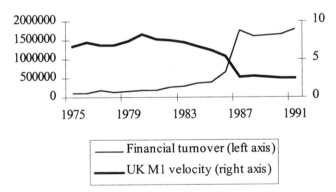

Sources: IMF, Bank of England.

The economics profession has trouble with this options demand for money because it is not very separable from other sources of money demand, because it is not measurable, and because it stands in opposition to the popular 'efficient market hypothesis' (EMS). The EMS, like most economic theory, assumes away the likelihood of significant information failure or indeed the likelihood of significant transactions costs of any kind.

Yet given 'the lack of information about either fundamental business prospects or about the magnitude and composition of an atypically large demand for immediate trading' during Big Bang, Grundfest's scenario might explain the behavior of the UK financial markets during the 1986–88 world stock market crash period.   The drop in velocity of certain monetary aggregates during this period, the rise in UK short-term interest rates by 1 percentage point shortly before the crash as money-liquidity demand was not accommodated by an increase in money supply, the subsequent crash, and the subsequent recovery and ultimate stability of financial markets as the money supply was increased – all fit into Grundfest's scenario.

As elaborated in Chapter 4, similar scenarios in the other G7 countries during 1986–88, especially the US, might well account for the worldwide nature of the 1987 crash.   Yet it was the UK Big Bang which provided the most obvious, sharpest money-liquidity demand due to information failure shortly before the 1987 crash.   Therefore the UK financial markets may have been the most culpable.

B. The German Case

Figure 3.1 shows how Germany's (m1) velocity began declining from its historic trend after 1981.   This break coincided with the major German liberalization of exchange controls in March 1981, and the one-year 1989–90 collapse corresponded with German reunification and the revolutions in Eastern Europe.   Germany's case study thus also seems to support the author's thesis that deregulation, internationalization and increased financial activity have driven declines in income velocity.

Figure 3.4 shows the inverse relationship between German financial activity as measured by stock market turnover versus income velocity over the chaotic 1989–90 period.   The 1989 revolutions in Eastern Europe and the full German monetary reunification on 1 July 1990 both resulted in information failure and confusion about fundamental business prospects.   An atypically larger demand for financial asset trading occurred as the new opportunities were figured out and reacted to, and this demand subsided in 1991 as the information environment improved.   Initially, money demand increased in order to reduce the risk of loss and in order to regain an optimal portfolio quickly once the information environment improved.   Therefore, income velocity collapsed before reversing its fall in 1991.

The increased German money demand and collapse in velocity from 1989 to 1990 were not accommodated by the Bundesbank with an expanded money supply, therefore a money-liquidity shortage occurred and interest rates rose rapidly.   The German money market rate rose from 4.0 percent in 1988 to 8.8 percent in 1991 whereas the government bond yield climbed from 6.1 to 8.6 percent – indicating a liquidity crisis especially in the more money-related side of the financial markets.

These high German interest rates in the context of the European Exchange Rate Mechanism (ERM) required overly restrictive monetary policies throughout Europe to stabilize exchange rates, which in turn led to the recessionary 1990s and the problems within the ERM. Germany's European partners could not tolerate such restrictive monetary policies for more than two years, and after 1991 most of them chose to lower interest rates and restore economic growth at the expense of ERM. The recessionary 1990– period is elaborated in Chapter 4.

Figure 3.4   The relation between financial market growth (marks billion) and (m1) velocity in Germany during the chaotic 1989–90 period

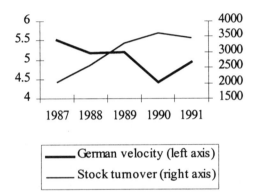

Sources: IMF, Bundesbank.

V.   THE RECENT HISTORY OF MONEY AND WEALTH

Back in the European Renaissance, gold, silver, and other precious metals were 'real money,' whereas paper IOUs, gold certificates, etc., that could be converted into precious metals, were 'quasi-moneys'. The bankers who were issuing these new quasi-money forms were often goldsmiths, because they had the best strongboxes.   Quasi-moneys were issued well beyond the amount that could be converted into precious metals all at once, and the money supply expanded.   The system of money creation could survive as long as the goldsmiths did not underestimate how much quasi-money their customers would want to convert into precious metals 'on the spot'. Goldsmiths took in gold and loaned it out, in paper form, for profit at what was eventually called the rate of interest.   The goldsmith-banker profited when his cost of taking in gold was low enough compared to the interest earned when he loaned it out.   The borrower also profited when the borrowed money was used in a venture that justified the interest expense.

The modern banking system advanced the 'money pyramid' further. When paper money was no longer quasi-money, but instead became accepted as real money, then it could be used as the 'monetary base' or 'high-powered money' for further money and credit creation. Regulators limited this process. A typical bank reserve requirement of ten to one, for example, meant that banks were allowed to create quasi-money-on-demand accounts up to ten times the value of what real money they actually held in reserve. Government agencies, i.e. the taxpayers, increasingly insured these demand-deposit-accounts, thus giving quasi-money a real money quality. For example, in the US savings and loan crisis of the 1980s, many thrift institutions attempted to profit on the creation and turnover of quasi-money by investing it in commercial real estate and other risky ventures, but many of these ventures failed. Consequently, as the lender of last resort, the US taxpayer funded approximately $130 billion to resolve the thrift crisis. Much of the quasi-money that could not be converted into real money on the spot by the thrifts, was instead, eventually, swapped for the real money of the taxpayer. In this case, growth in the US money supply was maintained.

In the 1990s, the money pyramid expanded even further. As documented in Chapter 1, electronic funds transfer (EFT) systems and other cybernetic advances expanded financial transactions faster than ever before. The measured value of financial transactions is now mostly in the form of electronic debits and credits. Electronic money credits can be converted to traditional currency, but most of these credits are never converted – they remain in the system to accommodate never-ending financial transactions and reconciliations between financial institutions.

Today's money: the synthesis. [Bank] reserves perch atop the money pyramid. Conventional money (the measured m's) is next [as the pyramid widens]. The e-transfers, or EFT as earlier known, follow. One level below is the newest kind of e-money: the smart card and computer cybermoney forms slowly taking shape. Free money, by definition without specific formal backing, and e-barter collect at the base of the pyramid.... As you get further away from the reserve base and the money that passes through banks, it becomes harder to track 'money'. This is especially true with bundling a lot of different corporate information or settlement in some kind of commodity account (e.g., oil or futures). The value of an aggregate-flows gross becomes supported by a dwindling reserve and money base relative to the expanded electronic blob as a whole (Solomon, 1997, p. 91, 95).

Given these developments, it is becoming difficult to separate the money stock (m) from its rate of use or velocity (v) as it recycles quickly through the system. 'The expanded electronic blob' of money transactions, or (m x v), remains measurable as an aggregate, but on electronic networks the two components coalesce. Thus, increasingly we do not really know what the underlying money stock is, and therefore how much money is being created.

Global money and monetary-processes are further complicated by the role of the dollar (and to lesser extent the yen, mark, euro, etc.) as the world reserve currency or 'high-powered money'. Just as quasi-money supplies can be created and destroyed on the basis of real money supplies within a national economy, 'soft-currency' supplies can be created and destroyed on the basis of their convertibility into the US dollar and other 'hard-currencies' in the world economy.

For example, the Mexican peso and the Thai baht functioned as quasi-moneys or soft-currencies during the recent financial crises in those two countries. Initially, increased dollar supplies in those two countries, often borrowed from abroad, or earned through trade, were used as the reserve currency upon which new peso and baht loans were issued. But, many new loans and money accounts were not used profitably. For example, too much commercial real estate was built with borrowed money, and it could not be rented or sold profitably.

People could not pay back their loans to the banks, and the banks had to 'write off' various accounts. The money supply held by the banks therefore declined, and they had less ability and incentive to continue creating money through lending procedures. The situation deteriorated until banks could not honor their own financial commitments. The Mexican and Thai governments themselves were 'banks' which had borrowed dollars and other hard currencies, and both governments lost the ability to honor their hard-currency debt. There was a general loss of confidence in the financial system. Many who could, transferred their local soft-currency into dollars and moved the dollars into safe-havens outside the country. But, just as gold notes may not fully convert into gold during a crisis, or bank deposit accounts may not fully convert into bank reserves, excessively-created quasi-money supplies of pesos and bahts did not fully convert into dollars.

A sudden currency devaluation (failure to fully convert) relative to the dollar, and a sudden drop in the monetary base in Mexico and Thailand were important components of their crises. International holders of pesos and bahts 'ran' on those currencies just as deposit holders typically run on a bank during a national financial crisis. National holders also ran on these currencies, demanding dollars, because the dollar was available domestically. Also, the most attractive thing to do with the limited supplies of dollars that could be obtained with the devaluing domestic currency was often to put the dollars in safe-haven accounts outside the crisis-ridden domestic economy.

More recently, at the end of August 1998, a run on rubles occurred in Russia as domestic and international holders of rubles rushed to convert them to dollars and then move the dollars out of the country. Perhaps $40 billion in dollars were then held domestically by Russians. Before the run, approximately $20 billion in rubles was held; at the end of the run in September the ruble had lost most of its exchange value and what rubles remained were worth less than $5 billion measured at international exchange rates. The Russian central bank canceled ruble–dollar trading on the Moscow Interbank Currency Exchange on August 27, and Russians lined up at their banks trying unsuccessfully to get all of their money out. Many bank accounts were frozen until November, and it was not clear how much money remained in the system. Since the beginning of July, the Russian central bank had sold $8.8 billion in dollars from its reserves, buying rubles, in order to support the exchange value of the ruble, but to no avail. Foreign dollar loans to Russia from the International Monetary Fund and other institutions were used in this process, but unsuccessfully. New supplies of dollars were often appropriated by the very fortunate or politically-connected parties who were thus allowed to convert their rubles into private dollar holdings.

Rubles are the quasi-money and dollars are the real money in Russia, despite long-standing attempts by authorities to implement just the reverse. When the run occurred, the dollar value of the quasi-money-rubles held by Russians dropped by more than 75 percent. The decline in ruble-wealth was much larger than the wealth that could be converted into dollars. Russians experienced a sudden decline in wealth – a decline in the dollar-based ability to purchase things, including their own products. More wages went unpaid, less work was done, money and goods were hoarded, incentives and means to coordinate economic activity deteriorated, and recessionary conditions worsened.

Mexico, Thailand, Russia and others suffered not only from a severe contraction of quasi-money supply, but the rush to convert local monetary wealth into dollars also involved a capital flight of wealth out of the country in order to best establish interest-earning dollar accounts. The US and other hard-currency countries thus gained monetary wealth at the expense of less-developed countries and other quasi-money users. Safe havens are also wealth havens. As discussed in Chapter 4, in the initial months, the 'Asian Financial Crisis, 1997–' was a net benefit to the US economy because of the monetary wealth transfer from Asia to the US.

In this section, case studies of the Great Depression, offshore financial markets, and monetary-wealth creation document this history of money and monetary wealth further.

A. The Role of Money in The Great Depression

The money supply times its velocity of use, (m x v), was called *effective money* by Gottfried Haberler in his 1937 book, *Prosperity and Depression*. Effective money can also be thought of as money liquidity or money flow, and it is somewhat like the total flow of water out of faucets under pressure. In the analogy, monetary velocity (v) represents water pressure – the greater the water pressure, the greater the water flow; the greater the monetary velocity, the greater the money flow. In other words, spendable money credits (m x v) is analogous to usable water, and it depends not only on some measure of the money supply (m = 'ground water'), but also on how fast it can be recycled under pressure through the system. If bank failures occur, and bad debts and other accounts are written off, then in the analogy there would be 'contamination' of the effective money supply, i.e. we would have to admit that there is less usable money in the system. Bad-loan problems tend to spread through the system like bacteria spreads through a water system, because some accounts are used to back up the credibility of other accounts. Therefore, when a crisis hits, authorities quickly try to find a lender of last resort to replace (or 'sterilize') bad money with good money. Otherwise, a process of bad-money 'contagion' can spread through the system and threaten the integrity of the money pyramid.

During the Great Depression in the US, from 1929 to the worst year, 1933, annual real gross domestic product (q) contracted 30.5 percent from \$203.6 to \$141.5 (numbers in billions of 1958-equivalent dollars), the money stock (m) contracted 25.2 percent from \$26.6 to \$19.9, and effective money (m x v) contracted 46.1 percent from \$102.96 to \$55.53. The general price level of GDP (p) declined 22.3 percent from 0.506 to 0.393 (p in 1958 equals 1.0), and the GDP-velocity of money (v) declined 27.9 percent from 3.87 to 2.79 – the money supply was recycled only 2.79 times in 1933 to accommodate and induce GDP. Thus, the decline in effective money (m x v), and therefore the equivalent decline in nominal GDP during the Great Depression was correlated with a drop in (v) that was even larger than the drop in (m). As a cause of the Great Depression, the slowdown in the rate of money-recycling was even more important than the decline in the stock of money available for recycling.

In the Great Depression, money (m) was being held outside the banking system and thus not circulating. Banks were failing (9,000 over a span of four years), there was less trust in financial intermediaries, and money was hoarded in private locations such as jars and safes. Some quasi-money created in the banking system based upon bank reserves was lost in bad investments. In addition, money did not circulate very fast out of jars and safes. In effect, financial markets, i.e. jars and safes, absorbed money away from the non-financial markets. Money did not circulate as fast through financial intermediaries, so there was less spendable money credits (m x v) in the system to pay debts and buy things. After dropping from 3.87 in 1929 to 2.79 in 1933, the GDP-velocity of money (v) ranged between 2.5 and 3.0 for the rest of the decade.

In the banking system, banks that were unable to honor their deposits due to bad loans, excessive credit creation, and the decline in effective money in circulation, had to close – they had to tell their depositors that 'we do not have so much money any more'. Without deposit insurance, the unhappy depositors had to 'agree that we did not have so much'. Secondly, in the stock market and other financial markets, a similar process occurred. The stock market crash in 1929 was a spontaneous agreement that 'we do not have so much money-wealth anymore'.

Stock market prices are maintained not only by the amount of effective money that is available and used to buy stocks, but also by various intangible assessments of the value of the real property that is being purchased. Mainstream economic theory agrees that stock prices reflect the expected stream of future earnings of the company, preferences for money-wealth now versus in the future (the discount rate), expected rates of return on alternative ways to store wealth (bonds, gold, money, other real property, etc.) and various other 'invisible expectations and preferences'. Stock market prices, and other real property prices, are a form of social consensus. Traders, armed with money-liquidity, negotiate with each other to determine how much monetary wealth an owner of, say, 100 shares of Microsoft is entitled to – in effect, there is an impersonal consensus on how much of the economic product he 'deserves'. Stock market valuations are a 'belief system' which allocates wealth through the institutions of the money economy.

The stock market run-up from mid-1927 to mid-1929, and the crash of 1929 which followed were not initiated by changes in the money supply (m) or the ability of institutions to handle money circulation (v). From mid-1927 to mid-1929 the money supply increased by approximately 3 percent and institutions were stable; but meanwhile the stock market doubled. Then, the crash in 1929 occurred despite continuing stability of effective money (m x v) – the general banking collapse and decline of (m x v) did not occur until 1930–31. Therefore, the invisible expectations and preferences were at play alongside tangible monetary conditions, and the changing social consensus dramatically increased and then dramatically reduced monetary wealth. Does this process sound irrational? It probably has both rational and irrational components – what Fischer Black, a President of the American Finance Association, distinguishes as 'information' versus 'noise,' respectively:

> The noise that noise traders put into stock prices will be cumulative, in the same sense that a drunk tends to wander farther and farther from his starting point. Offsetting this, though, will be the research and actions taken by the information traders. The farther the price of a stock gets from its value, the more aggressive the information traders will become. More of them will come in, and they will take larger positions. They may initiate mergers, leveraged buyouts, and other restructurings. Thus, the price of a stock will tend to move back toward its value over time...the farther the price of a stock moves away from its value, the faster it will tend to move back...[However], all estimates of value are noisy, so we can never know how far away price is from value' (Black, 1985, p. 532–3).

In other words, economic value or wealth as represented in stock prices can never be perfectly correlated with anything 'real'. Social consensus has not generated a fixed measure of value, therefore stock prices and other notions of value and wealth remain subject to changing belief systems. In the stock market, this indeterminacy can be thought of as 'the average investor trying to figure out what the average investor believes,' or 'the herd trying to figure out what the herd is going to do'.

B. Offshore Financial Markets

Eurodollars (dollars held in accounts outside the US), and many of the other new money accounts and forms that have been created since the 1970s, do not have reserve requirements in the banking system; therefore quasi-money and loans can be created based upon these accounts almost without limit. The rise of 'offshore finance' has encouraged this process, because offshore accounts usually do not have reserve requirements. Offshore finance can be defined as 'markets where operators are permitted to raise funds from non-residents and invest or lend that money to non-residents free from regulations and taxes'. Once money is raised, then without a reserve requirement it can be loaned, deposited, re-loaned, re-deposited, re-loaned, etc. in offshore markets without limits imposed by the banking system.

Offshore markets are generally categorized into three types: 'spontaneous' offshore sites, as in the UK and Hong Kong; 'International Banking Facilities' (IBF) as in New York and Tokyo; and 'tax havens' as in the Cayman Islands and Switzerland. London became an offshore site 'spontaneously' after the new Thatcher government abolished foreign currency exchange controls in 1979. In the UK, minimum reserve requirements were then abolished in August 1981 for onshore banks. The Bank of England wanted to maintain them, but the commercial banks lobbied successfully to abolish them so that they could compete in the Eurocurrency business with non-British institutions.

IBFs, which are more stringently licensed and controlled, were allowed in the US after 1980 in order to compete with London and the tax havens of the Caribbean. Tokyo followed suit with its IBF in 1984. All offshore sites can have tax advantages, but the typical tax haven is inhabited by 'letterbox' or 'brass plate' companies who exist mostly on paper, with the real activity taking place in a 'proper onshore' financial center. Tax havens struggle with respectability and anonymity in order both to attract deposits and avoid regulations. The Bahamas, for example, was identified by the IMF as the third largest international financial center in 1983 after Britain and the US, in terms of foreign liabilities, but after much publicity about drug trafficking and corruption it has now slipped to seventh place. The net worth of offshore markets is difficult to estimate, but it may be $5–6 trillion or 25 percent of world GDP.

By the 1990s, according to some estimates, 'as much as half of the world's stock of money either resides in, or is passing through, tax havens' (Kochen, 1991, p. 73). According to IMF data, the Caymans and the Bahamas together held approximately $400 billion in foreign liabilities in 1990, which compared with $1,073 billion in foreign liabilities held in the UK, $659 held in Japan, and $584 billion held in the US (of which the New York IBF held $333 billion). Much of the money in tax havens is held by 'residents,' and is therefore not included as part of foreign liabilities. The nine tax havens of the Caribbean are home to half of the world's insurance companies, and 14 percent of the world's merchant shipping companies. In addition, individual private savings of $500 billion was held in tax havens in 1993 – an amount of money approximately equal to the entire savings of the world's 'super-rich' (Norton, 1993). Thus, Lord Rees-Mogg warned:

> The world has never seen anything quite like this before. Governments are unlikely to recover their control of finance.... Any future attempts to restore capital controls or regain taxing power are quite implausible.... American and European welfare systems which depend on high tax may become insolvent. In the new world 'tax the rich' has ceased to be an option; the rich are not going to sit around waiting to be taxed (Rees-Mogg, 1993).

In the 1990s, when international trade data is added up for all countries, world export revenues fall short of import expenditures by approximately $100 billion per year. Economists agree that much of this $100 billion represents a true shortfall (not just measurement error) of money which is not repatriated, but instead is added to offshore finance. When combined with other flows that add to the stock of money in offshore markets, it may be that offshore markets now direct as much money as onshore markets.

Through the 1990s, approximately 60 percent of the world's official money reserves have been held in US dollars, 20 percent in German marks, and 10 percent in Japanese yen. More US dollars circulate outside the US than inside. (We will see how this dominance of the dollar, and this 90 percent dominance of the 'big three' changes as the euro now replaces the mark.) In offshore financial markets, compared to the entire global economy, the US dollar has an unknown, but significantly larger share of the *stock* of money reserves. What is possible to estimate is the yearly *flow* of foreign (non-US) savings of dollars. Table 3.1 shows a recent estimate of the annual sources and uses of US dollar financial flows outside the US, for 1992–96.

Table 3.1 estimates that there is a flow of more than $50 billion dollars per year into offshore financial markets from international transactions wherein money is not repatriated (or measured) through official national balance of payments statistics. This flow is then a non-US *source* of dollars that can be used for just about anything in the global economy, and it is increasing. The same comments apply to the separate category of capital flight, which also adds approximately $50 billion per year into the available supply of non-US-held dollars. By definition there is no firm data for capital flight, because it describes funds which leave a country in secret or disguised accounts to avoid taxes, political risks, inconvertibility risks, etc. Other sources of non-

US-held dollars, which are made available to the global economy each year, include dollars held in other countries which 'materialize' from private sources to buy dollar bonds, notes, direct and equity investments, and dollars which are 'freed-up' in other countries from official national reserve accounts. The grand total of non-US-held dollars, which are made available for use in the global financial markets each year, has been rising from an estimated $140 billion in 1992 to almost $300 billion in 1995 and 1996.

Table 3.1 Sources and uses of foreign savings in dollars ($billion)

	1992	1993	1994	1995	1996
Sources					
Accumulating in offshore financial markets	45	50	55	65	75
Non-US purchases of dollar bonds and notes	10	20	25	30	45
Capital flight	35	40	50	55	40
Direct and equity investment in the US	10	60	50	60	85
Net flows out of the reserves of:					
Industrial countries[1]	0	40	80	65	20
LDCs Fuel exporters	0	0	-20	10	5
Non-fuel exporters	40	30	15	10	15
Total	140	240	255	295	285
Uses					
Net financing in dollars by:					
Industrial countries (ex-US)	-35	-100	-20	-20	-25
LDC's Fuel exporters[2]	10	20	25	25	15
Non-fuel exporters	35	55	30	50	50
US direct and portfolio investment abroad[3]	60	160	70	80	90
US current account deficit	70	105	150	160	155
Total	140	240	255	295	285

[1]*Note*: Additions to the US Treasury's holdings of foreign currency subtract from this total.
[2]*Note*: Mexico is included under this heading.
[3]*Note*: US purchases of foreign currency bonds is added to this total.
Source: Brown (1996), p. 119.

Because of the rise of offshore finance, perhaps one-fourth of the world's money stock (m) is not subject to significant reserve requirements. Thus, quasi-money, loans, and effective money (m x v) can be created on the basis of a process of deposit-lending and added to the world system almost without limit – the offshore financial markets can expand as long as the players remain profitable. Many of the players are limited by national regulations where they do other business, and they cannot expand offshore business beyond a certain share of onshore business. However, some players have no such regulations, and they are the modern-day equivalents of private goldsmiths in the European Renaissance. Dollar-credits today, just like gold-notes in the Renaissance, can be issued almost without limit, i.e. as long as all private parties to the issuance profit from the use of those notes.

C. Monetary-Wealth Creation

Offshore financial markets and other innovations have given financial players a deregulated supply of money, and global networks, which can be used to exploit new opportunities. Some of this activity is reckless speculation and increases risk in the system, and some involves less risk and might even be arbitrage whereby the players simultaneously borrow at low interest rates and lend at high interest rates, or 'buy low and sell high' without risk. As part of this process, advances in information-processing technologies and market-driven institutional change have allowed a dramatic reduction in financial transactions costs for all participants. People have been able to find more favorable interest rates. In addition, less expensive ownership of stocks, commodities, and other property has been possible.

As discussed further in 'A New Political Economy of Money' in Chapter 5, in many cases these labors of financial operators can create wealth, because of the lower costs and greater economic efficiencies which they allow. Innovations which support, and arise within, the financial sector can in many cases be a win-win game, because they can also create and distribute new wealth. However, in some other cases, the labor of financial operators can appropriate wealth from other sectors of the economy in a win–lose situation, for example when financial institutions and players have inordinate political power. Alternatively, in the most pessimistic cases, as discussed in the case studies of Chapter 4, inappropriate labors of financial operators have resulted in lose–lose situations, for example if the supply of effective money or the 'money pyramid' is allowed to collapse, or if financial institutions and networks are destroyed by reckless activity.

Financial market participants, including central banks, can be the 'driving agents' whose actions may either increase or reduce the economic product of various nations. US Federal Reserve Board Chairman Alan Greenspan recently wrote:

The fiat money systems that emerged [after the gold standard system was abandoned in the early 1970s] have given considerable power and responsibility to central banks to manage the sovereign credit of nations. Under a gold standard, money creation was at the limit tied to changes in gold reserves. The discretionary range of monetary policy was relatively narrow. *Today's central banks have the capability of creating or destroying unlimited supplies of money and credit....* The changing dynamics of modern global financial systems also require that central banks address the inevitable increase of systemic risk. It is probably fair to say that the very efficiency of global financial markets, engendered by the rapid proliferation of financial products, also has the capability of transmitting mistakes at a far faster pace throughout the financial system in ways that were unknown a generation ago, and not even remotely imagined in the 19th century. Today's technology enables single individuals to initiate massive transactions with very rapid execution. Clearly, not only has the *productivity* of global finance increased markedly, but so, obviously, has the ability to generate losses at a previously inconceivable rate (Greenspan, 1998, p. 247, 249) [italics added].

The author would emphasize from Greenspan's quote that 'the capability of creating or destroying unlimited supplies of money and credit' is equivalent to 'the capability of creating or destroying monetary wealth'. Money and credit are 'stores of value,' as determined by social consensus within nations and between nations.

Regarding financial operators, innovations, and productivity, the author would use Joseph Schumpeter's classic definition (1934, p. 66) of 'innovation' to include the opening of new markets and the pioneering of new forms of business or commercial organization, as well as the development of new products and methods of production. Clearly financial operators have been innovative in each sense, perhaps especially with regard to new global forms of commercial organization. Schumpeter argued that clusters of innovations destroy many of the old ways of doing things, while simultaneously creating new ways to produce value – a process of 'creative destruction'. Economic development thus proceeds as an evolutionary process, with difficult 'transition crises'. Innovations are adopted in 'search and selection' processes as we proceed through transition periods.

Modelski and Thompson's work provides an excellent data-based account of these Schumpeterian processes over the long history of economic development. Regarding recent history, they argue that:

...the period since 1973, and lasting in our analysis until about 2000, is one of transition. The industries that have been the bearers of post-World War II prosperity – the 'auto-industrial' complex (including oil) and electronics (even including mainframe computers) – have become mature industries. They are no longer sources of rapid growth and major innovation...competition [worldwide in these industries] has brought unemployment, restructurings, and shocks to world trade balances.... In the meantime, the [1973–] information industries have been slow in making their impact felt. The large investment in the new technologies has not yet had noticeable effects on *productivity* [italics added]. This is a 'lag' that is characteristic of paradigmatic shifts in industrial organization. Early in this century, a similar delay, on the order of two decades, was seen in the impact of strong commitment to electric power equipment' (Modelski and Thompson, 1996, p. 223).

The word 'productivity' as it is used in the above two quotes, and as it is typically used in economics literature, means the rate of current production of merchandise and services (GDP) per unit of input (land, labor, tangible capital, financial capital, etc.). The author would call this statistic 'GDP-productivity'. An alternative statistic would be the rate of current production of wealth per unit of input – 'wealth-productivity'. 'Wealth' includes GDP, but it also includes the monetary value of financial assets, real estate, and other property. The *socially-agreed* value of the latter group, as discussed above, is affected by the flow of effective money (m x v), expectations of the future as well as assessments of the present, the influence of noise traders versus information traders, and other invisible conditions. To the businessperson, wealth-productivity is pursued through maximization of shareholder value, whereas GDP-productivity is pursued through maximization of net income. Economic models typically focus on net-income processes rather than shareholder value processes, although the latter is usually more important to the owners and operators of corporations.

The (1973–) information industries have not yet significantly increased GDP-productivity, as noted by Modelski and Thompson, but these industries have noticeably supported an increase in wealth-productivity. Financial operators, using these new information-technologies, and taking advantage of new opportunities in deregulated financial markets, have increased the monetary value of financial assets, real estate, and other property. Innovation has reduced the transactions costs of creating and transferring money, and innovation has reduced the transactions costs of owning and handling property. These reduced owning and managing costs of property give new-found value to the property, which is reflected in higher prices. People have been more able to enjoy a net benefit from property ownership; thus, increased demand for existing property has increased property prices and recognized values. This process has occurred mostly independently of what can be observed in GDP markets; instead we observe high stock and real estate prices, higher prices for bonds and therefore lower interest rates, etc.

Thus, the (1973–) information industries have already had the following economic impact: non-inflationary growth of GDP has been possible consistent with historical trends, while socially-recognized wealth and purchasing power accumulates faster than ever before in financial markets. This effect has been possible even if it is assumed (increasingly incorrectly) that the (1973–) information industries have yet to improve the 'good-old' physical productivity of people to bring forward tangible goods within the household, office, and factory. Of course, expectations of good-old GDP-productivity gains that will be realized from the (1973–) information industries also adds to current wealth-productivity.

To date, the entrepreneurs and innovators of the new information-age capitalism can primarily be observed realizing the fruits of their labors in financial markets, with stock options, arbitrage trading profits, global money and credit operations, etc. Those analysts who look only at the 'good-old' household, office and factory, and claim that 'the new technology is overrated,' might be unaware of this important arena within which capitalism reinvents itself, and within which capitalists maintain their ability to accumulate wealth. Globally, financial firms' information-technology spending is estimated to grow from almost $100 billion in 1995 to over $130 billion in 2000 to almost $200 billion in 2005.[7]

Wealth-creation as captured in financial markets is now, in turn, supporting GDP-productivity. Because the cost of obtaining financing has dropped, whether from loans or participating owners, and because the price of land and other real property has increased, there is an increased incentive to develop property for the market. Some of the wealth that has recently accumulated in financial markets is spent for these purposes, and an 'industrious revolution' occurs as resources are more fully exploited and more intensely used for further innovation – business investment increases. Also, accumulated wealth allows consumption spending to expand. For example, massive wealth-productivity from information industries realized itself in the mid-to-late-1990s in the US; the US stock markets boomed, household savings out of current income dropped close to zero as the extra wealth supported consumption; unemployment dropped to record lows and economic growth continued beyond all consensus forecasts. Government tax revenues collected from economic activity exceeded expectations and in 1998 the US Federal Budget moved into surplus. Inflation in GDP markets did not increase.

While creating the 'one world financial market' and forcing interest-rate and financial-strategy parities (Chapter 1) across international markets, deregulated, globalized, more innovative financial institutions have allowed a massive creation and transfer of effective money, and a massive revaluation of wealth between countries and individuals. There have been winners and losers, but the net effect of these 'paper tigers' (Mao Tse Tung's phrase) has, to date, been positive – positive as per the socially-agreed value of outstanding wealth.

For example, after 1983 the volume of international lending increased faster than any time in history, and average interest rates in the global economy were cut in half – primarily because low-interest-rate Japanese yen-based lending was allowed to increase from 3 percent to 10 percent of the total, and low-interest-rate German mark-based lending was allowed to increase from 5 to 10 percent of the total. Japanese and German financial institutions profitably expanded as their new global customers benefited from lower interest rates and lower transactions costs. Many US lending institutions were initially out-competed, but improved efficiencies eventually allowed the US institutions to maintain their global share despite lower interest rates and interest-rate-spreads. Also, the fall of the Japanese stock market after 1989, and the rise of the US stock market was a necessary convergence toward global price-earnings parity of approximately twenty to one – equity ownership wealth was transferred from Japan to the US and there was a net increase in total valuation.

To holders of tangible and intangible assets in the US or Japan, mostly oblivious to the 'why and wherefore' of this process, huge changes in wealth occurred. Wealth held in Japan, whether measured in yen or dollars, has been cut in half since 1989, while wealth held in the US has more than tripled. In just two years, from 1996 to 1998 the value of all US stock markets doubled from $6 trillion to $12 trillion. US stock markets account for approximately one-third of the 'market value of the US,' and the other components of US wealth, which are less transferable in the financial sector and less subject to revaluation, have not appreciated so fast.

Despite Japan's continuing recession and financial crisis, Japan's losses that can be attributed to financial innovation and globalization have been much smaller than US gains – thus a net gain to the global economy from the labors of financial operators involved with these two largest economies. The (1973–) information industries, together with financial industries, have increased wealth-productivity. The profit from these innovations, or what Karl Marx would call the labor surplus, has initially been appropriated not only by the information and financial industries, but also by the holders of financial assets. Bill Gates became wealthy with Microsoft, and so did (the other) holders of US stocks. The former is now entitled to approximately $40 billion in purchasing power, and the latter, $12 trillion, and both should thank financial operators as well as information-industry operators who labor in the new global economy.

These recent case studies are somewhat anecdotal. Therefore, in Chapter 5, 'a new political economy of money' is explained whereby the hard-currency-accumulating country can increase its wealth at the expense of capital-exporting countries at the periphery – a process of 'money-mercantilism'. Further definitions of 'wealth' and 'capital' are provided, so that the 'source of value' in the economic system can be more thoroughly identified.

VI. POLICY IMPLICATIONS

The structural changes discussed in Sections I–V have profound policy implications. As long as new, profitable opportunities arise in financial markets due to advancing technology, deregulation, and internationalization, and as long as a reasonable degree of confidence in the markets is maintained, money supplies can be increased faster than historical rates without overstimulating the markets for merchandise and services. Financial markets absorb the above-normal liquidity and add extra value to household, business, and government assets. Assuming that this extra wealth is used to buy foreign goods or that it is used sparingly to buy domestic goods, the financial side of the economy experiences a sustainable, profit-justified inflation without the necessity of GDP inflation. The author would call this phenomenon the 'golden egg'. Similarly, failure of financial institutions to support the circulation of effective money (m x v) can, *unnecessarily*, destroy monetary wealth and cause recessions – the golden egg can be 'dropped'.

As discussed next, the US in the mid-1980s and Japan in the late 1980s had the golden egg, but both countries dropped it. The US 'picked it up' quickly and still has it, but Japan did not pick it up and has consequently 'lost it'.

In 1986, the US Federal Reserve was substantially more accommodating than in previous years and allowed the (m1), (m2), and (m3) measures of the US money supply (m) to grow by 15 percent, 9 percent, and 9 percent, respectively. Yet the GDP price level (p), and real GDP (q) each increased by historically low rates close to 2 percent. As per the quantity equation, (m x v = p x q), and whether (m1), (m2), or (m3) is used as the measure of (m), there was a significant decline in (v) due to the structural changes.

Instead of stimulating GDP markets, the extra money supply was used to increase the prices and turnover volumes of financial assets. Interest rates dropped as bond prices increased, and as 1987 arrived, stock prices soared. Also, based upon financial strategy parities (Chapter 1) price-earnings ratios for US stocks were climbing toward international averages in the globalizing markets – some of the extra money supply was profitably absorbed for this purpose. In an unprecedented display of how fast money could be absorbed into financial markets, US household wealth locked up in the US stock market increased by more than $250 billion in January alone.

As argued in Chapter 2, it was largely the wealth effect of low interest rates and financial asset inflation that accounted for the historically low US savings rate of 3 to 4 percent in this period. Consumers spent a larger share of their current income on merchandise and services than at any time since World War II, without which there would not have been even the moderate 2 percent growth rate of real GDP.

Then in 1987 US monetary policy changed dramatically. Armed with the quantity equation, still believing in a stable value for (v), and thus unaware of the mostly positive effects of faster money growth, the Federal Reserve, as advised by many influential economists, began tightening the reins. Whether measured by (m1), (m2), or (m3), the annual growth rate of the US money supply declined by approximately 4 percentage points in the first five months of 1987, compared to its growth rate in 1986. And the reins were tightened further. The annual growth rate of (m1), which had been reduced to 11 percent in the first five months of 1987, dropped to 3.0 percent growth in June, 5.3 percent contraction in July, 2.1 percent growth in August, and 3.9 percent growth in September.

The Federal Reserve was reacting to a rising fear that GDP inflation was just around the corner, and that the dollar would fall precipitously, thus causing capital flight out of the US currency, further declines in its value and the erosion of investor confidence. Contractionary monetary policy was implemented to fend off these risks, and it was felt to be justified because the probability of a recession within the near future was slim.

Influential economists had actually been warning the Fed of impending inflation ever since an expansionary monetary policy was started in the US late in 1982. Instead of interpreting the collapse in velocity as a structural shift as per the author's equations in the Appendix, they emphasized as per Friedman (1988) that 'velocity fell because we were in a period of disinflation and falling interest rates'. But as emphasized by nationally syndicated columnist Warren T. Brooks: 'Every January since 1983, [these same] economists have been warning that soaring inflation would once again rear its ugly head. And every year they have been dead wrong'.[8]

For example, on 16 January 1986, Carnegie-Mellon Professor Allen Meltzer, one of the leading monetary economists and chairman of the prestigious Shadow Open Market Committee which monitors US Federal Reserve Bank policies said that 'we will see 8 percent inflation by the fourth quarter of 1986'.[9] Instead, inflation rose only 0.7 percent in the fourth quarter and less than 2 percent for the year. Citing the then-current 13–16 percent annualized rate of growth in the (m1) money supply as a key factor in his forecast, Professor Meltzer obviously did not foresee the 8 percent drop in the (m1) velocity of money that would occur in 1986.

Quoted in July, 1985 when the US inflation rate was over 3 percent, Milton Friedman predicted that inflation is 'more likely to go up than down. I think inflation will be higher than it is today – considerably higher. I suspect that the rate will reach 8–9 percent in 1987 or 1988 – but I have no confidence in that forecast'.[10] Actually, inflation was less than 2 percent in 1986 and less than 5 percent in 1987.

Writing in February 1986, Walter Heller, former chairman of the Council of Economic Advisors under Presidents Kennedy and Johnson agreed with the Reagan administrations forecast that real GDP would grow by 4 percent from the fourth quarter of 1985 to the fourth quarter of 1986. The actual increase was 2.0 percent. Heller also predicted that inflation would 'chug along at about a 3.5 percent rate for 1986', which eventually compared with the actual increase of less than 2 percent.[11]

And the 'dynamic mathematical model' developed by three economists at the Federal Reserve Bank itself in 1986, which used the entire floating exchange rate and price index history since 1973, predicted 6–8 percent inflation by the fourth quarter of 1987.[12] The actual rate was close to 4 percent.

The Federal Reserve's overly-restrictive monetary policies in 1987 due to these and other exaggerated warnings of inflation and capital flight caused a very costly reversal in the expansion of US financial markets – an expansion which had been occurring steadily in the mid-1980s due to advances in information-processing technology, deregulation and internationalization, each of which had given participants increased ability to make profitable investments. US interest rates were allowed to rise 2 percent in 1987 despite sluggish real GDP growth. The supply of effective money (m x v) collapsed – especially as demanded for financial market participation. The new-found profitability and store-of-wealth within financial markets could not be supported and investor confidence waned until the stock market finally sold off in October. The golden egg had been dropped.

Similarly restrictive monetary policy worldwide made the crash a global phenomenon. World stock market losses, which added up to more than the entire $900 billion debt of the Third World, might have been mostly avoided if central bankers had cooperatively maintained looser monetary policies in order to accommodate the natural expansion of the money centers. Instead, just when international monetary expansion was most needed shortly before the crash, West Germany raised its interest rates and prompted the confused central bankers to make their move in the opposite direction – to achieve what ultimately was the trivial and unobtainable goal of exchange rate stability.

Immediately after the crash, the US Federal Reserve dramatically lowered interest rates and expanded money supplies, and the monetary contraction and wealth destruction in the US was soon reversed before debt-deflation processes could become pervasive – the US picked up the golden egg quickly before it was lost. 'The Stock Market Crash of 1987' is elaborated in Chapter 4.

Japan, with its appreciating currency, non-existent GDP inflation, and massive exportation of capital, was the one G7 country that did not pursue restrictive monetary policies during this period. The average annual increase in Japan's domestically contained narrow-money supply during 1986–88 was 8 percent. Japan's massive capital and money outflow was buying foreign assets, and 'Japan Inc.' was expanding like an investment bank. Thus, it was the one G7 country that escaped the world stock market crash in 1987. Japanese stock prices increased by 45 percent in 1987, and then another 10 percent in 1988 and 20 percent in 1989. Land prices soared even faster in many regions.

Japan did not drop its golden egg until the 1989–90 period. Worried about the expansion of domestic credit and asset price inflation despite the fact that much of this increased wealth was used for foreign investment, the Japanese money supply was restricted to 2.4 percent growth in 1989 and 4.4 percent growth in 1990. Domestic credit was squeezed sharply with other directives, and the price of land and equities collapsed. Japanese stock prices dropped more than 50 percent over 1990–91, and real estate values declined in proportion but over a more extended period. Based upon financial strategy parities, price-earnings ratios for Japanese real property needed to drop toward international averages anyway in the globalizing markets (Chapter 1), but the restrictive monetary policy exaggerated this correction.

Japan soon lost its financial surplus and therefore its means to maintain record rates of foreign investment. Its net outflow of direct investment plus portfolio investment plus other capital (the identified capital outflow) dropped to $22 billion in 1990 from an annual average of $58 billion over 1986–1989. In 1991, temporarily, the Japanese money supply was once again increased significantly, by 9.5 percent, and the identified capital outflow jumped back up, to $72 billion. However, on balance monetary policy remained restrictive through the 1990s (real short-term interest rates of 4-to-5 percent), and Japanese land and equity price deflation spread to GDP markets. An economy-wide recession and large corporate failures are the result. Once the golden egg has been dropped, it is very difficult to pick up – especially, as discussed in 'Japan's Crisis, 1989–' in Chapter 4, if the Bank of Japan continues to 'fight the last war [against inflation]'.

Some research has confirmed the above scenario for Japan. In a paper presented at the annual conference of the Royal Economic Society in April, 1993,[13] Richard Werner of Oxford and the Bank of Japan suggests that GDP inflation and financial asset inflation can indeed be separated and linked to different uses of money. After disaggregating the Japanese money supply perhaps more successfully than Spindt's (1985) attempt in the US, Werner concludes that Japan's asset and land price inflation due to expanding money supplies in the mid-1980s provided the means to buy foreign assets. Furthermore, GDP inflation need not be risked.

Similarly, Robert Laurent at the Federal Reserve (1994, 1995) has shown that the Japanese crisis of the 1990s, like the Great Depression of the 1930s, can be explained by overly restrictive monetary policy, and indeed, the destruction of money and quasi-money. Taking issue with the Bank of Japan's view that monetary policy has been accommodative (Inoue, 1995), Laurent's statistical analysis shows that large loan losses and solvency problems for Japanese depositories can be linked to inappropriately tight monetary policies:

...the fundamental similarity between these two periods [US 1930s and Japan 1990s] was the severe stress experienced by money-creating depositories. The closing of insolvent depositories, the increased regulatory pressure, and increased capital requirements, all combined to weaken the normal stimulative impact of a given cut in short-term interest rates. Achieving the same growth in the broad monetary aggregates required even sharper cuts in short-term interest rates in these circumstances...the existence of deposit insurance in the more recent period is the most important difference between the more recent period and the 1930s. While deposit insurance has not rescinded the contractionary impact of depository stress on broad money, it has caused the impact to manifest itself in much different ways than in the 1930s. The presence of deposit insurance in the early 1990s also makes it clear that monetary policy in this period could certainly have offset the weakness in broad money growth [and therefore the current Japanese recession] (Laurent, 1994, p. 21-2).

In private correspondence with Laurent, the author realized that 'absorption of (m1) by financial markets and therefore a decline in (m1) income velocity' (the author's research), in times of financial distress, can also be measured by a 'weakness in broad money growth' (Laurent's research). Namely, expanded supplies of high-powered (m1) may not be able to serve as a base for expanded supplies of broad money (m1 plus CDs, credit, etc., and therefore economic growth) if the (m1) supplies are instead 'absorbed' by financial institutions to resolve bankruptcies, increase reserves, and meet other capital requirements. In this case, a decline in broad money and GDP would correspond to a decline in (m1) income velocity as (m1) is absorbed by (distressed) financial markets.

However, when depositories are well-capitalized and prosperous, (m1) and broad money would more likely grow or shrink together based upon monetary policies and normal credit-creation. Hence, if financial markets absorb money (for new profitable IRP and FSP activities), then the decline in (m1) velocity (which measures this absorption) would not be accompanied by a decline in broad money. This conclusion is exactly consistent with Laurent's work when he concludes (Laurent, 1994, p. 21) that broad money 'has seldom, if ever over the last 35 years, forecast real GDP as it did in the early 1990s (a time of financial distress)'. The author's equations in the Appendix thus capture the absorption of money by financial markets and institutions for reasons both of distress and prosperous liberalization, whereas Laurent's equations capture money-absorption only in times of distress. The author's equations might thus guide policy-makers in all periods rather than just in times of distress.

Werner's and Laurent's research thus supports the author's unconventional arguments. What was generally seen in the literature as a reckless and speculative expansion of domestic credit in Japan during the 1980s, an unsustainable bubble, can in the author's view be seen as a very successful form of economic imperialism. Japan printed the means to buy foreign assets and expand wealth domestically without accelerating GDP inflation. If overly restrictive monetary policies had not been used, the expansion could likely have continued but at a more moderate level in proportion to continuing but slower rates of technological change, deregulation, and international opportunities – as per the author's equations. 'Japan's Crisis, 1989–' is elaborated in Chapter 4.

The economics literature generally expects a monetary expansion to (a) increase GDP inflation via the quantity equation and (b) depreciate the exchange rate. The exchange rate would depreciate due to (c) lack of investor confidence in the inflating currency and country and withdrawals of foreign investment and (d) a larger trade deficit given the monetarily inflated, and therefore less competitive GDP prices. However, in Japan's case, just the opposite of each of (a–d) occurred during the 1980s monetary expansion due to the structurally new environment for monetary policy. During the monetary contraction period since 1989, these cause-effect relationships have also been persistently violated.

NOTES

1. 'Reserve's Policy Drifts As Its Officials Heed Different Indicators', *The Wall Street Journal*, 22 April 1988, p.1.
2. The author's research corroborates the work of others, that 'since (m1) comes closer than (m2) to approximating a medium-of-exchange concept of money, there is reason to expect that the demand for (m1) would be affected more by the volume of transactions than the demand for (m2), and that has turned out to be the case' (Friedman, 1988).
3. Much of the theory and statistical analysis of this chapter is elaborated in the author's 1989 publication (Allen, 1989).
4. Friedman considered the Dow Jones stock market index, a narrower aggregate but of course highly correlated.
5. 'Stakes High for Britain's Financial Firms in Freer Markets', *The New York Times*, 6 October 1986, p. 34.
6. 'London's Exchange Braces for Big Bang Set to Occur Monday', *The Wall Street Journal*, 24 October 24 1986, p. 1.
7. 'A Survey of Technology in Finance', *The Economist*, 26 October 1996, insert p. 3.
8. Ironically, the article is entitled: 'This Year, They May Be Right About Inflation', by Warren T. Brooks, *San Francisco Chronicle*, 27 January 1987, p. 32.
9. Brooks, Warren T. (1986), 'Why There is No Significant Inflation in Sight', *San Francisco Chronicle*, 2 December.
10. Friedman, Milton (1985), 'Is Hyperinflation Inevitable?', *The Commonwealth*, 8 July 1985, p. 1.
11. Heller, Walter (1986), 'Year to Reach for Economic Stars', *The Wall Street Journal*, 28 February 1986.
12. Brooks, Warren T. (1987), 'This Year, They May Be Right About Inflation', ibid.
13. 'Towards a Quantity Theorem of Disaggregated Credit and International Capital Flows with Evidence from Japan'.

APPENDIX   REGRESSIONS OF US (m1) INCOME VELOCITY AND RELATED VARIABLES

Quarterly Data, 1982:Q1–1998:Q2

(Equation A): $(r) = (9.42) - (3.41 \times 10^{-7}) \times (NEWFMK) + (2.36) \times (D96Q1)$
t-stat: (20.66)   (-7.35)   (3.29)

One-Period Moving Average: MA(1) coefficient = 0.76, t-stat = 10.08
Adj.R^2: 0.81
Durbin–Watson statistic: 1.20

(Equation B): $(v) = (6.78) - (3.67 \times 10^{-8}) \times (NEWFMK) + (1.20) \times (D96Q1)$
t-stat: (61.73)   (-3.23)   (6.71)

MA(1) coefficient = 0.70, t-stat = 7.34
Adj.R^2: 0.78
Durbin–Watson statistic: 1.20

Quarterly Data, 1980:Q1–1986:Q2

(Equation C): $(v) = (6.14) - (2.22 \times 10^{-7}) \times (NEWFMK) + (0.090) \times (r)$
t-stat: (10.78)   (-0.34)   (2.25)

MA(1) coefficient = 0.42, t-stat = 2.13
Adj.R^2: 0.56
Durbin–Watson statistic: 2.09

(Equation D): $(v) = (6.15) - (0.127 \times 10^{-2}) \times (NYSE) + (0.093) \times (r)$
t-stat: (7.98)   (-0.25)   (2.45)

MA(1) coefficient = 0.42, t-stat = 2.14
Adj.R^2: 0.56
Durbin–Watson statistic: 2.09

Quarterly Data, 1982:Q1–1995:Q3

(Equation E): $(v) = (6.91) - (5.68 \times 10^{-8}) \times (NEWFMK)$
t-stat: (77.1)   (-5.91)

MA(1) coefficient = 0.64, t-stat = 5.74
Adj.R^2: 0.74
Durbin–Watson statistic: 1.17

(Equation F): $(v) = (3.94) - (5.03 \times 10^{-8}) \times (NEWFMK) + (0.062) \times (r)$
t-stat: (4.85)   (-2.45)   (2.17)

$\qquad\qquad\qquad + (0.028) \times (INF) + (0.00136) \times (q)$
t-stat: (1.28)   (2.45)

MA(1) coefficient = 0.70, t-stat = 5.67
Adj.R^2: 0.83
Durbin–Watson statistic: 1.12

(Equation G): $(v) = (3.23) - (5.63 \times 10^{-8}) \times (NEWFMK) + (0.077) \times (INF)$
t-stat: (4.24)   (-4.73)   (6.16)

$\qquad\qquad\qquad + (0.0189) \times (q)$
t-stat: (4.08)

MA(1) coefficient = 0.91, t-stat = 13.38
Adj.R^2: 0.82
Durbin–Watson statistic: 1.08

Quarterly Data, 1982:Q1–1998:Q2

(Equation H): $(v) = (1.54) - (6.95 \times 10^{-8}) \times (NEWFMK) + (0.069) \times (INF)$
t-stat: (2.22)   (-6.70)   (5.19)

$\qquad\qquad\qquad + (0.0030) \times (q) + (0.48) \times (D96Q1)$
t-stat: (7.48)   (3.33)

MA(1) coefficient = 0.96, t-stat = 57.68
Adj.R^2: 0.86
Durbin–Watson statistic: 1.04

4. Financial Crises and Recession

Based upon the structural changes and cause-effect material of Chapters 1, 2 and 3, this chapter presents case studies of the 1982 world recession, the 1987 world stock market crash, the 1980s and continuing world debt crises, the slumps of the early 1990s, the 1994–95 Mexican crisis, the Japanese crisis after 1989, and the crises in various Asian countries beginning in 1997. Various common patterns are found, especially with regard to the increased international transfers of investment based upon interest rate and financial strategy parities (Chapter 1), the subsequent adjustments in international trade (Chapter 2), the decline and increased variability of monetary velocity, and the creation, loss, and transfer of monetary wealth (Chapter 3).

I. COMMON PATTERNS

Recent episodes of financial crises and recession in the global economy have common patterns. In most cases, a country or region initially benefits from expanded supplies of base money, new 'quasi-moneys' which are created from base moneys, and credit supplies – a financial liberalization phase. The financial sector expands as it captures profit from new efficiencies and opportunities allowed by globalization. The country or region, for a time, may be favored by international investors; thus the banking system, including government, is well-capitalized and able to expand money-liquidity. Assets increase in monetary value and interest rates are low, and this wealth effect encourages consumption, borrowing, business investment, and perhaps government spending. Productive resources are more fully utilized and economic growth is well supported. There is a 'boom', as measured by increased (a) monetary wealth held by private and public sectors of an economy, such as the value of stocks, real estate, currency reserves, etc., and/or (b) current production of merchandise and services (GDP).

Then, typically, the supply of base money (m) times its rate of circulation or velocity for GDP purposes (v) contracts, and so therefore does the equivalent nominal GDP. The decline in nominal GDP is usually split between its two components, real GDP which is the volume of current production measured in constant prices (q), and the GDP price level (p). By definition, the quantity equation requires $(m \times v = p \times q)$. When (q) declines for a sustained period (typically at least six months) we call it a recession, and when (p) declines we call it deflation. After this process starts, monetary policymakers may react by rapidly expanding (m), but this action may be too little too late – individuals and institutions may have unpayable debts, banks may even be failing, and international confidence in the country or region may already be damaged. In this pessimistic case, which is typical in less-developed countries with weak financial systems, the desperate increase in (m) may reverse the slide in (p) and even lead to hyper-inflation (destabilizing, rapid increases in p), but (q) would continue to fall. A weak financial system may be unable to maintain the circulation rate of secure currencies for productive activities, especially if people are hoarding money, and thus (v) would decline.

The initial contraction in 'effective money' (m x v) may be caused by monetary authorities or national and international investors draining money (m) from the country or region, or there may be a decline in (v) for reasons having to do with the inability of the financial system to direct money toward productive activities.   A contraction in effective money supplies or withdrawal of international investment may undermine equity markets, debt markets, bank capital, or government reserves, and monetary wealth is then revalued downwards. General economic or political uncertainty worsens the situation – the resulting austerity-mentality causes a contraction of spending and credit, and an increased 'risk premium' attached to business activity scares away investment. Interest rates rise, the demand for quasi-money and credit – i.e. the desire to hold and use the insecure 'monetary float' – declines and people try to convert the monetary float into more secure base money such as cash. No reserve-currency banking system is able to cover all of its monetary float with secure bank reserves if customers try to redeem all of the float at once, and thus 'runs' on banks can destroy the banks themselves.

A deteriorating banking sector may be unable to honor its deposits, bad loan problems surface and a 'lender of last resort' such as the International Monetary Fund (IMF) may need to be found.   The IMF concludes that approximately three-quarters of its more than 180 member countries encountered 'significant' banking sector problems of this type during the period from 1980 to 1995; of these approximately one-third warrant the definition 'crisis' (Lindgren et al., 1995).

More generally, these types of episodes can be called: (a) a financial crisis if there is a significant decline in monetary wealth held by private and public sectors, and/or (b) a recession if there is a significant decline in real GDP. Variations on these definitions can be found in the economics literature. Excellent reference works on the history and nature of economic crises include *Manias, Panics, and Crashes: A History of Financial Crises* (Kindleberger, 1989), *The Risk of Economic Crisis* (Martin Feldstein, ed., 1991), and *Marx's Theory of Crisis* (Clarke, 1994).

In the global economic system, the decline in effective base money (m x v) in a *peripheral* country or region may be initiated by the financial *centers* or dominant reserve-currency countries. The base money used in the periphery, which backs its less secure quasi-moneys and credit expansion, may even be the centralized global reserve currency – typically the US dollar. For example, the 1982– world debt crisis hit Latin America when the US dollar became scarce. Dollars had been loaned to Latin America in the 1970s at negative real interest rates, which provided the hard-currency monetary base for the dramatic expansion of local soft currency and credit – Latin America's financial liberalization and economic growth phase. Then, because of US monetary and fiscal policies in the early 1980s, dollar interest rates soared and dollars were both pushed and pulled out of Latin America into US deposits. Latin America lost the dollar reserves which were necessary to pay dollar-denominated debts; thus Latin America lost its internationally recognized 'source of value' which could maintain the 'redemption value' of local quasi-moneys. Policymakers desperately increased domestic currency supplies trying to reverse this process. Confidence in pesos, cruzados, and other soft currencies was lost, and they depreciated rapidly, i.e. inflation (p) surged even faster than the growth in (m); therefore the real money supply (m/p) declined; and a decline in real GDP (q) followed. From the quantity equation, (m/p = q/v), and (v) declined in many cases due to banking problems; therefore (q) had to decline. The 1980s became known as 'the lost decade' for Latin America.

These types of crises are generally more likely when excessive, risky speculation and investment is encouraged by the notion that 'if I fail, a lender of last resort or government institution will bail me out', i.e. the 'moral hazard problem'. In the Latin American case in the 1980s, many commercial lenders felt that, to a certain extent, they had an implicit guarantee from the US Federal Reserve Bank and other central banks to bail out any bad commercial loans that would arise from lending to the less-developed countries (LDCs). The famous quote from the Chairman of Citibank was 'countries do not go broke'. A similar moral hazard problem was identified between the US government and the US savings and loan institutions in the 1980s, which contributed to the savings and loan crisis. Deposit insurance and other Federal guarantees encouraged reckless use of funds, and US taxpayers ultimately paid $130 billion to resolve the savings and loan crisis. In the 1990s, shifting more of the bad-debt liability to the lender has been proposed to reduce the moral hazard problem, but authorities also want to maintain their lender-of-last-resort capability in order to prevent bad debt problems from spreading through the system (see Federal Reserve Bank of Kansas City, 1997).

The bankruptcy of a country or region can be similar to the bankruptcy of a bank. The failure results from an insufficient supply of high-powered base money or high-quality liquid capital to honor the redemption value of the less secure monetary forms which have been created in pyramid fashion from the secure base. Private goldsmith banks in the European Renaissance failed when they did not have enough gold to honor their gold notes; US thrifts failed in the 1980s when they ran out of hard dollar reserves to honor the soft dollar demand deposits which they had created; and Latin American economies failed when their monetary base proved insufficient to honor the monetary 'float' that had been created from that base.

In the nineteenth and early twentieth centuries, London was the secure financial center, and the US was more of a periphery that depended on the British pound to back dollar-expansion. As documented by Mishkin (1991), most of the financial crises in the US during this period began with a monetary-contraction and a rise in interest rates in the London markets, which then caused a contraction in US money-liquidity, a sharp rise in US interest rates, US bank problems and so on. In crisis episodes, the monetary contraction in the periphery is usually more severe than in the center, because the periphery uses the large monetary float which is sustained by the smaller monetary base in the center. Furthermore, if savings and monetary wealth in the periphery country are transferred to the financial center to take advantage of its higher interest rates, or for safe-haven purposes (typically when the crisis hits), then the periphery experiences an even greater contraction.

Since World War II, the dollar has been the dominant world reserve currency. Thus, recent financial crises and recession are typically initiated by dollar-monetary-contraction and increases in dollar interest rates. The negative effects can be especially severe at the periphery of the global economy if the contraction occurs suddenly and follows a more liberal dollarization period in the periphery. As discussed in this chapter, recent crises in less-developed countries and smaller countries especially follow this pattern.

II. THE 1982 RECESSIONARY PERIOD

Historically, national political leaders have entered office with a grand design for the economic future of their country. Significant changes in monetary and fiscal policies may be made in order to fight inflation, unemployment and other ills in the national economy. In addition, the new administration generally has an ideological slant in the way that it regulates business and labor.

In the early 1980s, just as the international financial markets began to expand rapidly and create the new global economy, French President François Mitterrand embarked upon an experiment in economic socialism. At the same time, newly elected leaders Margaret Thatcher in England and Ronald Reagan in the US were pursuing conservative policies aimed at restoring a more capitalist tradition. Each of these one-country economic experiments failed to recognize the new structure of the global economy, and as a consequence each experiment created severe economic hardships within one or two years.

A. The US Situation

The Reagan Administration came to Washington in January 1981, determined to stimulate the US economy with a 'supply-side' policy of large tax cuts, and a substantial increase in government defense spending which was to be more than offset by a cut in government non-defense spending. To reduce inflation, which was then 10 percent, the Federal Reserve Bank accelerated its recently enacted policy of restricting the growth rate of the US money supply.

As Table 4.1 shows, the Reagan Administration was successful in restraining government spending in its first few years. Government purchases of merchandise and services as a percentage of the economy's total, long-term trend purchases, called natural gross domestic product (natural GDP), declined from 18.6 percent in the first quarter of 1981 to 17.6 percent in the second quarter of 1983. It was actually state and local spending that accounted for this decline, as federal spending remained approximately constant – both are included in 'government spending'.

In its first few years the Reagan administration was also successful in reducing tax rates. Although the administration did not achieve its proposed 30 percent cut in total personal income tax rates, Congress did approve a 25 percent reduction – a 5 percent reduction on 1 October 1981 and two successive 10 percent reductions on 1 July 1982 and 1 July 1983. The first two of these three tax cuts are reflected in the first column of Table 4.1.

If everything else except these changes in government taxing and spending had remained the same in 1981–82, then the US economy might have expanded a little bit faster. The contractionary effect of the government spending restraints would have been more than offset by the expansionary effect of the tax cuts, particularly in late 1982 as the first of the two 10 percent tax cuts began to have its effect. However, everything else did not remain the same: between early and late 1981, as shown in Table 4.1, the Federal Reserve Bank reduced the money supply by approximately 6 percent relative to natural GDP.

This dramatic reduction in the money supply cut the supply of loanable funds in the US economy so much so that interest rates rose to historically high levels. As shown in Table 4.1, long-term interest rates increased from an already high level of 14.4 percent in the first quarter of 1981 to more than 16 percent in late 1981 and early 1982. It was these historically high interest rates that triggered the recession which began in late 1981 and lasted through 1982. The recession was characterized by a rapid slowdown in nominal GDP. The annual growth rate of this statistic slowed by 9.7 percent, from almost 13 percent in the third quarter of 1981 to just over 3 percent in the fourth quarter of 1982. Of this 9.7 percent decline, slightly more than half can be attributed to a reduction in inflation and slightly less than half to a reduction in real GDP. Real GDP, which had been increasing steadily since 1975 at an average annual rate of 3.5 percent, declined 2.1 percent from 1981 to 1982 before recovering to increase by 3.7 percent from 1982 to 1983 and 6.8 percent from 1983 to 1984.

Table 4.1 US monetary and fiscal policy and the 1982 recession

| Year: quarter | Ratio of personal tax pay-ments to personal income | Ratios to natural GDP | | | | Long-term interest rate |
		Gov. spending	Federal budget deficit	Money Supply	Actual GDP	
1981:Q1	15.9	18.6	1.3	14.4	97.1	14.4
1981:Q2	16.1	18.3	1.3	14.3	96.0	15.2
1981:Q3	16.2	18.3	1.8	14.0	95.8	16.3
1981:Q4	15.8	18.4	3.2	13.7	93.8	16.0
1982:Q1	15.8	18.1	3.3	13.8	92.8	16.1
1982:Q2	15.8	17.7	3.4	13.7	92.4	15.7
1982:Q3	15.4	18.0	4.7	13.6	91.5	14.7
1982:Q4	15.4	18.3	6.1	13.8	90.5	12.2
1982:Q1	15.1	17.8	5.2	14.0	90.4	12.0
1982:Q4	15.4	17.6	4.7	14.1	91.6	11.6

Sources: *Economic Report of the President* (February 1983), and *Survey of Current Business* (July 1983).

Table 4.2 shows the components of real GDP from 1981 to 1984, and it is clear that the components which are historically discouraged by high interest rates declined significantly from 1981 to 1982: namely, household purchases of durable products such as automobiles; non-residential fixed investment (business purchases of factories, machines and equipment); residential investment (housing purchases), and inventory investment (the change in inventories of final products that businesses keep on hand). Together, these purchases declined by $37 billion from 1981 to 1982 (1972 dollars). Likewise, these components of real GDP experienced a significant recovery from 1982 to 1983 and from 1983 to 1984 as interest rates changed course and declined dramatically, increasing by annual amounts of $43.7 billion and $89.1 billion.

Table 4.2 US GDP components and the 1982 recession (real GDP, 1981–84 in billions of 1972 dollars)

	1981	**1982**	**1983**	**1984**
GDP	1,515.2	1,480.0	1,543.7	1,639.0
Consumption	950.5	963.3	1,009.2	1,062.6
Durables	140.9	140.5	157.5	177.9
Nondurables	360.8	363.1	376.3	394.2
Services	448.8	459.8	475.4	490.6
Investment	230.9	194.3	221.0	289.7
Fixed Inv.	219.6	204.7	224.6	265.5
Residential Inv.	175.0	166.9	171.0	205.2
Non-residential Inv.	44.5	37.9	53.7	60.3
Inventory Inv.	11.3	-10.4	-3.6	24.2
Gov. Purchases	287.0	292.7	291.9	302.2
Net Exports	43.8	29.7	12.6	-15.5
Exports	160.2	147.6	139.5	145.8
Imports	116.4	118.0	126.9	161.3

Source: Economic Report of the President, 1985.

Because US tax rates had been reduced dramatically in the early 1980s, and because the recession reduced economic growth and the tax base, the US government collected less taxes. The Reagan administration in 1981 had forecast more balanced budgets, but in 1982 the federal budget showed a deficit of more than $100 billion (actual dollars – not 1972 dollars as in Table 4.2) for the first time in history, and in 1983 the deficit exceeded $200 billion. US fiscal policy thus required record amounts of government borrowing to cover these deficits, and it put upward pressure on US and world interest rates at a time when these were already high and the world was struggling to overcome the recession.

Historically, US net exports, defined as US exports minus US imports, have not declined significantly during a period of high US interest rates and recession. In fact, during a recession, US residents generally purchase fewer imports, and net exports may therefore increase. However, as shown in Table 4.2, US imports actually increased from 1981 to 1982. Also, because there was a simultaneous drop in US exports, US net exports fell, by 32 percent, from 1981 to 1982. A fall in US net exports reduces GDP because it reflects sales lost by US exporting firms as well as sales lost by US firms which produce import-competing products.

Why did US imports rise and US exports fall from 1981 to 1982 and therefore contribute to the recession? Most importantly, because the high US interest rates and restrictive US monetary policies, at a time when financial markets were globalizing, caused the exchange value of the US dollar to increase by 30 percent against major foreign currencies over these two years. Foreign exchange traders were accommodating new demand for US dollars by deregulated international investors who were attracted to the high US interest rates. Based upon the new interest rate parity conditions (Chapter 1), the 'net capital inflow' into the US from the rest of the world began to increase and the demand for dollars exceeded the supply.

The 30 percent increase in the value of the dollar over 1981 and 1982 caused US imports to be cheaper, in dollars, and US importers increased their total dollar purchases. Similarly, US exports became more expensive to foreign purchasers, in terms of foreign currency, so fewer US items were purchased by foreigners and the dollar value of US exports decreased. The decline in US exports can also be attributed to increased international competition from Japan and other newly developed countries such as South Korea and Taiwan, as well as to a reduction in US exports to many less developed countries that began using more of their dollar reserves to pay off their escalating international debts.[1]

How well did the leading economic forecasters predict the declines in US nominal GDP, real GDP and inflation? Table 4.3 shows the forecast errors computed as the difference between the actual declines and the declines which were predicted one year in advance.

It is clear from Table 4.3 that forecasters were too optimistic about the US economy. They predicted a fairly straight course – the growth rate of real GDP over this 15-month period was predicted to decline by only 0.8 percent from then-current levels rather than the actual decline of 3.8 percent from then-current levels. In other words, forecasters predicted that the economy would produce 3 percent more merchandise and services, $95 billion at 1982 prices, than actually was produced. From a workers' perspective, this error means that approximately two million more US jobs were lost than economists predicted, and expected US wages, salaries and profits amounting to $95 billion were not attained.

To understand why forecasters failed to predict the 1982 US recession one should first understand that econometric forecasting models generally require twenty to thirty years of data to identify the underlying structure of the economic system. Recent structural changes, including the increased international transfers of investment based upon interest rate and financial strategy parities (Chapter 1), the subsequent adjustments in international trade (Chapter 2), and the decline of monetary velocity due to deregulation, internationalization, and technological change (Chapter 3) were thus only marginally included in the forecasting models, and the models therefore failed.

Table 4.3 Actual versus predicted declines in the growth rates of US GDP and inflation, 1981:Q3 to 1982:Q4 (percentage points)

	Nominal GDP	Real GDP	Inflation*
Actual Decline	9.7	3.8	4.7
Predicted Decline	3.3	0.8	1.9
Forecast Error	6.4	3.0	2.8

* As measured by the GDP deflator.
Source: Robert J. Gordon, *Macroeconomics*, 3rd edn (1984), p. 408. The predicted decline is the average of predictions made by Data Resources, Inc., Chase Econometric Associates, Inc., the MAPCAST group at the General Electric Company, Wharton Econometric Forecasting Associates, Inc., and the median forecast from a survey conducted by the American Statistical Association and the National Bureau of Economic Research.

First, the increasing international transfers of investment allowed the increased US interest rates to have an unexpectedly strong negative impact on US net exports and therefore GDP via the trade effect discussed above. This trade effect, whereby high interest rates in a country cause that country's currency to increase in value, which in turn hurts its net exports, was not significant before 1971 when currency exchange rates were fixed administratively. Before 1971, national central banks kept exchange rates fixed by buying and selling currencies as well as redeeming currencies for gold at accepted prices.

After 1971, when fixed exchange rates and the gold standard were no longer maintained by the US and many other countries, economists had to begin including the trade effect of interest rate changes in their economic models. The trade effect was difficult for economists to estimate not only because of their limited experience with it, but also because interest rate changes affected currency values and, therefore, merchandise and services trade more strongly and unpredictably every year.

Every year, investors had better access to profitable opportunities in the world's major money centers, and there was an increased volume of money that was 'washing back and forth' in search of the best interest rates. A country which, for example, raised its interest rates as the US did in 1981–2 thus discovered an increased demand for its currency compared to historical periods; therefore a greater increase in the value of its currency; and therefore a greater reduction in its net exports. Econometric models which must use decades of historical data underestimated the significance of this trade effect.

Secondly, deregulation, internationalization, and technological change were behind the US recession of 1982 when policymakers underestimated the degree to which these structural changes would produce new financial market opportunities and absorb dollars away from the non-financial markets (Chapter 3). More dollars were suddenly kept on hand in the form of currency and checking deposits to accommodate these invisible transactions compared to the volume of dollars that were kept on hand to accommodate GDP transactions. Both types of transactions borrow dollars for a short period of time and then recycle them back into the economy to be used again.

The significance of this dollar-absorption by financial markets beginning in the early 1980s escaped most analysts. Therefore, they did not recognize the following fact: restricting the supply of US currency and checking deposits (m1) at a time when income velocity (v) was dropping because more of this spendable money was being used for financial transactions would more than proportionately reduce the amount of money which was being used for GDP transactions. Therefore, based upon the quantity equation (m1 x v = p x q), nominal GDP (p x q) would decrease more than expected following restrictive monetary policies. The decline in value of nominal GDP is usually split between a decline in the physical volumes of merchandise and services production, i.e. real GDP (q), and a decline in the GDP price level (p). As shown in Table 4.3, during the 1982 recession real GDP declined by 3.8 percent and the GDP price level by 4.7 percent.

Clearly, the forecasters who predicted that US nominal GDP would decline by 3.3 percent from the third quarter of 1981 to the fourth quarter of 1982 in the US due to restrictive monetary policies did not fully anticipate what was happening to the velocity of money. The actual decline in nominal GDP was a severe 9.7 percent. 'Forecasters missed the collapse of velocity almost entirely' (Gordon, 1984, p. 406).

B. The UK Situation

The British economic experiment of the early 1980s, like the American experiment just discussed, placed major emphasis on reducing the growth rate of the money supply in order to reduce inflation and, ultimately, interest rates. And, as in the US, these goals were achieved: between 1980 and 1983 inflation had been lowered from 18 percent to 3 percent and short-term interest rates had dropped from 16 percent to 10 percent. However, also as in the US, these goals were achieved at a tremendous, unexpected cost to the economy in terms of unemployment and lost output. During 1980, the first year of Thatcher's administration, the growth rate of the British economy plunged to -2.0 percent and continued to fall through 1981. In 1982, the unemployment rate had increased to 12.3 percent, the highest among the major industrialized countries.

Both Thatcher and Reagan made overly optimistic promises of economic performance which were not achieved due to widespread ignorance of just how powerful restrictive monetary policy had become. In the early 1980s, the financial side of the new global economy began absorbing an unexpectedly large supply of national currencies away from GDP markets. Therefore, GDP markets would have been faced with an unexpected liquidity crisis even without governmental moves to tighten credit. So destructive were the short-run effects of the UK's monetary experiment, that 364 university economists and nearly all of the retired senior economic advisors to past British governments issued an unprecedented public statement condemning the experiment:

> First, there is no basis in economic theory or supporting evidence for the Government's belief that by deflating demand [with restrictive monetary policy] they will bring inflation permanently under control and thereby induce an automatic recovery in output and employment; Secondly, present policies will deepen the depression, erode the industrial base of our economy and threaten its social and political stability; Third, the time has come to reject monetarist policies and consider urgently which alternative offers the best hope of sustained economic recovery.[2]

Fortunately for the British policy-makers, they did not highlight their ignorance of the new global economy, as did the Reagan economists, by setting specific targets for economic performance. The British promises were for the most part only generalized commitments for change, but even these were not attained. Large reductions in central government spending were not realized, and, as in the US, there was ultimately an increase in the central government's share of the economy – just the opposite of what both Thatcher and Reagan had promised their constituents. Thatcher's conservative mandate from the voters soon lost some of its momentum, and in a key power struggle with the National Union of Mineworkers the government halted its attempt to close down operations at redundant coal pits. Industry was not freed from 'the shackles of labor and government', instead, large loans and subsidies were given to British Steel, British Leyland, Rolls-Royce, British Shipbuilders, and British Airways.

C. The French Situation

While the American and British monetary experiments were combining with austere economic policies in West Germany to create a global recession in the early 1980s, François Mitterrand began implementing policies which were designed to stimulate the French economy.   Increased government spending, as mandated by Mitterrand's socialist revolution, allowed the French economy to grow by 1.7 percent in 1982, a year when economic growth in the US and West Germany declined by 2.1 percent and 1.1 percent, respectively.   Of the major industrial countries besides France, only Japan realized moderate economic growth rate in this recessionary year.

Instead of ushering in a period of economic prosperity or stability relative to its trading partners, France's attempt to buck the recessionary trend of the global economy soon ran into serious difficulties.   The strong French economy sucked in more imports while the weaker economies of other nations purchased fewer French products.   As a result, the French trade deficit almost doubled, from Fr 50 billion in 1981 to Fr 92 billion in 1982. This deterioration in the trade balance was unexpected, largely because policy-makers were unaware of just how much the French economy had become integrated into the new global economy.

The ballooning French trade deficit soon meant a loss of international investor confidence in the French franc and low levels of investment in French manufacturing firms.   Ultimately profit levels declined and jobs were lost.   In mid-1982, Mitterrand was forced to abandon his stimulative economic policies, and instead adopt the 'most deflationary postwar austerity package'.[3] Government spending was cut and taxes were raised to reduce the growing government budget deficit.   French travelers were allowed only $275 per year of foreign travel expenditures, and the foreign use of credit cards was banned.   Public utility rates were raised by 8 percent, and the money supply was tightened as in the US and Great Britain.   These reforms prompted Andre Bergeron, head of the moderate *Force Ouvrière* labor union to announce: 'today we have had a cold shower, and I assure you that our militants and members will not accept it'.[4]

The French austerity programs began to have their desired effect, in that they cut the trade deficit in half, from Fr 92 billion in 1982 to Fr 44 billion in 1983.   The French franc finally stabilized against the US dollar and the German mark, but at a very low rate.   However, the growth of the French economy slowed to zero in 1983, and Mitterrand's rating in the public-opinion polls sank to a low of 30–35 percent by late 1983.   Opposition parties began winning more local elections and seats in the French senate, and Mitterrand's main opponent, Jacques Chirac, substantially increased his political influence.

By 1986, Chirac had been elected Prime Minister, and his center-right coalition began remolding the economy somewhat in America's free-market image.   An unexpectedly popular $40 billion sell-off of government corporations to the private sector seemed to mark the end of the socialist revolution, a revolution which might have continued through the late 1980s and spread elsewhere if Mitterrand had not made his early mistakes.

France's failed attempt to act independently of the new global economy weakened its alliance with other members of the European Community (EC), who thought that France had more of a commitment to stability and moderation. As a member of the European Monetary System (EMS), France was expected to keep the value of its currency stable in relation to other EMS currencies, especially the German mark. However, when the franc began devaluing in the early 1980s, France did not immediately take corrective action with domestic monetary and fiscal policies as suggested by the EC. Instead, France attempted to maintain its one-country economic experiment, which meant blaming some of the currency problem on the Germans and threatening to pull out of the EMS. The integrity of the EMS was not restored until the mid-1980s when Mitterrand's socialist revolution became more moderate and 'middle-of-the-road'.

In the early 1980s, Mitterrand's socialist revolution had helped to define the 'left-wing' of the political-economic spectrum within the developed western world. At the same time, Reagan's and Thatcher's capitalist revolutions had helped to define the 'right-wing' of electable political-economic philosophies. But as the decade progressed, the more fervent ideological dogma faded from each of these revolutions; instead more globally pragmatic politics prevailed. These revolutions failed to maintain their original, more extreme, 'grandstanding' forms because these forms required monetary and fiscal policies which were not sufficiently compatible with average global trends.

The new global economy may thus have narrowed the political-economic spectrum of workable ideologies within the developed western world. It has become less practical for these major trading nations to pursue significantly different monetary and fiscal policies, and therefore it has become less practical for them to adopt significantly different monetary and fiscal philosophies. Where significantly different political-economic ideologies still exist, they are instead based more narrowly upon different types of business–labor relations, but even these contrasts are becoming less common due to the internationalization of corporations. As discussed in Chapter 2, the increased number of international joint business ventures and overseas production activities, as well as the increased international ownership of once-national corporations, is exposing business and labor everywhere to a more global blend of regulations and incentives.

III. THE STOCK MARKET CRASH OF 1987

As documented in Chapter 3, deregulation, internationalization, and technological change created the following trend which began in the early 1980s: more money-liquidity has been required by the US, UK, and other economies in order to support the simultaneous growth of nominal GDP and the new financial markets. How much more money-liquidity has been required? Despite the research of the author and others, the financial side of the new global economy has expanded too rapidly and unpredictably compared to GDP to allow for an accurate estimate as yet.

For example, in an unprecedented demonstration of how fast money can be channeled into the financial markets, so much money flowed into the US stock markets in January, 1987 that US household wealth locked up in these financial investments increased by more than $250 billion in just this one month.[5] Then, when the US stock market crashed 22.6 percent on 19 October 1987, $500 billion was lost in one day.

As another example, commercial lending by foreign banks, which captured 9 percent of the US market in the late 1970s, increased its share to 16 percent by the mid-1980s.[6] This foreign lending has added to the volume of US financial transactions, and, because it can quickly move in and out of the US money supply, it is very difficult to quantify its effect on the economy. The same thing can be said about foreign lending to the US government, i.e. foreign purchases of US government securities, which totaled $14.3 billion in just the first six months of 1986, compared to $10 billion in all of 1980.[7]

International financial transactions denominated in US dollars expanded to the point where dollar holdings by foreign investors reached $1 trillion by 1990, approximately 20 percent of the expected nominal GDP for that year. Predicting how these holdings will be used in the US economy in the future is very difficult.

Similarly in the UK, the 1986 Big Bang deregulation period allowed dramatic increases in both the profitability and turnover of financial markets. As shown in Figure 3.3, UK financial market turnover doubled from 1985 to 1986 and then doubled again from 1986 to 1987.

As the velocity of money continued its decline in the mid-1980s, most notably in the US and UK but also in other globalizing financial centers (Figure 3.1), expansionary monetary policies pursued by the major industrial nations had only weak positive effects on nominal GDP compared with historical periods. More of the expanding money was absorbed by the new, more international financial markets and less was used by people to boost their purchases of merchandise and services. Despite the mistakes of forecasters in 1981–82, this new structural environment for monetary policy was not yet fully understood. For example, scores of articles appeared in reaction to the expansionary monetary policy that was started in the US in late 1982, each expressing confusion at the minimal resulting increases in real GDP and inflation (p. 92).

Analysts can hardly be chastised for their confusion, because the structural environment for monetary policy changed very fast in the 1980s. Econometric forecasting models which must use decades of data cannot be expected to fully incorporate these structural changes. Also, direct measurement of the share of (m1) which is absorbed in the turnover of financial transactions and simultaneously unavailable for non-financial, GDP transactions is next to impossible, despite the well-respected work of Spindt (1985) and others. For example, how do we know the degree to which people see their negotiable order of withdrawal (NOW) accounts as interest-earning investments rather than as checking accounts for monthly shopping requirements?

These results of the 1980s, restrictive monetary policy more powerfully reducing nominal GDP and expansionary monetary policy less powerfully increasing nominal GDP, will be the overriding trends as long as financial markets continue to expand rapidly. The exact change in these 'multipliers' will be influenced by the rate at which financial transactions expand and absorb (m1). Clearly, this absorption has been unexpectedly great in the 1980s, as evidenced by the failure of economists to forecast nominal GDP – they have continually expected more nominal GDP than what actually occurs, and therefore more real GDP and inflation than what actually occurs.

In light of this new, frequently misunderstood environment for monetary policy, the unprecedented world stock market crash of 1987 can now be explained. On 19 October 1987, the Dow Jones Industrial Average fell an astonishing 508 points, or 22.6 percent, its biggest one-day percentage decline ever. This unexpected crash in the US market triggered panic selling in all of the world's major stock markets, which had become inextricably linked in the 1980s.

As shown in Table 4.4, from 25 August 1987, the record high for the US stock market, to 11 November 1987, the world markets declined anywhere from 43.4 percent (Australia) to 18.7 percent (Italy). After mid-November, the markets began a gradual recovery as fear-driven selling moderated, and as central banks dramatically (and finally!) increased national money supplies.

Why did the world's stock markets crash? The most commonly mentioned and commonly agreed-upon explanations seemed to be the following:

1. Speculation had driven stock market valuations too high relative to stock earnings, so that a major shift of funds out of stocks into bonds, other investments, and cash was overdue.
2. Investors lost confidence in the economic policies of the US government, especially its attempts to reduce the federal budget deficit and to maintain the foreign exchange value of the US dollar. Both of these conditions were felt to be necessary in order to insure healthy international financial markets.
3. Sudden fear that the US dollar would lose much of its value, especially after the announcement of an unexpectedly large US trade deficit, caused international investors to move much of their money out of the US stock market. As the US stock market crashed, fear spread through the other markets and they crashed as well.[8]

Table 4.4 World stock markets decline, 1987

Percentage change in each market between 25 August 1987, the record high for the US market, and 11 November 1987:

US	-27.8
Japan	-19.8
UK	-27.2
West Germany	-38.4
Canada	-28.4
France	-34.7
Switzerland	-30.5
Australia	-43.4
Italy	-18.7
Netherlands	-33.6

Source: Morgan Stanley Capital International Perspective.

4. Less mentioned, less agreed-upon, but more fundamental explanations attributed the world stock market crash to monetary policies. For example, on 22 October 1987, the editorial page of *The Wall Street Journal* carried two articles by prominent economists, one claiming that the crash occurred because monetary policy was too restrictive, and one claiming that the crash occurred because monetary policy was too loose.[9]

Although there are valid points in both of these WSJ articles, neither mentions the new structural environment for monetary policy that has been created by the deregulation, expansion, and globalization of financial markets. As discussed above, in the 1980s an increasingly larger money supply has been needed to support the rapid growth of financial markets as well as the normal growth of GDP. Recognition of this trend, combined with an examination of the relevant economic data, should make it clear that the world stock market crash occurred because monetary policy was too restrictive – not only US monetary policy, but also monetary policy in the UK and other countries which have participated in the expansion of international financial markets.

US monetary policy in fact became quite restrictive in 1987 in the time period leading up to the stock market crash. The annual growth rate of the US money supply, whether measured by (m1) or the broader measures (m2) or (m3), declined by approximately 4 percentage points in the first five months of 1987, compared to its growth rate in 1986. For example, US (m1) grew by 15 percent in 1986, a rate which allowed the globalizing US financial markets to expand and at the same time allowed US inflation and real GDP to expand at historically low rates close to 2 percent. Then, in the first five months of 1987, the US Federal Reserve Bank reduced the annual growth rate of (m1) to just over 10 percent.

After May, 1987, the US Federal Reserve Bank slowed the annual growth rate of (m1) even further, to 3.0 percent growth in June, 5.3 percent contraction in July, 2.1 percent growth in August and 3.9 percent growth in September, the last month before the stock market crash. The Federal Reserve Bank was reacting to the rising, but incorrect, expectation that inflation was just around the corner, as well as a mounting fear that the foreign exchange value of the dollar would fall precipitously, thus causing capital flight out of the US currency, further declines in its value and the erosion of investor confidence. Restrictive monetary policy was implemented to fend off these risks, and it was felt to be justified because the probability of a recession within the near future was slim.

Yet in the late 1980s, the probability of a short-run slowdown in economic growth was not the greatest danger created by restrictive monetary policies. The greatest danger, and one that central bankers failed to understand fully, was that many new profitable opportunities in financial markets could be destroyed, and with them hundreds of billions of dollars of wealth. Ultimately, the destruction of so much wealth when the 'golden egg' (Chapter 3) is dropped hurts economic growth as well.

Leading up to the October crash, contractionary monetary policies were being pursued in Japan, West Germany and England as well as in the US. From July to October, interest rates on 3-month Eurodeposits denominated in yen, marks, and pounds increased by 1 percent, while those denominated in US dollars increased by 2 percent. Somewhat tighter monetary policy was pursued in the US to defend the dollar, and to 'reassure financial markets by demonstrating that the Fed was on guard against inflation'.[10]

The short-term result of restricted money and higher interest rates was a very costly reversal in the expansion of the international money centers. This expansion had continued steadily through the mid-1980s thanks to deregulation, internationalization, and advances in information-processing technology, all of which had given the world's borrowers and lenders increased ability to make profitable investments. Higher interest rates despite continued sluggish real GDP growth around the world squeezed the new-found profitability and shattered investor confidence. Nervousness spread until the markets finally sold off.

World stock market losses, which added up to more than the entire $900 billion debt of the less developed countries, might have been largely avoided if central bankers had cooperatively maintained looser monetary policies in order to accommodate the natural expansion of the money centers. Instead, just when international monetary expansion was most needed shortly before the crash, West Germany raised its interest rates. The increase in West

German interest rates created fear that the US Federal Reserve Bank would have to raise interest rates even further to prevent a withdrawal of foreign investment from the US and a decline in the foreign exchange value of the dollar. Just when the US and other countries needed to lower interest rates and increase money supplies, Germany stubbornly encouraged the confused central bankers to make their move in the opposite direction, to achieve what ultimately was a trivial and unsustainable goal: exchange rate stability.

Germany's overly restrictive monetary policy, relative to the other major industrial countries, resulted in a 43 percent decline in the German stock market, measured from the beginning of 1987 to the end of 1987. While the other stock markets began recovering at the end of 1987 as central banks injected more money into their economies, the German market was less able to recover, making it the big loser of the world's major stock markets in 1987.

Interestingly, shortly after the crash, the US stock market was valued at roughly the same level as it was at the end of 1986. Also, the monetary reserves of the US banking system, an alternate measure of the amount of money-liquidity in the US financial markets, was at the same level shortly before the crash as it was at the end of 1986. With no extra money-liquidity available for the US financial markets over the first nine months of 1987, it is not surprising that the US financial markets ultimately maintained approximately the same valuation over this period.

As indicated by this case study of the crash in world stock markets, as of 1987 economists still had not learned the important lessons from their forecasting errors of the early and mid-1980s. Sufficient attention was still not being paid to the continuing deregulation, expansion and globalization of the money centers. Therefore, the continuing drop in the velocity of money in early 1987 was not expected, and monetary policy was made much too restrictive. The result was the destruction of hundreds of billions of dollars of wealth and the erosion of investor confidence.

Unlike the money-liquidity crisis of the early 1980s, which primarily deflated the then-relatively less profitable non-financial markets, the unaccommodated drop in velocity in the late 1980s deflated the then-relatively less profitable financial markets.

IV. THE WORLD DEBT CRISIS, 1982–

The economic integration of nations is pervasive and continues to be underestimated. As argued above, the recession of the early 1980s and the stock market crash of 1987 could largely have been avoided if economic policies had reflected a greater understanding of the rapidly evolving one-world financial market. Overly-restrictive, separately enacted, national monetary policies led to high interest rates, money-liquidity crises, and ultimately these two global events. US and UK monetary policies were especially responsible; the US and UK financial markets are dominant and require the greatest liquidity; and both crises began in the US and UK financial markets and rapidly spread to the rest of the global economy.

In this section, a further examination of economic policies in the US, UK and elsewhere places even more responsibility for global economic welfare at the feet of policy-makers. It is argued here that these economic policies were also the single most important cause of the 1980s world debt crisis.

The story starts in the early 1980s when the Reagan Administration cut US income tax rates by 25 percent to stimulate economic growth. Unfortunately, restrictive monetary policies in the US and UK due to the unexpected absorption of money by globalizing financial markets pushed up US, UK and therefore world interest rates to historically high levels. These high interest rates created the 1982 world recession, and the Reagan and Thatcher administrations did not achieve the supply-side economic growth that had been predicted.

The prime interest rate charged by US banks discounted by (i.e. over and above the rate of) US inflation increased from an average of 0.4 percent in 1975–79 to an average of 6.5 percent in 1980–86. In the UK, the equivalent rate was negative every year from 1975 to 1980, and then positive every year from 1981 to 1986 with an average value of 5.0 percent. The initial, 1979–1981 increases in these real costs of borrowing were due to the restrictive US and UK monetary policies; after 1981, and especially by 1983 the large US federal budget deficit was more to blame, as monetary policies were loosened somewhat.

How did these monetary and fiscal policies affect the world debt situation? Between 1972 and 1979, when interest rates charged on US dollars were only slightly above the rate of US inflation (as was typical in the developed world), the international indebtedness of the less-developed countries (LDCs) had increased at an annual average rate of 21.7 percent (Bogdanowicz-Bindert, 1985–86, p. 261). In this period price improvements in the LDCs (as on LDC exports) were higher than in the US, meaning that inflation-adjusted interest rates in the LDCs on US dollar loans were frequently negative, and considerable borrowing from the US could be justified. Also, the increasingly international, interest-rate-parity nature of financial markets implied that considerable borrowing from London, Frankfurt, Tokyo, and other money centers was similarly justified.

Then, in 1980 the money-liquidity crisis hit as the US, UK, and other developed countries pursued restrictive monetary policies. By 1982 the continuing liquidity crisis had created recessions in the developed countries, which in turn meant a collapse in the export markets for many of the products supplied by the LDCs. For example, 60 percent of Mexico's merchandise exports go to the US, and when the US economy 'caught a cold' in the early 1980s, many Mexican industries 'caught pneumonia' for this reason alone.

Higher US dollar interest rates and lower prices for LDC exports, both of which were largely due to the liquidity crisis and recession that began in the US, soon made it impossible for many LDCs to continue paying back their loans. The US prime interest rate discounted by the price on non-fuel exports of the LDCs increased from 5.7 percent in 1975–79 to 19.5 percent in 1986.[11] This 13.8 percent increase in the real cost of financing non-fuel production and exports was devastating to the LDCs. Many of the old loans were variable and soon reflected the higher US prime rate and London Interbank Offer rate. New loans, even when needed only to service the old debt, could rarely be justified in the private marketplace. Virtually all new private lending to the LDCs stopped.

Before long, the 13.8 percent increase in the real cost of financing non-fuel production and exports in the LDCs meant that (approximately) a 13.8 percent increase in the growth of these export industries would have been necessary to maintain the same ability to service foreign debt. Such growth would not have been possible even without the global recession. The world debt crisis had been created, primarily by US and UK economic policies.

The situation for major fuel exporters, such as Mexico, was the most devastating. By the time world oil prices had fallen by $18 a barrel from 1981 to 1986, oil-dependent Mexico had lost tens of billions of dollars of export revenues. A one-dollar drop in the world oil price reduces Mexico's export earnings by a half billion dollars per year. The LDC debt crisis cannot be blamed upon an independent collapse of OPEC and oil prices, however. Brazil's economy is not so significantly affected by changes in oil prices, and Brazil became the biggest and perhaps the most heavily-burdened LDC debtor. Also, the inability of OPEC to maintain high US dollar-denominated oil prices was significantly influenced by the drop in US dollar-demand for oil due to the restrictive dollar monetary policies and world recession.

The story continues in the mid-1980s. The US federal budget deficits continued to exceed $100 billion and even $200 billion per year after 1983 and there was still a bias toward restrictive monetary policy in the US and elsewhere. Consequently, US interest rates remained high, and in the rapidly integrating world financial markets these high interest rates began to pull international funds into the US at an unprecedented rate. The net flow of international funds into the US exceeded $100 billion per year by 1984 and, directly or indirectly, began financing about half of the US federal budget deficit.

By the mid-1980s, US government borrowing in and of itself was no longer significantly adding to the liquidity crises in the US nor exerting significant upward pressure on US interest rates – fortunately for US fiscal policy, the net inflow of foreign funds both responded to and exceeded the volumes of new US government borrowing. Unfortunately for many LDC debtors, however, some of the more than $100 billion per year, net, that was being pulled into the US came from their already cash-short economies.

Therefore, some of the liquidity crisis was effectively transferred from the US and other developed economies to the LDCs in the mid-1980s, thus compounding the LDC debt crisis.

For example, despite attempts to channel Mexican loans into productive investments for the Mexican economy, it has been estimated that one-half of Mexico's foreign borrowings in the late 1970s and early 1980s instead left Mexico as capital flight, with the US and Switzerland as the primary safe havens for this cash. Sizable capital flight has also been a significant problem for Brazil, Venezuela, Argentina and others (Figure 4.1). In the more globalized financial markets, capital controls used by the LDCs could not prevent the ultimate transfer of wealth to the most attractive international investment opportunities, which increasingly were in the US.

Figure 4.1 Capital flight from Latin America (1977–87, $billion)

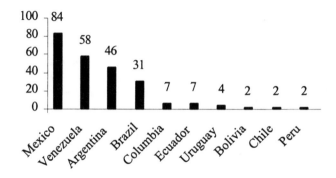

Source: Morgan Guaranty Trust Co.

Back to US economic policies: US Treasury Secretary James Baker, who presided over US economic policies in the early and mid-1980s, proposed the Baker Plan for dealing with the debt crisis in 1985. The primary emphasis of this plan was to protect the short-run solvency of US banks. There was no call for debt reduction or any other effective means of ultimately reducing the debt burden in the LDCs; instead Baker called for new loans to service existing LDC debt so that US banks could continue to receive normal payments and not have to classify a significant portion of their LDC debt as bad debt. As reigning Federal Reserve Board chairman Paul Volcker stated years later about this period, 'we make a choice as to what to protect and what not to, and the strategic element to protect is essentially the banking system' (Feldstein, 1991, p. 178).

Indeed, the solvency of many US banks was at stake when the debt crisis hit in the early 1980s. For example, as shown in Table 4.5, the nine major US banks had 176.5 percent of their capital in heavily debt-burdened Latin

American countries at the end of 1982. This ratio means that 176.5 percent of the entire stock-market value of these banks had been loaned to Latin America as of year-end 1982. Having to write-off a majority of this debt might therefore have left the major US banks with insufficient capital to remain in business.

Protecting the solvency of the major US banks during the 1980s required one or both of the following: either significant write-offs in LDC debt had to be avoided, or the stock market (capital) value of the banks had to significantly increase. As it turned out, the Baker Plan insured the former in the short run, until the rapidly globalizing financial markets and US monetary and fiscal policy had insured the latter.

As shown in Table 4.5, the total stock market capital value of the nine major US banks increased from $29.0 billion to $46.7 billion to $55.8 billion at year-end 1982, 1986, and 1988, respectively, thus lowering the percentage of their total capital in Latin America to 110.2 percent at year-end 1986 and 83.6 percent at year-end 1988. By the late 1980s, therefore, the major US banks were no longer in danger of being insolvent if major write-offs of Latin-American debt occurred, and US policymakers could turn their attention to broader issues, such as the ultimate resolution of the debt crisis, and the overall health of the US and international financial markets. For example, the (new Treasury Secretary) Brady Plan in 1989 finally formalized and encouraged several ways in which private markets were already writing-off LDC debt including resale discounts of this debt in the secondary markets.

Question: what accounted for the increased stock market capital value and, therefore, the return to secure solvency of the major US banks from 1982 to 1988, despite the obviously negative effect that the debt crisis must have had upon their stock market values over this period? Answer: the net flow of foreign funds into the US financial markets of more than $100 billion per year by 1984. As discussed previously, these funds allowed for a non-inflationary expansion of the US bank money supply, the longest post World War II expansion in US economic growth, and the tripling of US stock market values from 1982 to 1988 even considering the stock market crash of 1987.

The story now takes an ironic turn. As discussed in the previous section, the 15 percent increase in the US money supply during 1986 was perfectly reasonable given the inflow of foreign funds and increased absorption of money by financial markets. However, excessive concern about inflation and lack of cooperation between the developed countries in 1987 led to restrictive monetary policies in the US and elsewhere, which in turn caused the stock market crash of October 1987. It was truly a world stock market crash in that the value of assets in the LDCs declined in proportion to the developed country losses shown earlier in Table 4.4.

Table 4.5 Money flows into the US financial markets in the 1980s and saves US banks from bad foreign debts

	End-1982	End-1986	End-1988
Nine Major US Banks			
% of bank capital in:			
-Developing countries:	287.7%	153.9%	108.0%
-Latin America:	176.5%	110.2%	83.6%
All Other US Banks			
% of bank capital in:			
-Developing Countries:	116.0%	55.0%	32.2%
-Latin America:	78.6%	39.7%	21.8%
Total Bank Capital			
(billions of dollars)			
-Nine major US banks:	$29.0	$46.7	$55.8
-All other US banks:	$41.6	$69.4	$79.8

Source: Federal Financial Institutions Examination Council, 'Country Exposure Lending Survey', 25 April 1983, 24 April 1987, and 12 April 1989.

Table 4.6 shows the discount rates at which banks were able to sell off the debt of various developing countries before and after the October 1987 world stock market crash.   These discount prices represent private market perceptions of the ability of countries to repay debt and thus indirectly the prices represent the income potential of country assets.   As an example, Brazil's foreign debt sold for 62–65 cents per dollar of face value in May, 1987, indicating that 35–38 cents on the dollar of Brazilian debt could be written-off during debt-equity swaps in that month.   In November, 1987, one month after the money-liquidity crisis caused the crash in world stock markets, Brazil's debt sold for 37–41 cents on the dollar, indicating write-offs of 59–63 cents.

Reduced selling prices from May to November, 1987, for the debt of all of these developing countries verifies the truly global impact of the stock market crash. The crash reduced the average market value of developing-country investments as per Table 4.6 just as much as it reduced the value of investments within the richer nations as per Table 4.4.

As discussed in the previous section, stock market losses in the developed countries, which added up to more than the entire $900 billion debt of the LDCs, might largely have been avoided if central bankers, especially in the

US and UK, had cooperatively maintained looser monetary policies in order to accommodate the natural expansion of the money centers.

Table 4.6 Foreign debt prices, before and after the stock market crash (in cents per dollar of face value)

	May, 1987	November, 1987
Argentina	58–60	33–37
Brazil	62–65	37–41
Chile	67–70	50–53
Colombia	85–88	72–76
Ecuador	52–55	31–34
Mexico	57–60	48–52
Peru	14–18	2–7
Philippines	70–72	55–60
Venezuela	72–74	49–53

Source: Shearson Lehman Brothers Inc.

Now for the whole, ironical, sequence of events: high interest rates in the developed world in the early 1980s, especially caused by US and UK monetary policies, created a global recession and the LDC debt crisis. Continuing high interest rates during the mid-1980s in the developed world, still primarily due to monetary policies, but then also because of the US federal deficits, pulled newly-loaned global funds out of the LDCs as capital flight. This capital flight did not reduce the official LDC debt, but instead made it harder for LDC countries to generate the economic growth that would allow debt to be serviced.

Then, capital flight funds (actually, larger amounts of monetary wealth) were destroyed by the world stock market crash, itself caused primarily by US and European monetary policies. There has been much less channeling of funds into Latin American LDCs since the 1980s, but instead, poorer developed as well as developing countries have continued to send more than $100 billion per year, net, into the US (an amount approximately equal to either Mexico's or Brazil's total foreign debt).

These global funds have maintained the capital strength of the major US banks, allowed the US government to maintain large budgets through the 1990s for national defense, social welfare and other purposes, and paved the way for a continuing non-inflationary expansion of the US economy.

V. THE EARLY 1990s RECESSIONARY PERIOD

Recessionary conditions in the early 1990s can, as in 1982, be blamed on overly strict monetary policies given the continually increasing money-liquidity and capital needs of the global economy. For example, Japan's 8 percent average yearly money growth from 1986 to 1988 was slowed to 2.4 percent in 1989 and 4.4 percent in 1990. The result was the destruction of Japan's financial surplus and long-term capital outflows that had helped sustain economic growth in Europe and the US. The wealth lost domestically in Japan as its stock market fell 60 percent from 1989 to 1991 temporarily slowed growth there. But, unlike the US, Germany and others, Japan had the fiscal means in the early 1990s, including a $120 billion fiscal stimulus package in mid-1993, to avoid recession. As elaborated below, restrictive monetary policies in Europe and the US, together with Japan's 'turning inward' contributed heavily to the early 1990s global recessionary conditions.

The global regions hit especially hard by recessions in the early 1990s were those that lost international capital. The timing of recessions in the US and Europe demonstrates this fact. Also, the probability of early-1990s recessions in the developed countries increased due to the return of international investment to the LDCs. Net inflows of foreign direct investment into LDCs averaged $13 billion per year from 1985 to 1989, then jumped to $18 billion in 1990 and $31 billion in 1991.[12] Unlike in the 1970s, Asian LDCs rather than Latin American LDCs were receiving the major part of this direct investment. As direct investment to the LDCs soared in 1991, developed countries saw their average inflows shrink by one-fifth.

A. The European Situation

The late 1980s was a time of strong economic growth for Germany and others within the European Community. The Single European Act signed in 1987 to 'complete the internal EC market by 1992' began abolishing border controls and other technical barriers to trade including inconsistent health, safety, and environmental regulations; it commenced opening up public procurement, most significantly in energy, telecommunications, transportation, and water supply; and began creating a unified market for financial services.

The perceived efficiencies of 'Europe 1992' led to a cross-border European investment boom beginning in 1987, not only in the internal European market, but also from the European affiliates of US, Japanese, and other foreign firms. For example, majority-owned foreign affiliates of US companies increased capital spending in Europe from $15.4 billion in 1987 to $18.8 billion in 1988 to $21.1 billion in 1989. And by 1989, 411 Japanese manufacturers had opened or made plans to start production in Europe, thus tripling the number of Japanese plants since the early 1980s; the Toyota plant constructed in Great Britain in 1990 was the largest foreign investment ever in Britain. The French, who had long been one of the most protectionist against Japanese trade and investment, reversed their stance in April, 1989, when Industry Minister Roger Fauroux said that the French government has decided that 'it is better to have Japanese (factories) than to have unemployment'.[13]

Aided by international capital and internal efficiencies, economic growth for all of western Europe averaged over 3 percent per year from 1987 to 1990. As the biggest exporter of capital goods within Europe, West Germany gained the most from Europe 1992, achieving economic growth rates of 4 percent in both 1989 and 1990.   Able to export more easily to its strengthened neighbors, West Germany's trade surplus within the EC widened from DM32 billion in 1985 to DM94 billion in 1989. Thus, 60 percent of West Germany's trade surplus was with the rest of Europe by 1989.

German reunification was forwarded in the hope that the late-1980s EC economic growth rates would continue through the 1990s.   Under this assumption the German economy would have been able to absorb the estimated cost of successful reunification without severe hardship.   The DM94 billion ($55 billion) West German trade surplus with the EC in 1989 equaled 4.6 percent of its total economic output. Therefore, if growth rates had continued and all of this trade surplus with the EC was instead directed toward East German investment without any immediate return, the West German economy would have been in a minor recession, and East Germany would have had $350–$400 billion necessary for modernization before the year 2000.

Unfortunately, not only has the initial forecast of $350–$400 billion necessary for modernization of East Germany proved to be too low, but also the EC growth rate has slowed. Foreign firm-to-firm investment into East Germany since reunification has been slower than expected, given legal tangles over ownership of real estate and business assets, dilapidated transportation   and   communication   systems,   and   the   general uncompetitiveness of East German industry compared to international standards.   Only 30 percent of East German companies were capable of competing in the EC market, 50 percent needed overhauling to survive, and 20 percent were doomed to bankruptcy.[14]

The inability to compete within the EC led to substantially increased unemployment within East Germany after the full monetary union of 1 July 1990. Obliged to conduct all business in newly-issued West German marks after that date,[15] East German firms were thrown into many of the rigors of what the EC labor and product markets could stand, but how to compete when the output per worker in East Germany was 40 percent of the output per worker in West Germany, approximately equivalent to West Germany in the late 1960s?[16] Unemployment doubled in July to 270,000 workers, and three times as many East Germans were placed on reduced work time.[17]

Closing this productivity gap between the two Germanies has required a continuing $70–80 billion per year transfer to East Germany from the global economy through the turn of the century rather than the $50 billion per year originally estimated. Perhaps DM200 billion ($118 billion at $1 to DM1.7) has been necessary to restore the roads and railways, link the canals to West Germany's, and build a new international airport in East Berlin.[18] On 20 June 1990, a DM55 billion ($32 billion) plan to modernize the East German telephone system was unveiled, DM30 billion of which West Germany's state-run telecommunications group, Bundespost Telekom, expected to raise from the capital markets by 1998.[19] Further governmental expenditures will be required for postal and telecommunications systems, and other public works, and even greater rates of private investment are necessary.

Attracting enough international capital to Germany to help support the $70–80 billion per year necessary for successful reunification, especially given initial pledges not to raise taxes, required high German interest rates. The German 'identified capital flow' with the rest of the world (direct investment plus portfolio investment plus other capital), which had been a net outflow of $70 billion in 1988 and 1989, began turning inward to a net outflow of $50 billion in 1990 and a net inflow of $11 billion in 1991.

As is now well known, the high German interest rates and capital inflows in the early 1990s led to the effectual breakup of the EMS and the delay of other economic efficiencies of Europe 1992. In addition, the restrictive monetary policies of the other EMS countries through mid-1992 as they tried to maintain EMS interest rate and exchange rate parities with Germany led to recessionary conditions.

Economic output of the EC's twelve member states declined slightly in 1993, the first shrinkage since 1975, and the EC unemployment rate rose to 11 percent. Clearly, Germany's restrictive monetary policies and fiscal requirements put it at the center of the early 1990s EC crisis. Declining competitiveness and confidence in Germany due to the appreciating mark and, still, high interest rates, escalating costs of reunification and widespread Eastern European problems scared some international capital away from Germany. Pre-reunification German capital outflows returned, and the German economy contracted 1.2 percent in 1993. In mid-1993 German unemployment rates reached 7.5 percent in the West and 15.3 percent in the East.

B. The US Situation

The official US recession, as dated by the National Bureau of Economic Research (NBER), occurred during the last two quarters of 1990 and the first quarter of 1991. More generally, US economic growth averaged less than 1 percent from the beginning of 1989 to 1993, as compared to 2.3 percent from 1973 to 1989. Compared to a hypothetical 2.3 percent growth rate continuing (the 'natural potential rate of growth'), during 1989–1991 there was a $225 billion loss in potential GDP, approximately half of which was a decline in consumption and half a decline in fixed investment. Aside from these figures, a small increase in net exports was balanced by a small decrease in inventory investment and a small decrease in net government spending.

At the American Economic Association (AEA) meetings in January 1993, the main conclusion seemed to be that established models have been unhelpful in understanding this US recession. In papers given by Robert Hall of Stanford and the NBER (1993), and Olivier Blanchard of MIT (1993), there was only the general consensus that consumers may have lost confidence about the future. From Hall:

> A spontaneous decline in consumption would probably result in unusual behavior of consumption during the recession relative to its pre-recession values and relative to real disposable income... There was a considerable swing in consumption at much lower than a recession frequency from 1987 to 1991. At the same time, survey measures of consumer confidence fell from record high to somewhat subnormal levels. Although a sharp spontaneous contraction of consumption was not part of the story of the recession, changes in consumption not associated with changes in disposable income may be an important part of a bigger story about the late 1980s and early 1990s.

And from Blanchard:

> By far, the main proximate cause of the recession was a 'consumption shock', a decrease in consumption in relation to its normal determinants. Because the effects of such shocks are long lasting, this also explains why, in contrast to previous recoveries, the last recovery was a slow and weak one...

What is especially revealing about assessments of this US recession is the scant attention paid to global conditions including increased international transfers of investment based upon interest rate parity (Chapter 1), the subsequent adjustments in international trade (Chapter 2), and the structural decline in monetary velocity (Chapter 3). Presumably reflecting the research of the NBER as it advises the US government, Hall's (1993) paper devotes only a few sentences to the rest of the world:

> It appears unlikely that events in the rest of the world contributed to the recession...net exports grew a little during the recession. It would be almost impossible to tell a story in which events in world markets caused a US recession but US net exports rose... There was no outside force that concentrated its effects over a few months in the late summer and fall of 1990...

As per the explanations of earlier financial crises and recessions in this chapter, the reader might already understand the author's skepticism about the above quote. In fact, one only needs to look at Figure 4.2 to find an international force that adversely affected the US economy beginning in 1990. As shown in Figure 4.2, the identified capital inflows to the US for direct investment, portfolio investment, and other investment (monetary authorities plus general government plus banks plus other sectors) collapsed in 1990. Aggregating these categories shows a net identified capital inflow to the US of close to $100 billion per year until the sudden drop to $13 billion in 1990 and $30 billion in 1991. After 1991, the net inflow rose again to average over $100 billion.

The net identified capital inflow shown in Figure 4.2 excludes the very suspect 'statistical discrepancy' account which reconciles differences between measured commerce and payments for that commerce. The statistical discrepancy is generally considered part of the Capital Account balance; however, there is no way to verify exactly how much of the statistical discrepancy reflects actual flows of capital. In 1990, the statistical discrepancy account had a $64 billion credit position, its largest imbalance ever. The author's view is that some of this $64 billion did not actually flow into the US, which thus contributed even more to the US credit crunch and recessionary conditions.

From 1989, the last pre-recession year, to the depth of the US recession in 1990–91, the US economy was thus receiving approximately $100 billion/yr less net foreign investment, and the NBER and others claim that there was no outside force that concentrated its negative effects on the US economy in 1990–91! Certainly the $225 billion loss in potential GDP during 1989-1991 could be completely accounted for by this decline in net foreign investment once one figures out the reduced US income, monetary wealth, and therefore reduced consumption that would occur combined with the immediate loss of fixed and inventory investment. Based upon the timing lags and cause-effect material discussed in Chapter 2, the author's position is that the collapse in foreign investment inflow initiated the recession, rather than vice-versa.

German reunification was pulling international funds into Germany, and Japan's money-liquidity crisis was pulling international funds into Japan – independently of US domestic economic conditions. Also, the approximately $100 billion/year reduction in net foreign investment into the US could certainly account for the depreciation of the dollar during the recession against, especially, the Japanese yen – Japanese foreign investment especially dried up during 1990. In turn, the depreciating dollar and reduced US income (therefore more competitive US exports and less US demand for imports) could certainly account for the small rise in US net exports during the recession. Yet, in direct contrast to this scenario Hall (1993) claims that:

Figure 4.2   Explaining the 1990–91 US recession: the decline in net
identified capital inflows (by category, $billion)

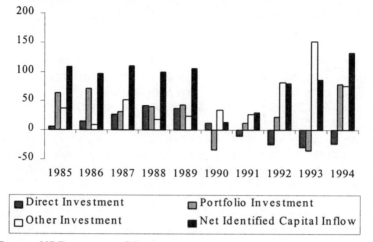

1985 1986 1987 1988 1989 1990 1991 1992 1993 1994

■ Direct Investment	▥ Portfolio Investment
▢ Other Investment	■ Net Identified Capital Inflow

Source: US Department of Commerce.

Any force that decreased the volume of resources going to capital formation would
raise the volume going to other purposes, especially consumption...it would be
almost impossible to tell a story in which events in world markets caused a US
recession but US net exports rose.

Obviously Hall among others did not acknowledge the possibility that
international flows of finance based upon interest rate and financial strategy
parities can be an initiating, profit-seeking force that drives changes in trade
and GDP growth among affected countries.

Hall's (1993) regression models, which are based largely on domestic
income trends, do not explain the drop in US consumption during the
recession period when foreign investment into the US collapsed, nor do they
explain the surge in US consumption during 1987 and 1988 when
international investment into the US reached record inflows: 'it is worth
mentioning, however, that consumption exceeded its predicted value by a
large margin ($41 billion) in 1987 and by over $20 billion in 1988'. This
under-prediction of consumption during 1987–88 provides further evidence
that the international flow of investment is a missing variable.

The US economy went into its 1990–91 slump at the same time that the
identified capital inflow collapsed, and the US dollar subsequently
depreciated to its lowest level.   Then, these trends began to reverse
themselves somewhat in 1991 and 1992 as the identified capital inflow began
to improve. Also, in the first two quarters of 1991 the US received 'official
unrequited transfer' net inflows of $17.45 and $7.61 billion respectively – a

current account line item reflecting in this period payments from allies due to the US Persian Gulf actions. The official unrequited transfers balance of the US is generally negative. Its annual balance over 1987–1992 was –$12.49, –$13.01, –$13.28, –$20.25, $20.98 (in 1991), and –$17.56 billion, respectively.

The $35–$40 billion improvement (more payment inflow) in this one current account category in 1991 plus the $50 billion increase in identified capital account inflow to the US in 1992 (Figure 4.2) initiated the weak US economic recovery and dollar appreciation in 1991–92. Once again financial flows were driving changes in GDP and trade. The US current account balance, which had dropped close to zero in 1991 due to the Persian Gulf contributions, weak US economy import demand, and low US dollar, began to deteriorate again in 1992 (Figure 2.2) as the capital inflow resumed.

Thus, a stronger US economy, as in the 1980s, remains associated with a larger US trade deficit. This result is contrary to most economic adjustment literature as discussed in Chapter 2. Also, it helps explain why the economics profession has had trouble modeling the early 1990s US recessionary period.

Economic models also failed to explain the early 1990s US recession because, as with 1980s financial crises and recession, insufficient attention was paid to the income velocity of money. US (m1) velocity fell 3 percent from 1990 to 1991 at the same time as the Federal Reserve Bank was restricting the growth rate of monetary aggregates. The result, as in 1982, was a contraction of nominal GDP from its growth path, and this was split between its two components, real GDP and inflation.

Instead of adjusting the money supply to maintain nominal GDP along its growth path, which would have appropriately been 6.5 percent as in 1988–90, the Fed seemingly returned to money-supply targeting and over-concern with inflation in late 1990. While Hall (1993) among others discusses the collapse of nominal GDP below its 6.5 percent growth path, velocity is not discussed, nor does the collapse in nominal GDP seem to worry him. He excuses Fed policy as a source of the recession because he does not find that the Fed consciously adopted a lower nominal GDP target, and because US interest rates remained low and even fell during the recession.

US interest rates did decline during the recession, but not until the fourth quarter of 1990 when the Fed began reducing the discount and federal funds rates. Also, the cut in these short-term rates midway into the recession was not followed by a significant fall in long-term rates, such as the 30-year Treasury bond, until a year or two later. The yield gap between the discount rate and the 30-year government bond thus approached 4 percent at the end of 1991, a gap seen before only during the 1982–84 LDC debt crisis period when US bank solvency was threatened.

Such a gap, twice as large as normal, helps re-capitalize banks and restores their profitability, because banks can borrow at the discount rate and lend at the 30-year bond rate. A joke going around in the early 1990s was of a 10-2-4 club. Bankers would take in short-term 3 percent deposits or draw-downs at the Fed discount window at 10:00 A.M., invest these funds in long-term 7 percent T-bonds at 2:00 P.M., and then hit their private clubs at 4:00 P.M. Presumably they had not managed to loan money to businesses or households in the process.

When domestic yield-gap re-capitalization is occurring, domestic borrowing may suffer, which was the case during the early 1990s US recessionary period. In effect, banks were subsidized as intermediaries between domestic monetary and fiscal policy, and the rest of the economy felt a money-liquidity crisis from being 'left out of the loop' despite rapidly declining short-term rates.

Longer-term US interest rates are more subject to the international interest rate parity conditions than the shorter-term interest rates. The shorter-term interest rates can be set more directly by the Fed via changes in the discount and federal funds rates. The high international interest rates in 1991 in Germany and elsewhere kept US longer-term rates high, and the Fed's move to reduce short-term US rates in 1990–91 probably encouraged the US capital outflow and dollar depreciation.

In contrast, at the end of the 1982 recession the US began receiving big increases in net foreign investment due to the structural changes associated with globalization (Chapters 1 and 2). Unlike the early 1990s recessionary period, the 1982–84 capital inflow soon made up for the shortfall in domestic investment. The US in 1983 and 1984 was thus able to have strong economic growth while at the same time capitalizing its banks. Coming out of the 1990–91 recessionary period, recovery was slower; not until 1994 did the net capital inflow rise above the pre-1990 levels (Figure 4.2).

VI. THE 1994–95 MEXICAN CRISIS

The 1980s Latin American debt crisis appeared to be resolved by the late 1980s, and economic growth in Mexico and elsewhere had returned. Financial liberalization and globalization in Mexico, and less uncertainty regarding its economic and political prospects, led to rapid credit and quasi-money expansion and inflows of foreign investment. From 1990 to 1993, Mexico received $91 billion in net capital inflows, which was approximately one-fifth of all net inflows to developing countries. Bank credit extended to the private non-financial sector increased from 10 percent of GDP in 1988 to more than 40 percent in 1994. Oversight by the National Banking Commission in this period was weak, partly due to the rise of offshore finance (Chapter 3) and other complicated international monetary channels that directed funds into Mexico. Dollar-denominated bonds – *tesobonos* – which were guaranteed by the Mexican government based on its dollar reserves, expanded rapidly and were classified by the Mexican government as domestic debt. By late 1994, there were $18 billion in *tesobonos* held by foreigners, and $11 billion in *tesobonos* held by Mexicans – all of which were short-term and coming due in 1995.

Unfortunately for Mexico, contractionary monetary policies began in the US in February 1994, which were reciprocated in the other hard-currency money centers. From 1 February to 1 August 1994, interest rates on ten-year government bonds increased by the following percentage point amounts: 1.4 percent in the US, 0.9 percent in Japan, 1.4 percent in Germany, 1.6 percent in France, and 2.4 percent in the UK – severe increases given the absence of any general rise in inflation or economic growth rates.

Given these increases in interest rates in the money centers, flows of international investment into Mexico could not be sustained. Furthermore, Mexican investment was discouraged by increased political and economic uncertainty in Mexico following the Chiapas uprising (which began in January 1994 to coincide with the North American Free Trade Agreement), the assassination of Presidential candidate Colosio, and the corruption charges against President Salinas and his family. Subjective perceptions can be extremely important in the marginal decision-making of international investors, who flirt with small deviations in expected rates of return on investment between countries. An internal memo issued to the Emerging Markets Group of a major US bank, dated 13 February 1995 read, in part:

> While Chiapas, in our opinion, does not pose a fundamental threat to Mexican political stability, it is perceived to be so by many in the investment community. The government will need to eliminate the Zapatistas to demonstrate their effective control of the national territory and of security policy (Hawkes, 1996, p. 189).

National and international investors also knew that the Mexican economy had been slowing and that inflation had outstripped productivity growth, yet the Salinas administration had not allowed a devaluation of the peso to reflect these trends. As of early December 1994, a majority of investors did not believe that these trends required a devaluation. Capital inflows into Mexico had been mostly curtailed six months earlier, yet the Bank of Mexico had pledged to support the peso with expenditure of its dollar reserves. Dollar reserves had thus been declining, yet the Bank of Mexico had been slow to admit the extent of the decline. However, in December, when the Mexican government released data indicating that a major devaluation was likely, traders rushed to get out of the peso. Furthermore, they removed their US dollar holdings out of Mexican institutions. These dollar holdings were very liquid, because debtors had issued short-term dollar bonds that promised redemption at face value. On 21 December 1994, $29 billion of *tesobono* short-term liabilities were for sale, $18 billion of which were the responsibility of the Mexican government, and this news made the front page of *The Wall Street Journal*.

Just like a run on a bank, investors ran on Mexico:

> Like small savers who see their neighbors lining up outside a bank and join the queue to withdraw their deposits before the bank's cash reserves are exhausted, investors in government bonds have an incentive to liquidate their holdings when others do likewise and they fear that the government's limited foreign exchange reserves will be exhausted...the magnitude of capital flows can leave a government facing a debt run, like a bank facing a run by its depositors, no choice but to suspend payments, regardless of the damage to its creditworthiness. On the eve of the crisis, the Mexican government was responsible for more than $18 billion of dollar-denominated and dollar-indexed liabilities, roughly triple its foreign exchange reserves. Once investors began to liquidate their holdings, the authorities were at their mercy (Eichengreen and Portes, in Federal Reserve Bank of Kansas City, 1997, p. 195).

Unlike the Latin American debt crisis of the 1980s, which involved large loans from money-center banks, this time stocks and bonds were the vehicles for much of the foreign investment into Mexico. Selling of these liquid securities was thus immediate, and it could not be slowed by negotiations between government officials, the IMF, and large financial institutions. When the Mexican finance minister presented his economic crisis management program at the Federal Reserve Bank of New York on 21 December 1994, various mutual fund and hedge fund managers were present, who represented only a subset of the exposed investors – if Mexican officials had wanted to renegotiate terms with its creditors, they would have had trouble even identifying them. As the peso and the Mexican stock and bond markets crashed in December, the market pushed short-term peso interest rates above 100 percent at an annual rate. Many Mexican banks and other firms, which had debt obligations in foreign currency, and which owned stocks and bonds, experienced a rapid decline in net worth and creditworthiness. In 1995, Mexico would have its worst recession in decades – real GDP would fall 6 percent, and the industrial output portion would fall more than 10 percent.

Much of the transfer of Mexican monetary wealth into dollars and out of the country went, initially, into offshore financial markets. This data is mostly not reported in balance of payments statistics, but Table 3.1 estimates what was happening at least with 'LDC fuel exporters' and offshore dollar markets – Mexico can be presumed to account for the major share of these flow-changes between 1993 and 1994. As shown in Table 3.1, in 1992 and 1993 the LDC fuel exporters did not accumulate or lose dollars reserves, but in 1994 there was a $20 billion loss (this portion of the data is fairly reliable as reported to the IMF). This loss in reserves occurred despite $20 billion in 'net financing in dollars' by LDC fuel exporters in 1993 and $25 billion in 1994 (still reliable data). Where did these monetary reserves and credit supplies of dollars held by LDC fuel exporters go? Table 3.1 estimates that, from all sources (not just LDC fuel exporters) there was flow of hidden dollar income into offshore centers and tax havens of $50 billion in 1993 and $55 billion in 1994, and additional 'capital flight' into the dollar is estimated at $40 billion in 1993 and $50 billion in 1994 (unreliable data now). Industrial countries (excluding the US) were accumulating dollar reserves in this period (an additional $40 billion in 1993 and $80 billion in 1994); therefore they were not likely to be contributing dollars to offshore financial markets. Likewise, the US was receiving a massive inflow of dollars in all investment categories. Therefore, the LDCs, especially Mexico, probably accounted for a majority of the dollar flows into offshore markets, which in turn were mostly transferred to the US and other industrial countries (see 'uses' of foreign savings in dollars in Table 3.1).

By early 1995, the only solution to avoid Mexican government insolvency, and bankruptcies across the Mexican economy, was to find an international lender of last resort. On 31 January, the rescue package was finalized when the IMF agreed to provide $10 billion in five-year loans on top of the $7.8 billion in credit it had already promised Mexico. Additionally, by executive order, US President Clinton approved $20 billion in loans with terms of as much as ten years by tapping the US Treasury's Exchange Stabilization Fund (normally used to support the dollar); major industrial nations contributed $10 billion in short-term credit through the Bank for International Settlements; Canada pledged $1 billion and Latin American nations pledged $1 billion. The US and IMF conditions for these loans included strict targets for money supply, domestic credit, fiscal spending, and foreign borrowing. Furthermore, unprecedented international collateralization was obtained – Mexico's oil export revenues can be held by the Federal Reserve Bank of New York to guarantee US loans. The total rescue package thus amounted to approximately $50 billion, which was enough to stabilize the Mexican economy. Foreign investors, who had seen their Mexican holdings reduced 45 percent by the depreciation in the peso since December, drove the peso up 18 percent on 1 February and stock prices rose 5.2 percent.

VII. JAPAN'S CRISIS, 1989–

The story of the recent Asian economic crisis should begin with Japan's crisis, which hit in 1989. By the mid-1990s, most Japanese real estate as well as stock market prices had dropped 50 percent from 1989 levels, economic growth was stagnant, and the 'Japanese miracle' was over. The author's position is that the monetary contraction allowed by the Bank of Japan under Governor Mieno, beginning with interest rate increases in May and October of 1989, was a mistake which caused much of the crisis.

A reduced valuation of Japanese land and equity prices was coming anyway in the early 1990s given 'the law of one price' for real property that was quickly being established across the global economy due to integration and globalization of markets (see the discussion of 'interest-rate-parities' and 'financial-strategy-parities' in Chapter 1). For example, price-earnings ratios in the Japanese stock market would naturally drop closer to the 20/1 global averages from their historic levels of 50/1, as newly-deregulated investment funds could leave Japan in search of more favorable price-earnings ratios elsewhere. In 1989, given this investment outflow which was required by the law of one price, a 'hollowing-out' of the Japanese money and investment base, and GDP-deflation, were more of a risk than inflation – restrictive monetary policy turned the risk into reality.

The Bank of Japan's restrictive monetary policies continued through the early 1990s, despite the asset deflation and the increasing consensus by international investors that Japan faced deflationary risks similar to what happened in the US during the Great Depression after the 1929 stock market crash. According to many influential foreign investors, 'Governor Mieno was a general fighting the last war [against inflation]' (Brown, 1996, p. 24). Taking account of the shift in private consumption towards discount outlets, the GDP price level in Japan was probably falling by 2 percent or more by 1995, yet Japanese money-market interest rates were kept up at two to three percent – a historically high real rate of 4 to 5 percent. The high real interest rates deepened the recession, and Japanese banks began having troubles with non-performing loans. This recessionary deflationary-debt spiral continues to worsen at the end of 1998 as this book is written.

The author's position is that the 1990s 'hollowing-out' of the Japanese economy could have been largely avoided with more accommodative monetary policies. Instead, Japan lost its financial surplus and therefore its means to maintain record rates of foreign investment. Its net outflow of direct investment plus portfolio investment plus other capital (the 'identified capital outflow') dropped to $22 billion in 1990 from an annual average of $58 billion over 1986–1989. In 1991, temporarily, the Japanese narrow money supply (m1) was once again increased significantly, by 9.5 percent, and the identified capital outflow jumped back up, to $72 billion. However, monetary policy remained restrictive on balance through the 1990s (real short-term interest rates of 4–5 percent), and Japanese land and equity price deflation spread to GDP markets as the Bank of Japan continued to 'fight the last war against inflation'.

As elaborated in Chapter 3, 'absorption' of base money by financial markets and therefore a decline in its rate of circulation for GDP purposes (v), in times of financial distress, can also be measured by a weakness in the growth of broad money. Namely, expanded supplies of high-powered money may not be able to serve as a base for expanded supplies of broad money if the high-powered money supplies are instead consumed by financial institutions to resolve bankruptcies, increase reserves, and meet other capital requirements. In this case, a decline in broad money would correspond to a decline in the velocity of high-powered money as it is absorbed by distressed financial markets rather than being used to support growth in GDP. As shown in Figure 3.1, Japan's (m1) velocity began dropping significantly in the early 1990s.

Figure 4.3 also shows this scenario for Japan. A dramatic decline in the growth of Japan's broad money supply (m2 + CDs) was allowed in the 1990s which correlated with declines in the stock market, real estate values, and real GDP (in July 1998 a GDP recession began). Maintaining the growth of the narrow money supply (m1) has not prevented deflation and recession, because more of the (m1) is absorbed by distressed financial institutions. Elaborating this situation further, research in 1998 indicated that:

Figure 4.3 Negative consequences of restrictive Japanese monetary policy after 1989

The dramatic decline in Japan's broad money supply growth rate (m2 + CDs) in the 1990s was correlated with declines in the stock market, real estate values, and real GDP. Maintaining the growth of the narrow money supply, (m1), has not prevented deflation, because more of the (m1) is absorbed by distressed financial institutions. Japan's monetary contraction has contributed to Asian and worldwide monetary deflation and recession. (Annual percent rates of change, 1975–1997).

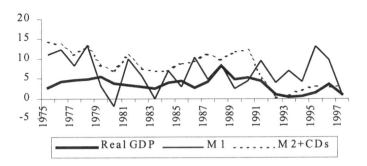

Source: IMF

A central bank *in a deflationary situation with troubled banks* must avoid interpreting low [nominal] interest rates as an indicator of an expansionary policy. When monetary growth is low and default risks are high as in Japan today, low interest rates reflect expectations of both low (or negative) inflation and rates of return. In such a situation, *the appropriate focus of monetary policy is on money and not interest rates* [broad money supplies should be expanded despite low interest rates] (Federal Reserve Bank of St. Louis, p.1).

Thus, what was initially seen in the literature as a reckless and speculative expansion of domestic credit in Japan in the 1980s, an unsustainable bubble, was instead increasingly seen as a more sustainable form of economic growth based upon monetary expansion.   As shown in Figure 4.3, monetary expansion in the 1980s was not high compared to the 1970s. In the author's view, Japan in the 1980s printed the means to buy foreign assets and expand wealth domestically without accelerating GDP inflation. If overly restrictive monetary policies had not been used, the expansion could likely have continued but at a more moderate level in proportion to the new international investment opportunities that were being found by 'Japan Inc.' in the global economy. While beyond the scope of this book, econometric work as per Chapter 3's analysis of the US is needed in order to identify the linkages in Japan between monetary growth and the rate that non-inflationary economic growth can be supported in this current period which is characterized by technological change, deregulation, and new international opportunities.

VIII. Asia's Crisis, 1997–

The investment flows out of Japan in the mid-1990s found 'homes', primarily, in the rest of Asia as well as the US. Japan became the major source of bank loans to every major country in Asia except Taiwan and the Philippines. Japan's outstanding loans to South Korea, Taiwan, Thailand, Indonesia, Malaysia and the Philippines, combined, rose 76 percent from the end of 1993 to the end of 1996, including a doubling of lending to South Korea and Thailand. Also, by 1996 Japan accounted for more than 40 percent of all bank loans to Hong Kong and more than 30 percent to Singapore. Japan's monetary outflow thus helped support what was essentially a monetary-investment expansion in the rest of Asia during the mid-1990s.

Global investment inflows into this region during this period were further encouraged by the deregulation and internationalization of capital accounts and foreign exchange transactions in all Asian countries, privatization, and by government commitments to support Asian exchange rates against the dollar (Haggard and Maxfield, 1996). US and European companies were setting up factories in Asia (direct investment), and the portfolio investment inflows from the US and Europe exceeded those from Japan. The World Bank estimates that total international capital flows to 'emerging markets' increased from $50 billion in 1991 to $250 billion in 1996, with the majority going to Asia. Total capital formation (corporate, housing, and government investment) in Asia excluding Japan increased 300 percent from 1990 to 1996, which compared with much lower increases of approximately 40 percent in the US and Japan and 10 percent in Europe.

Perhaps Thailand was the most obvious home for international investment funds in this period. Technocrats had even manipulated interest rates and currency exchange rates with a formula designed to bring in international capital:

> Since 1987 the Thai authorities have kept their currency locked to the US dollar in a band of baht 25–26 [to one dollar] while maintaining domestic rates 500–600 [basis] points higher than US rates and keeping their borders open to capital flows. Thai borrowers naturally gravitated towards US dollar borrowings and the commercial banks accommodated them, with the result that the Thai banks now have a net foreign liability position equivalent to 20 percent of GDP. The borrowers converted to baht with the Bank of Thailand the ultimate purchaser of their foreign currency. Fuelled by cheap easy money, the Thai economy grew rapidly, inflation rose, and the current account deficit ballooned (*HG Asia, 1996*).

Because this Thai formula was so successful in attracting capital, it was soon copied by the central banks and finance ministers in the Philippines, Malaysia, and Indonesia. The International Monetary Fund and the World Bank praised these policies, especially the elimination of barriers between domestic and global financial markets. As late as the second half of 1996, the IMF cited Thai policymakers for their 'consistent record of sound macroeconomic management policies' (Chote, 1997).

In this optimistic financial liberalization phase, Thailand received large-scale international investment inflows mostly from private sources, including offshore financial markets. In 1994–96, offshore banks (Bangkok International Banking Facilities) were allowed to borrow funds internationally and lend them to Thai residents without limit. Unlike most banks, these banks were not required to disclose asset mixes (such as the extent of real estate loans) or non-performing loans, and they were allowed to purchase finance companies. In 1994–96, Thailand received a net inflow of approximately $25 billion in portfolio investment and another $50 billion in loans to Thai banks and enterprises. The latter mostly found its way into the stock market, consumer financing and, especially, real estate. Commercial banks and finance companies were estimated to have 40 percent of their loans into real estate.

Thus, the mid-1990s was a financial liberalization phase for Asia as supported by the dollar, yen, and other hard currencies. Local currency and credit supplies were expanded dramatically based upon confident convertibility into the hard currencies, and the 'money-float' or 'money-pyramid' encouraged some reckless speculation.   The IMF and other government agencies encouraged financial deregulation and free-market 'dollarization' of these economies, and the presence of these optimistic 'lenders of last resort' increased the moral-hazard problem whereby 'even if something goes wrong the agencies involved have an interest in bailing me out'.

Then came dollar-flight, dollar-contraction, and crisis, as discussed below.

At the core of the global financial economy is the dollar, which accounts for approximately 60 percent of the world's money supply, and at the core of this 'dollar-float' is the (m1) in US circulation, and at the core of this core is the money-reserves of US depository institutions. The US Federal Reserve has significant control over the growth of these latter two statistics, and is thus a powerful driver of the high-powered money base of not only the US economy but also the world economy. Figure 4.4 shows the growth rate of both statistics from 1988 to a peak in 1992, and then a decline after 1992. Fears of inflation across the developed world were exaggerated after 1992 and translated into contractionary monetary policies and interest rate increases of 1–2 percentage points for the hard currencies. As discussed above in 'The Mexican Crisis, 1994–95', these increases in interest rates pulled money out of Mexico which contributed to its crisis.

Viewed from the high-powered dollar core of the world economy, the mid-to-late 1990s period was thus characterized by extremely restrictive monetary policies and even 'dollar-destruction'. Further evidence for this view is provided by dollar-currency-appreciation and capital-flight to the dollar relative to virtually all other world currencies, the historically high inflation-adjusted US dollar interest rates, and the dramatic decline in virtually all commodity prices measured in US dollars.

Regarding currency exchange rates, the dollar appreciated 20 percent against the German mark (and therefore most of the European currencies) and the Japanese yen, measured from the beginning of 1997 to the middle of 1998. Japan tried to maintain some stability between the yen and the dollar in mid-1997 to avoid further 'crises of confidence' in the Japanese economy, but these policies proved untenable by early 1998.   This free-market appreciation of the dollar against the other hard currencies was required by supply-demand conditions as effected by the restrictive US monetary policies.

There was even more dramatic and sudden appreciation of the US dollar against the other Asian currencies over the same time period. As discussed above, Thailand and the others had a policy of keeping domestic exchange rates fixed against the dollar, and as part of this strategy, they were expanding domestic currency supplies based upon a guaranteed convertibility into the dollar. In other words, small Asian countries were conducting a normal reserve-currency process of credit expansion with the dollar serving as 'real-money' and the Thai bhat and other local currencies serving as 'quasi-moneys' that are floated beyond an amount that could all be converted into dollars at once.

Unfortunately for Asia, by mid-1997 the restrictive US dollar monetary policies and supply-demand imbalance between the dollar and Asian currencies could no longer be denied. Asian monetary authorities no longer had enough reserves of US dollars to intervene with (by selling them to the private markets) in support of their fixed exchange rates (by buying local currencies off the private markets).

Figure 4.4 Negative consequences of restrictive US monetary policy after 1993

> *Both US (m1) and bank reserves increased rapidly in 1992 and 1993, and thus contributed to a worldwide dollar-based monetary expansion; then, after 1993, both declined rapidly and contributed to restrictive worldwide monetary conditions and high US dollar real interest rates. High US dollar real interest rates attracted international investment into the US, especially as deposited in broad-money accounts (m2 and m3). The US experienced a broad-money expansion after 1993 and strong economic growth, but many other countries experienced a contraction in broad-money supplies as investment flowed to the US. Financial crises in Mexico (1994–95) and Asia (1997–) were affected by this reversal from expansionary to contractionary dollar-based policies. (Annual percent rates of change, 1989–1997)*

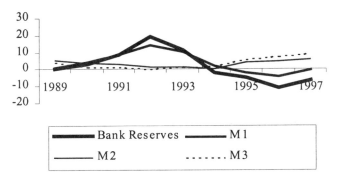

Source: Federal Reserve Bank.

The crisis hit. The impossible rush to fully convert local quasi-moneys and credit into dollars happened first in Thailand with flight from the Baht, and then the rush to convert was immediately copied in the Philippines, Malaysia,

South Korea and elsewhere. Ultimately Indonesia was the hardest hit with the biggest decline in dollar-value of its domestic currency, a decline that continued after the end of 1997 despite some recovery by the other Asian currencies as international bailouts were arranged. South Korea, for example, received $21 billion in credits from the IMF, and other international groups and nations provided the rest of a $57 billion package.

The currency devaluation process not only reduces the dollar-value of domestic currencies, but it reduces real (dollar-measured) domestic wealth including the ability to maintain production and consumption. Recession, and even depression in the case of Indonesia, were immediate and devastating. Despite a $40 billion lender-of-last-resort plan led by the IMF for Indonesia, abject poverty rose to 40 percent and political instability led to the ouster of President Suharto.

Regarding capital flight to the dollar, not only Asia but also the rest of the world rapidly 'de-dollarized' their economies after the mid-1990s. US dollar short-term interest rates were maintained at approximately 5 percent by the US Federal Reserve from 1996 through 1998, despite declining inflation in the US economy. US GDP-inflation dropped from 2–3 percent in the mid-1990s to as low as 0–1 percent in 1998. Real interest rates, or the real rate-of-return from short-term investing in the US economy thus climbed from 2–3 percent in the mid-1990s to 4–5 percent in 1998. Four to five percent is an extremely high real return, and it exceeded any other short-term safe return in the global economy. International investment thus poured into the US.

Official statistics identify key turning-points in the late 1990s when worldwide financial flows began to favor the US. Foreign institutions and individuals increased the rate at which they were purchasing US financial assets from $563.4 billion in 1996 to $733.4 billion in 1997. This record inflow in 1997 came especially in the third and fourth quarters as US real interest rates increased and the Asian financial crisis hit – inflows of $182.5 and $219.5, respectively. Then, in the first quarter of 1998, this inflow slowed to a more normal $90.5 billion, reflecting deteriorating Asian balance sheets and the subsequent need by Asian banks to repatriate foreign assets. For example, Japanese banks reduced their assets in the US from $358 billion in 1997 to $289 at the end of March, 1998, and there were similar percentage declines in all other Asian bank assets in the US except Taiwan which had mostly escaped the crisis.

Similarly in the late 1990s, US institutions and individuals reduced the rate at which they were purchasing foreign financial assets, but this reduction did not occur until the Asian financial crisis became widespread and threatened other regions of the world early in 1998. US purchase of foreign financial assets was $368.8 billion in 1996, $478.5 billion in 1997, and then only $47.4 billion in the first quarter of 1998. Combining foreign purchases of US financial assets, and US purchases of foreign financial assets, yields the 'net identified financial flow' between the US and the rest of the world, which was thus a net inflow into the US of $194.6 billion in 1996, $254.9 billion 1997, and $43.1 billion in the first quarter of 1998. These net inflows into the US were much higher than in previous years, wherein transfers of $100 billion per year were normal.

As discussed in Chapter 3, the rise of offshore financial markets makes this data unreliable, because financial flows through offshore international banking facilities, 'spontaneous offshore sites', and 'tax havens' are difficult to measure. Aggregate worldwide data shows that monetary flows into official country accounts are systematically less than outflows, and economists believe that much of this difference adds to offshore financial markets. In the case of the US, what is called the 'statistical discrepancy' between monetary inflows and outflows (product trade as well as finance) amounted to $59.6 billion (an excess of measured outflows over inflows) in 1996, $99.7 billion in 1997, and only $5.2 billion in the first quarter of 1998. However, flows into offshore markets have as their major counterpart (often unmeasured) inter-bank transfers of dollars to the US economy.

These hidden dollar transfers to the US are most likely to show up in what the Federal Reserve measures as 'overnight and term Eurodollars (net)' held by US institutions. (A Eurodollar is a US dollar owned by a non-US citizen or institution.) Overnight and term Eurodollars (net) held in the US, which decreased steadily from $117.0 billion in 1988 (year-end) to $66.3 billion in 1993, then increased steadily to $80.8 billion in 1994, $88.6 billion in 1995, $109.2 billion in 1996, and $145.3 billion in 1997. In early 1998, these holdings began dropping once again, and stood at $136.3 billion in June. These changes in Eurodollar holdings in the US correspond to what would be expected based upon the rise in US dollar real interest rates after 1994, and the capital flight to dollar-havens (first offshore markets and then the US) as Asia and other regions 'de-dollarized' their economies in 1997. It is thus likely that a certain amount of hidden net dollar transfers to the US should be added to the officially measured net inflows in recent years – a further sign that monetary policies, institutions, and perceived risk-adjusted return have favored the dollar and the US at the expense of other currencies and regions.

Further proof that US dollar monetary policies have been quite restrictive, with worldwide consequences, is provided by the recent collapse in virtually all commodity prices as measured in dollars. Fewer dollars available for transactions in international markets means that fewer dollars are swapped for the same volume of commodities, i.e. there is dollar-deflation in international commodity markets. According to the global commodity index published by *The Economist*, from end-July 1997 to end-July 1998 the decline in dollar prices of all commodities was 22.2 percent, the decline in dollar prices of food items was 20.6 percent, the decline in dollar prices of industrial commodities was 24.1 percent (including metals), and the decline in dollar price of crude oil was 34.8 percent.

These price declines mirror the percentage by which the dollar appreciated on currency markets against a trade-weighted basket of the world's other currencies over the same time period.   Of course, country-by-country consequences of worldwide dollar-price-deflation and the related dollar-flight to dollar-havens vary considerably based upon the degree to which countries export or import commodities, the degree to which they rely on domestic dollar supplies for monetary stability as discussed above, etc.

What is clear to the author, then, is that restrictive US dollar monetary policies in the mid-1990s in the core of the global economy have been an important cause of the recent world financial crisis, especially because these policies came so swiftly on the heels of the more accommodative monetary policies and liberal worldwide dollarization in the early 1990s.   On 4 August 1998, US Federal Reserve Chairman Alan Greenspan stated: 'In the Spring of 1998 the Federal Open Market Committee was convinced that a rise in inflation was the primary threat to the continued growth of the US economy'. Later, in late September, he stated that the Federal Reserve had become evenly split in mid-August as to whether the major threat to the US economy was inflation or, alternatively, deflation and recession.

In conducting its monetary policies for the primary purpose of stabilizing the US economy and promoting its non-inflationary economic growth, the Federal Reserve contributed to a worldwide monetary contraction, financial crises and recession in the mid-1990s. Unlike in the 1930s, more US dollars now circulate outside the US than circulate inside, and the US dollar is now responsible for a majority of the 'high-powered money' or monetary-base upon which world supplies of money and credit are maintained. Even more than in the 1930s, it is thus necessary that the Federal Reserve cooperate with other hard-currency countries including Western Europe and Japan to maintain worldwide, and not just US, supplies of money and credit. If broad-money supplies continue to shrink worldwide, measured in US dollar terms, then the risk of debt-deflation, recession, and even depression increase.

Policy-makers and analysts rightfully note that, while US (m1) and bank reserves were declining after restrictive narrow-money policies were implemented in 1994, broad measures of money-liquidity in the US were increasing, such as m2 (m1 plus retail money-market funds, savings deposits and small time deposits) and m3 (m2 plus large time deposits, Eurodollars, and institution-only money-market funds).   Figure 4.4 shows these trends. Part of the disjunction between (m1) and the broader aggregates after 1994 is appropriate and due to the increase in (m1) velocity after the SEC reduced the securities-funds-settlement time for (m1) to be made available (Chapter 3).

However, it is likely that the net inflow of financial investment into the US from the rest of the world is significantly responsible for the growth in (m2) and (m3) since 1994.   International investment largely shows up in US money supplies as money-market fund deposits, large time deposits,

Eurodollar deposits, etc., which are included in (m2) or (m3) but not (m1). For example, net foreign purchases of US government securities dramatically increased from $100 billion in 1993 and 1994 to $200 billion in 1995 to almost $300 billion in 1996 and 1997. US government securities holdings in the financial system are often the wholesale funding base for retail money market fund and large time-deposit accounts. Also, as discussed above, offshore financial markets have been sending a lot of Eurodollars and large institutional funds to the US, which are funding sources for these accounts.

Thus, the Federal Reserve has tolerated a reduction in US (m1) and bank reserves, in effect 'sterilizing' or removing base money from circulation, as the US economy runs on an increased (m1) velocity of money and foreign-supported broad money (m2) and (m3). At the end of 1998, US interest rates, especially short-term rates paid on the scarce narrow-money accounts remained high. Longer-term interest rates, such as those paid on the broad money accounts which are heavily demanded by foreign investors, were not so high. In some cases, long-term rates were even lower than short-term rates – an inverted 'yield curve' – which is a very rare occurrence. In this case, a likelihood of economy-wide deflation was signaled, and it would be largely transmitted to the US economy from international markets.

As this book is being written in late 1998, the US Federal Reserve has just reduced its short-term interest rates and eased credit conditions in order to begin a monetary-expansion process and prevent worldwide deflationary conditions from hitting the US. How US (m1), (m2), and (m3) will be affected in the long run remains to be seen, but it appears that 'reflation' of US monetary aggregates is sufficient for the purposes of the US economy. The danger, of course, as recently experienced by Japan, is that, at some point, US (m1) growth may not be able to translate into broad money growth and thus help prevent financial crises and recession. This danger is more likely if the net flow of foreign investment into the US subsides.

NOTES

1. The 'Case Study of US-Foreign Trade, 1981–' is discussed in Chapter 2.
2. 'The 364 Economists' Attack on Government Policy', *Barclays Review* 56, May 1981, p. 27.
3. *Business Week*, 4 April 1983, p. 67.
4. Ibid.
5. 'While Investors are Acting on Their 'Wishful Thinking...', *Business Week*, 2 March 1987, p. 24.
6. 'Banking's Balance of Power is Tilting Toward the Regionals', *Business Week*, 7 April 1986, p. 56.
7. 'Financing US Deficit Abroad', *The New York Times*, 7 November 1985.
8. An excellent summary of various potential causes of the crash, especially the trade deficit announcement, is contained in: Mark Mullins (1989), 'Meltdown

Monday or Meltdown Money?: Causes of the Stock Market Crash', *International Economics and Financial Markets*, Chapter 3, Oxford: Oxford University Press.

9.   'Monetary Policy Caused the Crash...Not Tight Enough...Too Tight Already', *The Wall Street Journal*, 22 October 1987, p. 34.

10. Ibid.

11. United Nations, *World Economic Survey*, 1986.

12. 'Economic and Financial Indicators', *The Economist*, 20 June 1992, p. 108.

13. 'The Triumph of Capitalism', Topical Study #17, Prudential-Bache Securities, 1 August 1989, p. 14.

14. 'Spontaneous Union, a Survey of the New Germany', *The Economist*, 30 June 1990, p. 12.

15. In 10,000 booths and banks around the country, East Germans had one week to exchange 4,000 East German marks (more for the old, less for the young) at a rate of one-to-one into West German marks. Most of the remaining East German marks were traded in for only half as many West German marks. Most prices and wages were converted at one-to-one. This monetary union went smoothly in a macro-economic sense in that the increased supply of (West German) marks reflected the value of East German production. Therefore, West German inflation did not significantly increase, and the mark maintained its value on foreign exchange markets.

16. 'Spontaneous Union, a Survey of the New Germany', ibid.

17. 'Just a Question of Time', *The Economist*, 11 August 1990, p. 25.

18. 'Spontaneous Union, a Survey of the New Germany', ibid.

19. 'Bundespost to Raise DM30bn For E German Phone Network', *Financial Times*, 21 June 1990, p. 1.

5. International Adjustments and Political Responses

As per the more personal notes in the Introduction, the author originally decided to write this book due to his dissatisfaction with the typical textbooks in international economics, macroeconomics, and the related subjects that he teaches. These textbooks do not present the major structural changes and recent events in the global economy to his satisfaction; insufficient attention is given to financial market globalization, new trade patterns, new forms and uses of money and changes in its circulation, monetary wealth processes, and recent financial crises and recessions. Hopefully in Chapters 1–4 the author has been able to enhance the reader's understanding of these topics.

It is not only the conventional economic theory regarding these topics with which the author is dissatisfied. He also finds (and dare he say) that the major 'players' who work very closely with the evolving markets – the Group of Seven (G7), central banks, the World Bank, the International Monetary Fund (IMF), various national policymakers, etc. – also seem somewhat naïve or at least too dismissive about these particular topics.

For example, in a review of the first edition of this book, a member of the Federal Reserve Board concluded that the author 'grossly overstates [that financial globalization] is the principle cause and explanation of various events that Allen exaggeratedly refers to as "crises"'.[1]   This comment was made in full light of the 'lost decade' and 50 percent decline in standard of living during the 1980s in much of Latin America due to its international debt crisis, and in full light of the 50 percent decline in Japan's monetary wealth from 1989–94 due to international capital revaluation, etc. Perhaps now that 'Asia's Crisis, 1997–' has occurred, and now that an additional five years of historical perspective on the severity of the 'events' of Chapter 4 has been digested, it is possible for more policymakers to admit economic 'crisis' into their thinking and lexicon.

As another example, there is a recent book co-authored by Paul Volcker, chairman of the US Federal Reserve System from 1979 to 1987, and Toyoo Gyohten, former vice-minister for international affairs in the Japanese Ministry of Finance, which provides a sweeping history and analysis of international monetary affairs. The book, *Changing Fortunes: The World's Money and the Threat to American Leadership*, does not once mention the early 1980s decline of (m1) income velocity, nor does it cite this decline as the reason why monetary policy was too restrictive in hindsight. When discussing causes of the early 1980s world recession and the inability of Mexico and others to repay foreign loans, Volcker states that:

> the general level of interest rates reached higher levels than I or my colleagues had really anticipated...interest rates moved still higher, with the commercial banks' prime lending rate reaching the unheard-of level of 15.25 percent in early February 1980...we at the Fed saw no alternative to tightening again given the growth in the money supply (Volcker and Gyohten, 1992, p. 170–71).

As discussed in Chapter 4, this targeting of money supply based upon inflation goals and inattention to changes in money velocity, as is typical of the monetarism school, resulted in the worldwide money-liquidity crises of the early 1980s. Similar policy inattention to or misunderstanding of changes in velocity help explain the 1987 world stock market crash and the early 1990s slumps.

As of 1998, money supply targeting is much less common. Economists and policymakers now admit difficulties in predicting more volatile monetary velocities, and they admit increased difficulties even measuring the new high-tech global money supplies. Consequently, monetary policy has become even more of an *ad hoc* art which responds to changes in economic growth, financial valuations, and a wide variety of market conditions.

Various anomalies to mainstream economic models, such as the monetary velocity puzzle might eventually be worked out as per the author's equations in Chapter 3 – this book has quibbled enough already. An even more important debate looms: to what degree is the new global economy inherently unstable, and to what degree are the types of crises discussed in Chapter 4 avoidable? These concerns are raised forcefully by Simon Clarke:

> ...the whole of economic theory is built on the premise that the capitalist system is self-regulating, the principal task of the theoretical economist being to identify the minimal conditions under which such self-regulation will be maintained, so that any breakdown will be identified as the result of exceptional deviations from the norm... For all their mathematical sophistication, the explanations of crises offered by today's economists are no different from those that were being put forward at the beginning of the nineteenth century. It was always recognised that a large external shock, such as a war or harvest failure, might precipitate a temporary disruption in the relations between branches of production, or in the international economic relations of the national economy, but the cause of such a crisis [economists typically argue] lies outside the capitalist system, and it was assumed that stability would soon be restored by the normal processes of market adjustment... For Keynesians, as for the classical economists, the tendency to crisis is not inherent in the capitalist mode of production, but is a result of the inadequacy of institutional arrangements and policy responses... After two hundred years of repeating this nonsense one would have expected that the economists would have begun to smell a rat (Clarke, 1994, p. 1–3).

The business of Chapter 5, then, is twofold. First, Clarke's critique is addressed, and the author provides 'a new political economy of money'. Secondly, the author tries to provide useful analysis and suggestions for the policymakers and 'players'. In the future perhaps world financial crises and recessions can more easily be avoided and nations can pursue more appropriate economic policies within the evolving structure of the global economy. However, the author does find economic crises to be endemic in the current structure of the global economy.

I. A NEW POLITICAL ECONOMY OF MONEY

It is unfortunate for the purposes of this book, as the author addresses himself to international policy-making, that much of the international relations and international political economy literature uses game theory between rational, 'utility maximizing' nation-states as a central tool of analysis. Typically, this literature strives to predict when nations will choose certain cooperative versus competitive strategies (Axelrod, 1984; Keohane, 1984; Oye, ed., 1986). Based upon the payoffs and costs of cooperation versus competition, one might then attempt to explain political decisions and economic outcomes. Rational nations could presumably seek win–win gains with other nations or deliberately impose slumps on other nations in win–lose games.

The author would cite four problems with the use of rational nation-state models to explain recent financial crises and recession.

First, the financial crises and recessions as discussed in Chapter 4 were, generally speaking, too impoverishing for too many nations to be the predictable results of utility-maximizing strategies by game-playing nations, even if competitive game-playing models are used (even though lose-lose games are allowed in these models).

Secondly, there is some ignorance on the part of policy-makers about what political-economic game they are playing in the evolving global economy, and what the costs and benefits of various actions are. Rational game-playing strategies are less likely to occur when ignorance or confusion is present. Major structural changes have occurred too recently, and they have created a more dynamic and chaotic global economy than has been possible to predict. Even in those cases where winners and losers can be found, the gains to the winners were most likely accidental and greater gains could have been achieved without imposing such costs on others if policy-makers had indeed understood what was going on. For example, the US and other capital importers did gain at the expense of the LDCs and other capital flight countries during the 1980s. However, when the early 1980s US Comptroller of the Currency spoke to the author's class several years ago, he had this to say about the financial deregulations which he, Volcker and others carried out: 'we believed in the principle of free market finance, but we could not have possibly imagined the long run consequences [including the massive US capital inflow which this deregulation helped allow]'.

Thirdly, the globally integrated nature of financial and, increasingly, non-financial markets does not allow national policymakers to control the allocation of imposed costs and benefits on a country-by-country basis. This fact would be true even if policymakers had full working knowledge of the new global economy. For example, probably less than 30 percent of G7 stock markets is owned by individuals loyal to a particular nation, and thus it is not clear how policy-makers identify their national interest. As elaborated in Chapter 2, the increased international ownership of corporations, combined with the increase in overseas production and joint ventures, and in trade as a share of G7 economies makes protectionism and other competitive trade strategies impractical.

Fourthly, private markets rather than national governments increasingly determine economic outcomes. For example, global financial markets can now reposition more than $3 trillion between different countries from month to month. Of this $3 trillion, $2 trillion is so-called 'stateless' money that is virtually exempt from the control of any government or official institution, but available for use by all countries.[2] Private capital flows can swamp the resources of central banks, making central bank intervention to stabilize exchange rates or interest rates ineffective.

Having cited these four problems with the use of rational nation-state models, the author would thus call for 'a new political economy of money'. The remainder of this section develops elements of a new framework, which emphasizes the importance of semi-autonomous financial processes. Increasingly, 'money is wealth' as determined by social consensus. Also, to the limited degree that nations or international institutions can rationally direct international monetary flows to suit the interests of their constituents, the author would call the process 'money-mercantilism'.

A. Money, Wealth, and Social Consensus

Based upon the findings of previous chapters, the author's framework allows for the possibility that wealth can be initially *created* in financial markets – not only, as commonly believed, through the production of merchandise and non-financial services. Independently of the efforts of labor in non-financial markets, financial market participants might reduce owning and handling costs of property, revalue existing financial assets upward, create new financial assets, establish new forms of ownership over new resources, and translate this new-found, socially-accepted wealth into sustainable purchasing power over time, without GDP-inflation. Likewise, financial market participants also have the power to reverse these processes, and reduce wealth and real purchasing power over time. There need not be any other initial drivers of these changes in monetary wealth than the labors and social consensus of financial market participants.

Regarding the role of 'social consensus', the author's position is that invisible 'belief systems' can engender wealth independently of physical processes, and this kind of wealth can be first represented and distributed through the institutions of finance. 'Wealth', which the author would define to include 'purchasing power, production power, and a wide variety of social powers' is thus recognized to have transcendental (subjective, unobserved) content as well as empirical (objective, observed) content. In other words, invisible expectations, preferences, and social consensus, as incorporated into the ideologies and institutions of finance, can be 'where the action is', and where differential economic power is determined across the world system. The author would like to make clear that he is not advocating, as a matter of ethics or social policy, transcendental notions of value over empirical notions, but rather he finds that transcendental, belief-system processes have driven changes in empirically-observed phenomenon, as well as vice versa.

Autonomous, transcendental notions of value need not reflect, or even be compatible with, the observed empirical world. For example, the purely transcendental 'law of compound interest' is a social agreement which may or may not correlate with the way that the physical economy grows. Growth in the physical economy is subject to thermodynamics, biological growth processes, capacity of infrastructure, endowments of resources, sunlight and rain, etc. Perhaps debtors as a group, who are required to pay *exponentially* increasing interest under this transcendental law, can generate goods and services and therefore economic revenues only in *arithmetically* increasing increments over time. It has been hypothesized that some debtors might have to fail, and yield their economic resources to the others, so that the others can meet their obligations.

Whether or not this type of debt-repudiation crisis is systemically required in modern capitalism has been debated. Mainstream economic thinking is generally confident that 'hard-to-qualify' lending-restrictions and other microeconomic policies, as well as macroeconomic management of the business cycle, wherein all parties are conscious of systemic risk, can avoid over-lending and debt-failure. In contrast, Marxists (see Clarke, 1994) and others, such as Frederick Soddy (1933), are convinced that these crises are endemic to capitalism, and cannot be prevented with common Keynesian or monetarist policies. Kindleberger, in his well-respected book on the history of financial crises, takes a somewhat middle road between these positions by arguing that mainstream economics is incomplete, but it can be strengthened if appropriate consideration is given to various invisible expectations and social agreements, i.e. transcendental notions:

> The heart of this book is that the Keynesian theory is incomplete, and not merely because it ignores the money supply. Monetarism is incomplete, too. A synthesis

of Keynesianism and monetarism, such as the Hansen-Hicks IS-LM curves that bring together the investment-saving (IS) and liquidity-money (LM) relationships, remains incomplete, even when it brings in production and prices (as does the most up-to-date macroeconomic analysis), if it leaves out the instability of expectations, speculation, and credit and the role of leveraged speculation in various assets (Kindleberger, 1989, p. 25).

As documented in Chapter 4, massive debt-repudiation crises continue to happen in the world system. Therefore, we have not yet been able to avoid over-lending and periodic disjuncture-crises between, on the one hand, the belief system which includes mathematical compound interest, and on the other hand, the ability to generate money from tangible 'real world' processes. The author's position is that some borrowers and lenders are conscious risk-takers who know that periodic failures are required in 'casino capitalism' (Keynes' phrase), whereas other borrowers and lenders underestimate systemic risk and allow over-lending based upon a mistaken ideology regarding the stability of capitalism. Thus, on both accounts, debt crises are likely to remain with us.

Invisible belief systems, including those of money-gamblers and optimistic market capitalists, have supported a money economy based on exponential interest payments, and an easing of lending restrictions. The acceptance and growth of offshore finance, as discussed in Chapter 3, without reserve requirements or other significant regulations, is an example of how belief systems – in this case free market capitalist ideology – drive institutional change. Offshore market institutions, such as the Bangkok International Banking Facility, encouraged unsustainable over-lending, excessive unprofitable construction of real estate, etc., and ultimately contributed to the risk of crisis, recession and misery throughout Asia. Transcendental belief systems and their supporting institutions can thus be important drivers of change. Much of the economic wealth that was initially created through deposit-lending, as it exercised itself in production power, consumption power, and power to change institutions, was destroyed in the recent Asian crisis; but it nevertheless did exist as a broad social agreement. Also, less wealth would have been destroyed if financial capitalists had been more patient in accepting lower, less risky rates of return which were more compatible with the ability of human populations working with the physical environment to yield economic growth.

Reversing the causality of Karl Marx's materialism-philosophy, it is increasingly true that autonomous, invisible financial processes drive changes in the physical relations of production, rather than vice versa. As part of this process, central banks and other financial market participants can (haphazardly) increase or reduce wealth independently of any initial changes in the production of GDP or other 'real' economic prospects. Money is *not* a neutral driver of the real economy over space – especially across the wide spaces of the global economy. Furthermore, the author's econometric work as in Chapter 3 confirms that financial markets can absorb money so that the money is not contemporaneously available to support and induce the real economy, which shows up as a decline in the GDP-velocity of money. This absorbed money-power might be used at a later date to command production or consumption, or it might be destroyed in an economic crisis before its title-holders can use it. Therefore, monetary-wealth is also not a neutral driver of the real economy over time.

Depending on the magnitudes of the transfers, re-valuations, and creation of monetary wealth over (how much) time and space, serious real effects can be produced over time and space. These processes, generally not accepted by either mainstream or Marxist economics, can nevertheless help to explain what the mainstream has understood as 'business cycles' or 'debt-deflation crises' (Fisher, 1933) and what Marxists have understood as crises of 'underconsumption', 'overproduction', and 'disproportionality' (Clarke, 1994).

To the author, 'money is wealth' in the sense that it gives the holder a claim on the entire social product. The 'social product' includes not only consumption power and production power, but also the power to direct and control large social processes – such as those which are dependent on (gaining access to) the institutions of government, courts, communications, culture, and so on. The accumulation of monetary assets, or what Marxists would call the accumulation of finance capital, represents a social-power-claim that becomes a key driver in the evolution of the world system. Once monetary-wealth is understood as power-claims over the social product, then monetary wealth is 'real', and it is limited only by the degree to which power can be exerted over others. Presumably this limit would only be found in the unlikely event that an all-encompassing global monopoly has maximized its differential power.

In the author's framework, social agreements are 'real' and they can therefore *create* real value and distribute this value in financial markets quite independently of what is happening in tangible GDP markets. In fact, it is essentially a social agreement that determines, to a significant degree, the importance of tangible GDP processes compared to the importance of intangible belief systems and social agreements – both are capable of determining who has differential power and who has the incentives, rights, and privileges to command production and consumption. To a significant degree, especially once we are beyond basic subsistence needs, whether the growth of GDP itself compared to other economic, political, and social goals is more 'valuable' rests upon belief systems.

A reviewer of the first edition of this book advanced the Marxist belief that 'the labor of financial operators [and accompanying social agreements] cannot produce value but is a channel through which value is appropriated from those sectors of the economy where value is produced...[whereas] for

Allen the financial sector can create value' (Carchedi, 1996). Who is right? The author would submit that, philosophically, either can be right depending upon the self-justifying definition of value which is chosen; but, for the purposes of explaining differential economic power across the recent global economy, his own framework is preferred.

Some current research in the field of international political economy is consistent with the author's notion that monetary-wealth, or what Marx would call 'unproductive finance capital' (as opposed to physical capital or capital goods such as machines and factories) can represent the first-round appropriation of broad social powers. This research has not quite (but almost) taken the author's next step to claim that finance capital can also be the first-round creation of new (rather than appropriation of fully existing) social powers:

> Drawing on the institutional frameworks of Veblen and Mumford, our principal contribution is to *integrate power into the definition of capital*. Briefly, the value of capital represents discounted expected earnings. Some of these earnings could be associated with the productivity (or exploitation) of the owned industrial apparatus, but this is only part of the story. As capitalism grows in complexity, the earnings of any given business concern come to depend less on its own industrial undertakings and more on the *community's overall productivity*. In this sense, the value of capital represents a *distributional* claim. This claim is manifested partly through ownership, but more broadly through the *whole spectrum of social power*. Moreover, power is not only a means of accumulation, but also its most fundamental end. For the absentee owner, the purpose is not to 'maximize' profits but to 'beat the average'. The ultimate goal of business is not hedonic pleasure, but *differential* gain. In our view, this differential aspect of accumulation offers a promising avenue for putting power into the definition of capital... In the eyes of a modern investor, capital means a *capitalized earning capacity*. It consists not of the owned factories, mines, aeroplanes or retail establishments, but of the present value of profits expected to be earned by force of such ownership (Nitzan, 1998, p. 173, 182).

Building upon this quote, Nitzan argues that wealth accumulation processes allowed by monetary capital have favored pecuniary business activities and owners over tangible industrial productivity and working consumers. He argues that, increasingly, 'the causal link runs not from the creation of earnings to the right of ownership, but from the right of ownership to the appropriation of earnings' (p. 180). This causality is consistent with the historic writings of Thorstein Veblen, who insisted that the 'natural right of ownership' conferred by society to various people (initially to own slaves, then animals, land, and in Veblen's time, capital), can be used coercively or even as a form of sabotage to obtain further social powers at the expense of others:

For the transient time being, therefore, any person who has the legal right to withhold any part of the necessary industrial apparatus or materials from current use will be in a position to impose terms and exact obedience, on pain of rendering the community's joint stock of technology inoperative for that extent. Ownership of industrial equipment and natural resources confers such a right legally to enforce unemployment, and so to make the community's workmanship useless to that extent. This is the Natural Right of Investment... Plainly, ownership would be nothing better than an idle gesture without this legal right of sabotage. Without the power of discretionary idleness, without the right to keep the work out of the hands of the workmen, and the product out of the market, investment and business enterprise [as distinguished from other economic activity or forms of organization] would cease. This is the larger meaning of the Security of Property (Veblen, 1923, p. 65-7).

In the global economy, 'the natural right of ownership' is now being conferred by society on various people over new resources and new ways to gain differential power which compete with old resources and old ways to gain power. Examples include ownership rights, where none had existed before, over airwaves and bandwidths, various intellectual properties, and new electronic moneys – these newly recognized assets are to a certain degree 'created out of thin air', and so are the ownership rights over them. Monetary wealth, even more so than other property ownership, might especially be created as well as transferred by social agreement.

B. Money-Mercantilism

Based on wealth creation and transfer processes, the author's research confirms that the US and the 'hard-currency-core' of the current global economy can benefit from what he would call 'money-mercantilism' at the expense of the 'soft-currency-periphery'. Because of the way that the international monetary system works with the US dollar as the dominant reserve currency, over time various monetary-wealth transfers from the periphery to the core have occurred without any other inherent instabilities in the real economy. 'Dollarization' of the periphery might increase the wealth of the periphery without necessarily affecting the core (a financial liberalization-globalization phase for the periphery), but then dollar-flight out of the periphery back to the core might appropriate new-found wealth from the periphery back to the core. The core might end up wealthier than before the dollarization phase, and the periphery might end up poorer. If world supplies of the dollar are excessively restricted by the Federal Reserve Bank and other financial institutions in the core, as in 1981–2, then both the periphery and the core might suffer a slump, but the core might still gain 'differential wealth' relative to the periphery.

Monetary-wealth transfers to the core need not translate proportionally into GDP inflation; they need not be inflationary at all. Whether inflation is affected depends on the production capacity which is currently available in the core, the capacity which can be added, the 'thickening' and 'commodification' of markets as new activity or non-market activity becomes part of the income-expenditure flow, the degree to which new-found monetary wealth is spent domestically, etc.

These remarkably successful labors in the core by the Federal Reserve Bank, the 'Wall Street-US Treasury complex' (Bhagwati, 1998), and the millions of international financial market participants, as allowed by the dollar-based international monetary system, need not be conscious or conspiratorial, but they have favored US dollar havens. Because the dollar is a preferred 'store of value' and not neutral (which is a social agreement), dollar havens are wealth havens. Wealth havens are power havens where production power, consumption power, and social-process-power are gained relative to non-havens. As documented in previous chapters, global monetary-capitalism currently supports institutional arrangements whereby dollar havens gain monetary wealth from 'dollar colonies'. The net flow of investment into the US from the rest of the world was $194.6 billion in 1996, $254.9 billion in 1997, and is expected to be more than $250 billion in 1998.

Regarding the US as a 'winner' due to international transfers of monetary wealth, and some other countries as 'losers', the author would like to be perfectly clear about this somewhat unconventional position. Capital outflows, devaluation, and use of soft currencies in the 'periphery' of the global economy has pushed those regions into relative poverty and pushed the dollar-haven 'core' of the global economy into relative wealth. The periphery has certainly included Latin America and Africa since the early 1980s, but in the 1990s the capital-losing periphery has widened to include much of Eastern Europe and Asia. The Japanese yen has also given way to the dollar, not in terms of the unit-to-unit currency exchange rate, but in terms of the share of the world's wealth which is denominated in yen. From 1989 to 1999, the share of the world's wealth denominated in yen has dropped approximately 50 percent. Ronen Palan, among other international political economists familiar with offshore finance, began grappling with this issue in the mid-1990s:

Indeed [after WWII] a hierarchy was produced as the new global currency [mainly the dollar] became the core currency of 'hard' to which all other currencies, 'soft' currencies were attached. The 'off-shore' financial markets may be understood as a reproduction of one of the central features of the post-war international financial system, namely, this hierarchy among currencies... The whole off-shore market then operates, whether intentionally or not, as a huge transmission mechanism, transferring the accumulated capital of the old periphery to the financial centers of the 'core'.

...about 30 percent of third world debt has found its way into tax havens. The figures rise sharply concerning Latin America. By 1981 five of the havens considered by the Caribbean Task Force report (Bahamas, Bermuda, Liberia, the Dutch Antilles and Panama) had approximately 14.3 percent of the total estimated investment stock which had flowed from OECD to all developing countries, although the economies of these five accounted for less than 0.3 percent of the total GNP of all developing countries... With current third world debt outstanding at US $1.6 trillion, these figures imply a net [accumulated] inflow of US $500 billion into the tax havens. Such figures quite simply dwarf anything traditional theories of third world's exploitation and unequal exchange have managed to come up with. This is arguably the saddest of all aspects of third world plight (Palen, 1994).

Where do tax havens invest and transfer this wealth? Swiss banks, the earliest modern tax havens 'rarely squander it [money accumulated from the periphery] or speculate with it. They invest it prudently and cautiously in the rich Atlantic world' – the big three Swiss banks actually made a policy decision in 1957 to invest only in the 'first world' (Fehrenbach, 1966, p. 126). More recently, as shown in Table 3.1 as backed up by Brown (1996), flows into tax havens and other offshore markets have as their major counterpart inter-bank lending into the US.

The author would call these processes 'money-mercantilism'.

Historically, 'mercantilism' is the use of restrictive trade policies and colonial empires, especially by the European *ancien régime* of the seventeenth and eighteenth centuries, in order to accumulate precious metals centrally. Various nineteenth-century German historians, especially Georg Friedrich List, gave coherence to mercantilist notions of how wealth is accumulated, and they critiqued the *laissez-faire* economics of Smith, Ricardo, and Say. The institutional advantage used by powerful and hegemonic European states to appropriate unequal win–win or even win–lose gains from international commerce was recognized by the German Historical School as an important determinant of 'the wealth of nations' – perhaps a more important determinant than the decentralized 'invisible hand' interactions and efficiencies of supply and demand. More recent defenders of the mercantilist perspective include the Caribbean School and the World-System School (Hopkins and Wallerstein, eds., 1982).

What the author would add to the historical mercantilist perspective, in order to make it 'money-mercantilism', is the notion that extraction of money-wealth from the periphery, through institutional advantage, does not require GDP trade flows – instead, it only requires dominance in financial affairs. In the *ancien régime* period, there was an international financial system, but it was associated more with national debts rather than with commercial finance. Hence, it was easier for France and England and others to extract money-species from the colonies through favorable trade and exports of goods and services rather than more directly through commercial finance. However, in the current period, well-developed international commercial financial markets allow various trade channels to be bypassed.

The current 'mercantilists', who are typically financial intermediaries, are less government-affiliated, and thus mercantilism is not so intentionally associated with nationalism, but the wealth-enhancing effects obtained for the home country or its currency bloc are mostly the same as with the old mercantilism. The official government 'players' in this process might act as direct or indirect agents or partners for the private financial intermediaries and thus maintain much of the nationalism or core-regionalism that is historically associated with mercantilism. For example, case studies of 'The World Debt Crisis, 1982–' and 'Mexico's Crisis, 1994–95' in Chapter 4 elaborate the degree to which official US institutions were able to protect the solvency, profits, and capital inflows to private US financial intermediaries. The 1985 US 'Baker Plan' and IMF 'austerity requirements' generated new revenues (often from Latin American populations) and loans to service existing LDC debt so that US banks could continue to receive normal payments and not have to classify a majority of their LDC debt as bad debt.

More recently in April 1997, US Treasury Department Secretary Robert Rubin headed a meeting by the finance ministers of the G7 largest industrial countries which issued a statement 'promoting freedom of capital flows' and the deregulation and opening of the financial markets of newly industrializing countries in Asia and elsewhere. Efforts were simultaneously made to amend the charter of the International Monetary Fund so that it could also promote 'capital account liberalization' of its member countries. These efforts are increasingly seen in both academic and business circles as aggressive efforts to promote and protect the business interests of US financial firms and their multinational affiliates in foreign markets (Wade, 1998-99; *The New York Times*, 1999). Furthermore, the 'net dissaver' US economy benefits from unrestricted access to international savings.

Since the Asian financial crisis, there is increasing opposition to 'financial liberalization' in Asia and elsewhere by many who see it as a win-lose game favoring the stronger US and G7 institutions and exploiting the less developed countries. For example, the $57 billion restructuring bailout of South Korea in late 1997 did not require US banks with the bad loans to put up significant new money or write off bad debts, but Citibank, J.P. Morgan, Chase Manhattan, BankAmerica, Bankers Trust and others were allowed two to three percentage point higher interest rates and government guarantees that passed the ongoing risk of default from their shareholders to Korean taxpayers. The main 'burden' accepted by the U.S. banks was an extension of these risky loans for up to three years. As stated by Milton Friedman:

> The effort is hurting the countries they are lending to, and benefiting the foreigners who lent to them... The United States does give foreign aid, but this is a different kind of foreign aid. It only goes through countries like Thailand to Bankers Trust (*The New York Times*, 1999).

The dollar's dominance in international finance since the US-dominated Bretton Woods agreements after World War II has attracted some recognition of what the author would call US money-mercantilism. Charles de Gaulle complained that the international reserve role of the dollar 'enabled the United States to be indebted to foreign countries free of charge'. Unilateral devaluations of the dollar, as long as the dollar remains the international currency of choice, unilaterally devalues US foreign debt – a privilege enjoyed by the US as the only major country whose foreign debt is mostly denominated in its own currency.

Over 50 percent of all international notes and bonds are denominated in dollars as of 1998, and 45 percent of all cross-border bank loans are in dollars. Economists such as Richard Portes and Helene Rey estimate that this dominance in debt markets gives dollar-issuers such as the US government a 'liquidity discount' or reduced transaction costs of 25 to 50 basis points (hundredths of a percentage point). Non-US holdings of US government debt amount to $2 trillion, which means that the US government saves $5–10 billion per year in interest expense on its debt due to the liquidity discount. *The Economist* estimates that an additional $5–10 billion per year may be 'earned' from other countries by the US due to seigniorage, which is the profit earned by the monopoly issue of coins and notes.[3] That is, other countries give up real goods and services to holders (and therefore issuers) of dollars in order to obtain dollars for their reserve accounts.

In the author's view, these widely acknowledged money-mercantilist 'profits' are only part of the money-mercantilist benefits that currently accrue to the US. The current $200–$250 billion annual net investment inflow into the US, mostly channeled through private markets, is of course approximately matched in the balance of payments accounts by a similarly large US current account deficit in goods and services. However, as discussed in Chapter 2, a majority of the US current account deficit is intra-firm or reflects critical component and sub-assembly transfers between global affiliates, and thus the majority of this current account deficit should not be seen as a net profit or wealth loss to the 'real' sector of the US economy – unlike the *ancien régime* period when trade deficits between more separate national economies could more clearly be identified with non-competitiveness and wealth outflows.

In the current period, virtually all of the capital-usage and monetary-wealth enhancement benefit of the $200–$250 billion annual net investment inflow supports the US economy; yet some of the monetary outflow due to the current account deficit (an outflow which is actually less than the size of the deficit – see chapter 2) enhances US multinationals, or at least remains denominated in dollars and builds up the non-US dollar core of the global economy. As elaborated in Chapter 2, US current account deficits are increasingly not bad for US economic interests, and might even be good due to overseas production, international joint ventures, and international ownership arrangements – it depends on how firms have 'gone global'.

US money-mercantilism is achieved via favorable terms (as per the liquidity-premium and seigniorage) on more initiating capital account surpluses, which are recycled through more accommodating current account deficits. On both accounts, but especially on the dollar-rigged financial side, US multinationals and their dollar-based affiliates benefit. In contrast, *ancien régime* mercantilism was achieved through institutionally-rigged current account surpluses that were then used to expand the political-economic power of the regime.

Whichever type of mercantilism is identified, the essential element is the disproportionate accumulation of monetary wealth which is obtained by the institutionally more powerful country or region through international commerce. How does this monetary wealth accumulation from international commerce enhance the domestic economy of the mercantilist country? In a work edited by the author, Daudin (2000) answers this question for the *ancien régime* of eighteenth-century France. Not only did France use political and military power to exploit wealth from the colonies, but the inflow of precious metals (monetary-wealth) actually allowed France a more-than-proportionate increase in domestic economic growth and wealth. Under this mercantilist revision of mainstream economic thinking, France was well justified in sacrificing various free-trade efficiencies in order to accumulate centrally precious metals that could serve as hard-currency. The accumulation of gold and silver as reserve currency allowed a non-neutral (wealth-favorable) expansion of quasi-moneys and credit which in turn intensified and coordinated economic activity and further enhanced French economic growth and power relative to the (capital-exporting) rest of the world. During the eighteenth century, there was no real banking system in France, and most money creation was done by commercial agents who issued bills of exchange and promissory notes based upon reputation. The estimated 0.8 percent growth per year in circulating metallic money during 1715–1788 made it possible for commercial operators to reliably circulate a much larger volume of commercial paper and exchangeable notes.

Daudin's mercantilist analysis is further supported by Clark (1998), who identifies in great detail how the industrial revolution in Britain was more of a monetary-capitalist-driven top-down 'industrious revolution' supported by the appropriation and use of foreign wealth rather than a bottom-up industrial revolution initially driven by new technologies and greater productivity of the average worker. Enhanced transactions systems brought, especially, under-utilized rural labor into the formal economy in Britain as well as France.

In both the mercantilist *ancien régime* and in present-day mercantilist US, economic growth might thus be largely driven by a 'thickening' and 'commodification' of domestic markets as social agreements and institutions allow foreign and newly-created domestic monetary wealth to be spent domestically. Following this pattern, in the 1990s the US economy boomed ahead with unexpectedly great work force participation and 'stressed-out' industriousness despite no significant increase in the per-hour productivity of the average worker. Furthermore, new wealth derived from the international labors of financial operators and from the innovations of the post-1973 information industries accumulated first in US financial markets, which then allowed greater US investment in fixed capital and consumerism and differential economic power within the world system.

II. THE ROLE OF THE G7

The meeting of finance ministers and central bank governors at New York's Plaza Hotel in September 1985 is commonly mentioned as an important event in international monetary economics. It was the first time that such a meeting was announced in advance and a communiqué was issued afterwards. With such publicity, the G-5 countries of the US, Japan, Germany, France, and the UK soon expanded and formalized themselves into the G7 with the inclusion of Italy and Canada.

Also, despite no mention in its communiqué about intervention to drive down the value of the dollar, the Plaza accord was widely known to be a concerted effort to do so. By the end of the first week after the Plaza meeting the G5 had sold 2.7 billion dollars (Volcker and Gyohten, 1992, p. 255). Also, during that week the Japanese yen, German mark, French franc, and British pound did appreciate against the dollar by 11.8, 7.8, 7.6, and 2.9 percent, respectively. However, before the meeting the dollar had already declined more than 10 percent from its record February 1985 heights, and the Plaza meeting did not seem to change the long-run rate of decline which continued in a linear fashion.

As argued in Chapter 1, in this period the major driving forces were the rapidly globalizing financial markets, the logic of interest rate and financial strategy parities, and flows of private investment. The 2.7 billion dollars sold by the central banks in the week after the Plaza accord is a small number compared to $150 billion in foreign exchange trading that was then occurring on an average day or the hundreds of billions of US dollars that were held by private non-US investors.

What the Plaza accord did establish was quite a precedent for concerted efforts by central banks and government treasury departments to realign exchange rates via direct intervention and interest rate policy. And at a time when the private markets were uncertain which way the dollar was headed, the financial officials did have important psychological influence via their strong announcements and impressive coordination.

Central bank coordination continued for a year or so. For example, economic historians were quite impressed by the beautifully choreographed, simultaneous cuts in US, Japanese and West German central bank interest rates in May, 1986.[4] But as discussed in Chapter 4, the lack of cooperation in October 1987 when Germany and Japan publicly indicated that they would not follow US international policy initiatives helped cause the 1987 stock market crash. Shortly before the crash, these three countries engaged in somewhat competitive rather than cooperative interest rate increases to maintain currency alignments. But this goal was not achieved as the dollar's long-term decline continued.

Since the late 1980s, especially given the lack of full cooperation, the effect of G7 action on interest rates and exchange rates increasingly appears to be more psychological than real. Private capital flows increasingly dominate central bank intervention, as Europeans relearned during the partial breakup of the European monetary system (EMS) late in 1992. Foreign exchange turnover during the EMS crisis reached $1 trillion per day, and discretionary central bank intervention on behalf of a major currency was rarely as much as $10 on a given day or $50 billion, net, over the whole crisis episode.

When G7 cooperation is not available, even the US Fed now has difficulty reversing trends in the private markets. For example, just before Christmas in 1989 the Fed's Open Market Committee voted nine to two to push US interest rates down. On 20 December, the Fed bought Treasury bills, provided more credit to the banking system, and lowered its closely-watched short-term interest rates, thus telegraphing its desire to push general interest rates lower. Historically, when the Fed pushed short-term interest rates down by half a percentage point, this led to a decline of perhaps one-tenth of a percentage point in longer-term interest rates.

Unfortunately for the Fed in this case, however, in early 1990 interest rates were rising in Germany due to the liquidity crisis there and the capital needs of reunification. In addition, interest rates were rising in Japan because of exaggerated fears of inflation and the restrictive monetary policies which were soon to destroy Japan's financial surplus. Therefore, the massive private flows of funds moving between countries in search of interest-rate parity left dollar-denominated assets, raised longer-term US interest rates, and created recessionary conditions in the US. Two and one-half months after the Federal Reserve attempted to reduce US interest rates, yields on 30-year Treasury bonds were three-quarters of a percentage point higher than before the Fed acted.

Economists debate the degree to which central banks should use their resources to fix interest rates and exchange rates. Because of the rise of offshore finance (Chapter 3) and other private market growth, the author's position is that specific rates cannot generally be sustained even with G7 cooperation, and huge trading losses by the central banks are likely. When private speculation within the EC erupted on 8 September 1992, within 24 hours the Italian lira had lost 10 percent against the German mark, the British pound had lost 9 percent, and the Spanish peseta had lost 8 percent. The monetary authorities intervened with over $70 billion of various currencies, including the use by the Bank of England of approximately one-third of its reserves (Joffe, 1992–93, p. 37). The Bank of England reportedly lost more than $5 billion on its unsuccessful attempts to support the pound.[5] Britain left the EMS without committing itself to a return date. Similarly during this crisis, Sweden had to abandon the peg between its krona and European currencies after massive and costly intervention by the Sveriges Riksbank failed.

Official institutions should not be encouraged in the direction of unsustainable goals and trading losses – increasingly, attempting to fix exchange rates between major currencies with direct market intervention falls into this category. Instead, the author would propose various other directions for G7 policy, which include: (A) reducing the number of currencies in the world, as per the introduction of the euro as a single currency in Europe; (B) greater development of forward-looking markets for interest rates and exchange rates so that a fuller spectrum of inexpensive hedging opportunities is available; and (C) maintaining sufficient money-liquidity across the global economy. Each of these proposals should be designed so that the US and other global reserve currency countries do not benefit excessively from 'money mercantilism' at the expense of other countries.

A. Proposal 1: Reducing the Number of Currencies

The case studies of this book indicate that economic crises typically occur when one or more of the major currencies, after having been *de facto* but not *de jure* reserve currency for a particular country, suddenly leaves the country through private channels. The national monetary authorities thus, typically, have no means to create or replace the lost high-powered money supplies except by costly, *ad hoc* international borrowing. Because of the dominance and volatility of private capital, inevitably this type of crisis will occur, and it will occur with higher probability to the degree that 'foreign' currency is used domestically without appropriate central bank to central bank arrangements.

Of course more formalized use of a foreign global reserve currency requires central bank-to-bank policy cooperation and other institutional cooperation, and to a certain degree these arrangements are already occurring. However, they should be encouraged further, and supported with greater central bank-to-bank funding and reconciliation of the relevant currencies. For example, the Mexican government had $18 billion of dollar-denominated *tesobono* debt classified as domestic debt in 1994 before its crisis. When the crisis hit and threatened the region, an emergency rescue package of $50 billion was cobbled together to resolve the crisis, but it did not prevent a severe one-year recession in Mexico (Chapter 4). In the author's view, a similar funding transfer could have been provided more automatically and more quickly with lower cost for both sides based upon central bank reserves and international discount rates.

A similar *ad hoc* emergency line of credit of approximately $40 billion was provided for Brazil in November 1998, but only after Brazil's dollar reserves had declined from approximately $60 to $30 billion and international investor confidence in Brazil had seriously deteriorated. By February 1999, even the $40 billion rescue package proved unable to stabilize the Brazilian *real* against the dollar, and authorities were forced by the markets to abandon their monetary regime and allow the *real* to depreciate rapidly.

These types of dollarization and lenders-of-last-resort arrangements are happening anyway; it is time to formalize them through central banking rather than through cumbersome executive-branch and legislative-branch one-shot deals. Last-minute deals are often too costly and ultimately ineffective as in the case of Brazil. Transitionary period dollarization should aim at the establishment of global reserve currency 'currency boards' to fix small country exchange rates, as per Hong-Kong (fixed since 1983) and Argentina (fixed through the 1990s).

The author recommends that currency-board transitionary periods should be followed by consideration of new more regional currencies. Regional currencies and supporting institutions, patterned after the euro and new European Central Bank could be developed for Asia, Latin America and elsewhere. Thus, there need not be concerns about 'money mercantilism' or 'dollar-hegemony' as discussed earlier in this chapter, but only 'dollar hedge-money' as discussed below in Proposal 2.

The introduction of the euro is a good model for other regions. It is expected to reduce liquidity-premiums on debt for participating countries and therefore bring about lower financing costs. The use of a common currency of course wipes out exchange rate risk and various speculation and hedging flows between the participating currencies. The euro-11 countries' share of international trade outside the new euro area is expected to be 19 percent, which compares with the US's share of international trade outside the dollar area of 17 percent. Thus, elimination of the 11 national country currencies brings trade-exchange-rate risk way down to the level enjoyed by the historically more self-sufficient US. Debt and equity markets need not become completely unified, however, because differences in tax rates, corporate productivity, political and legal risks, etc. remain across the euro area. The European Central Bank decides euro monetary policy with the primary goal of price stability, whereas fiscal policy, economic growth concerns, etc., are mostly left up to the member governments. A valid concern is therefore that economic development may remain uneven or even become more unequal when national governments lose the monetary levers to inflate their regional economies independently (Feldstein, 1998).

In Latin America, Africa, Asia and elsewhere, the introduction of regional currencies should join similarly productive and similarly competitive countries so that regional monetary policy can inflate or deflate participating countries fairly. 'Convergence criteria' entry requirements into the union help solve these types of problems. In addition to European-style convergence criteria based mostly upon price stability such as interest rate, budget and trade deficit levels, criteria based upon productivity levels and stages of development are important in developing country blocs. The European Union has historically had Union-wide programs to equalize development, and similar fiscal-policy unions should accompany new monetary unions. Very few of these precautions are currently being taken in the LDCs as they dollarize their economies in *ad hoc* fashion; therefore the IMF and World Bank are often brought in, also in *ad hoc* fashion, for crisis and poverty management. The author would thus agree with Jeffrey Sachs (1998) that a G16 group including developing countries could be convened to work on regionalization of the international monetary system including an increased role for ASEAN in South-East Asia, Mercosur in Latin America, and SADC in Southern Africa.

The introduction of a regional currency requires assets and liabilities to be denominated in the new currency, and can thus be destabilizing if not done carefully and gradually. However, in order for the new currency region to gain liquidity premiums, reduced transactions costs, seigniorage benefits, and to protect itself against the money-mercantilism of the US and others, these risks seem worth taking. In the euro's case, euro-enthusiasts such as Fred Bergsten think that ultimately 30–40 percent of world financial assets will be denominated in euros and 40–50 percent in dollars. This outcome would require the one-time transfer and retirement of $500 billion to $1 trillion of dollars into euros, or an equivalent devaluation of the dollar of perhaps 40 percent. This outcome is probably too euro-optimistic, because, according to the IMF, US international assets and liabilities total $3.5 trillion and $4 trillion, respectively, and private investors associated with these accounts will probably continue to prefer the dollar compared to a Bergsten-size transfer into the euro.

Reducing the number of currencies and money-creating central banks is not a radical proposal – there were approximately 50 independent central banks at the end of World War II, 100 in 1970 and now there are approximately 170. Independence of central banks from political pressures is important, but so is accountability to elected politicians and public debate, and these issues must be balanced. Whichever balance is chosen requires the central banks to win public trust, and thus the author would recommend 'transparency' of the banks, including timely publication of minutes and reports to elected officials. Unlike the Federal Reserve and the Bank of England, the new European Central Bank has currently chosen not to publish minutes of policy meetings.

B. Proposal 2: Developing Forward-Looking Financial Markets

With a fuller spectrum of forward-looking financial markets, the 'covered interest rate parity' strategy discussed in Chapter 1 is then more able to remove interest rate and exchange rate risk from international business. Businesspeople and governments would thus be more able to assume whatever levels of risk are appropriate for their activities, and only those traders willing and able to assume high risk would have to – not most of us as is currently the case.

For example, a conspicuous feature of the recent Asian crisis is the extent to which financial institutions, enterprises and governments were exposed to foreign exchange risk through the holding of foreign currency liabilities. Soesastro (1998) estimates that, based on a post-crisis exchange rate devalued to Rp10,000 to the dollar, currency losses had entirely wiped out the aggregate net assets of all companies listed on the Jakarta Stock Exchange. Private sector foreign debt in Indonesia was approximately $70 billion, and 83 percent was unhedged; an additional $27 billion in foreign currency had been obtained from domestic banks. This story has repeated itself over and over, as in the 1982– world debt crisis and the 1994–95 Mexican crisis (Chapter 4).

Financial authorities who are dissatisfied with the current floating exchange rate system do not seem to recognize and/or support the potential for forward-looking financial markets to remove interest rate and currency risk from international business: 'What is wrong with the current non-system is its lack of stability and predictability in exchange rates, which seems to hurt the stable growth of trade and investment' (Volcker and Gyohten, 1992, pp. 303-4). Instead of supporting forward markets and encouraging hedging, central bankers, treasury departments, and other financial authorities devote considerable resources to their historically unsuccessful attempts at stabilizing exchange rates and interest rates:

> The strength of the G-5 or G-7, to my mind, rests on its informality and flexibility… What seems to me possible within that framework is the development of some reasoned and broad judgments about what range of [spot market] exchange rate fluctuation among the regions is reasonable and tolerable, and what is not…governments should stand ready to support a broad and agreed range by more than just intervention in currency markets. They would have to be prepared to support their agreements in the short term with changes in monetary policy, and in the medium and longer term by a willingness to alter the basic orientation of their fiscal policies as well (Volcker and Gyohten, 1992, p. 300).

In contrast, the author would argue that, with further institutional development, it would be more efficient and reliable to remove interest rate and exchange rate risks from international business with private forward contracts than with trading and direct intervention by governments. By the late 1980s one out of four US companies surveyed were trading foreign currencies as a hedge against foreign exchange losses,[6] and that number has increased. Via forward-looking hedging operations these companies are increasingly able to know with certainly what their long-term rate of return on international operations will be – regardless of wild swings in spot-market rates. Nevertheless, much greater development and subsidization of forward arrangements by the G7 should be encouraged.

Forward-looking market instruments include the forward exchange market, the futures market, the options market, and a wide variety of private swap and derivative arrangements. These financial arrangements are available in various time structures for the major currencies, but much less available in lesser currencies. Nevertheless, it would be quite easy for financial authorities of a non-G7 country in cooperation with the G7 to sanction forward-looking markets for the lesser currency. In the major currencies, forward exchange contracts, futures, and options are widely available in liquid markets only for horizons up to a year or so. Contracts longer than one year should also be encouraged better to mirror business and investor planning horizons.

Various financial authorities have traded in forward markets – this is rare and should not be encouraged. For example, the central bank of Spain was widely believed to have informally encouraged the writing of forward-looking 'put' and 'call' options on the peseta in early 1993 via the large Spanish banks. Its motivation was probably to support the peseta during this EMS crisis period and thus considerable risk was involved for the bankers doing the underwriting. Currency targeting with forward-looking market instruments is no more likely to succeed than the traditional means of direct intervention in the spot markets. However, a benefit of underwriting forward contracts is to provide the means whereby many risk-averse holders of pesetas could find mutual advantage with risk-seeking speculators as the forward market develops.

The author would argue that financial authorities should not directly underwrite forward-looking market contracts. Instead, they should create a regulatory environment whereby transactions costs associated with forward contracts could be lowered. Private pension funds, mutual funds, insurance companies, and others are already far more involved in these strategies than most individuals are aware, but there are substantial 'knowledge gaps' and regulatory lags as with most new markets.

For, example, many investors are aware of the opportunities to have 'portfolio insurance' against fluctuations in the value of their stocks. But only about $200 billion of the $5 trillion in US exchange-listed stocks were covered in the early 1990s; instead, more sophisticated hedging and speculation strategies called 'derivatives' have become popular. The general public remains ignorant of derivatives, yet the US Federal Reserve estimated as early as 1993 that its member banks held $7 trillion of privately negotiated derivatives. The Bank for International Settlements estimates that over-the-counter trading in derivatives, worldwide, was $1 trillion in 1995, based upon outstanding contracts worth $40.7 trillion. In addition, daily turnover of exchange-listed interest rate and futures contracts was even higher, based upon outstanding contracts worth $16.6 trillion.

The current need is to formalize what private traders are doing with derivatives and other forward-looking market arrangements and to increase investor knowledge and access. For example, the central bank of Mexico in alliance with other Mexican institutions and the G7 could set brokerage fee structures for forward arrangements and subsidize those fees sufficiently until, initially, a sufficient number of the typical 30-day, 60-day, and 90-day contracts would be available for most types of investors. If currency targeting by the official institutions is still desired, changes in the fee structure, including asymmetries between buying and selling, would be a more efficient vehicle to expose the official institution to less risk compared with traditional methods of intervention. Eventually, if the private forward-looking market institutions are sufficiently mature, then the fee structure could be deregulated as per Britain's Big Bang. Markets for contracts longer than one year would develop more slowly.

The real question is: 'Why should the Mexican government be bearing full spot market currency risk on its dollar-denominated debt, when for a sufficient fee various private underwriters would be happy to bear that risk? And isn't that fee (even when contracting parties consider the moral hazard problem and other game-theory strategies) less of a burden on the Mexican government and economy than the cost of recurring currency crises?'

C. Proposal 3: Maintaining Money-Liquidity

The G7 should ensure that there is sufficient money-liquidity in the global economy to support the new financial markets. As per the author's money-velocity equations and discussions in Chapter 3, the new financial markets, many of which are not affiliated with any nation, absorb money away from non-financial markets. The risks of GDP inflation and exchange rate volatility have been exaggerated relative to the risk that new money-liquidity needs are not accommodated by the G7.

The author's equations in the Appendix of Chapter 3 quantify how much money-liquidity is required by financial and non-financial market turnover in the US, and thus might be a starting point for world money-liquidity targeting. Combined identified balance of payments deficits of the G7, greater identification of flows through offshore markets, etc. should be compared with international financial market volumes, just as national money supplies should be compared with national financial market volumes. This type of international money-liquidity research should be encouraged.

Supplying a growing international economy with money-liquidity has always been an important theoretical and practical concern of economists. However, growth since the 1980s, especially in the financial side, has been so dramatic that even the best international monetary arrangements face difficulties.

From World War II to the late 1960s, it was the US dollar and gold that served as the main international means of payment and source of value for the growing international economy. Increased gold production and increased supply of dollars by the US Federal Reserve system were frequently necessary, especially as oil and other primary product trade expanded and denominated itself in dollars. The dollar became the international currency, and the main avenue for increasing the supply of dollars in foreign hands was a deliberately-planned US balance of payments deficit.

One problem with this dollar-based international monetary system, as forcefully put forward by Robert Triffin in his book *Gold and the Dollar Crisis: The Future of Convertibility* (1961), was that the US balance of payments deficits would eventually undermine confidence in the value of the dollar and therefore the system itself. However, if the US eliminated its overall financial deficits with the rest of the world and restored world confidence in the dollar, there would not be sufficient gold or other money-liquidity to finance the growing world economy.

This dilemma came to be called 'the Triffin dilemma' and it eventually led to the late 1960s break-up of the Bretton Woods international monetary system based on gold and the dollar. By 1968 the dollar was felt to be overvalued by the system, insufficient gold was available to maintain confidence in the value of the dollar, and President Nixon could find no solution other than to stop selling gold at its fixed dollar price. Attempts were made for several years to re-establish a fixed dollar-gold link and create other supportive international currencies such as the IMF's Special Drawing Rights, but these attempts failed. Also contributing to the breakup of the Bretton Woods system were 'money-mercantilist' arguments by President de Gaulle of France and others that the dollar system gave the US an unfair advantage by allowing the US to freely finance itself around the world and then settle its obligations in dollars without limit.

The author would use a Triffin-type situation to describe the late 1980s and early 1990s international economy. The money-liquidity needs of the global economy expanded faster than the G7 anticipated, and the US dollar supplied much of the new global liquidity needs. Yet, because of difficulties in data collection, the G7 remain somewhat unaware of the size of world dollar-expansion. For example, in 1990, a chaotic year of Eastern European revolution and Persian Gulf crisis, the US Department of Commerce recorded a 'statistical discrepancy' credit of $64 billion within the US Capital Account. Therefore, $64 billion of unidentified capital was assumed to come into the US based upon traditional double-entry accounting. However, the author doubts that most of this capital came to the US; instead it added to cash balances within Eastern Europe, the Middle East and elsewhere.

The dollar remains the dominant safe haven for capital flight and international savings. Any world traveler knows this. International capital flight and savings conversion to non-US holdings of dollars in 1990 was probably unprecedented, and therefore much of the $64 billion statistical discrepancy was probably a US balance of payments deficit to accommodate this conversion. Dollars can easily be held outside the US and created in offshore markets (Chapter 3), and in order to maintain the US money supply the Federal Reserve and deposit money lenders have expanded the world dollar supply more than most analysts realize.

As long as new foreign demand for dollars from the foreign exchange markets matches new supply, dollar depreciation is not likely. In fact, during the early 1980s this demand exceeded supply and contributed to dollar appreciation. However, in the late 1980s and early 1990s the reverse was more likely as statistically-hidden US balance of payments deficits and offshore deposit creation expanded dollar supplies faster than demand. The dollar thus depreciated.

Since the mid-1990s, as discussed in 'Asia's crisis, 1997–' in Chapter 4, the reverse has happened as identified and unidentified capital flows have favored the US, and as world dollar demand has exceeded supply. The dollar appreciated 20 percent against the yen and mark from the beginning of 1997 to the middle of 1998 due to restrictive Federal Reserve Policy, US balance of payments surpluses, and worldwide capital flight to the dollar. The worldwide dollar shortage and dollar flight from Asia was a dominant cause of Asia's crisis. This time, authorities erred not on the side of dollar-liberalization and the Triffen dilemma, but on the other side – dollar restrictions and US money-mercantilism.

Going into the next millenium, the author would recommend less double-entry accounting use of the statistical discrepancy to direct attention away from identified capital flows, better monitoring of offshore markets and other historically unidentified capital flows, and greater use of Japanese, German, and other G7 balance of payments deficits to supply new money-liquidity needs within the global economy. Moving in the direction of more than one dominant world currency does not guarantee a reduced monetary cycle of boom and bust, as we found out in the 1920s and 1930s, when the British pound and the US dollar had an equal role. However, the author's view is that currency supplies should more closely match each country's share of economic activity. In the period after 1994, the US Federal Reserve conducted monetary policy with the main goal of maintaining non-inflationary growth in the US economy rather than concerning itself with world money-liquidity, and world money-liquidity shortages increased the risk of crises. This possibility is less likely if the dollar is less dominant globally.

A greater international monetary role for the other G7 would reduce the US ability to unilaterally inflate its way out of foreign obligations, and therefore reduce the likelihood of Triffin-type crises of confidence. It would also reduce the likelihood of US money-mercantilism, and worldwide money-liquidity crises.

The dollar accounts for 60 percent of world money reserves, the mark 20 percent, and the yen 10 percent. But the US only accounts for 25 percent of world GDP, whereas Germany accounts for 7 percent and Japan for 16 percent. Realigning world money reserves in the direction of world GDP, especially with a greater role for the yen and the new euro, and a lesser role for the dollar should be a cooperative goal of the G7. Reduced US balance of payments deficits and increased Japanese and European ones are necessary for this.

III. THE ROLE OF THE WORLD BANK AND THE IMF

The World Bank is owned by more than 150 of the richer countries, and it is the biggest international source of aid for more than 100 of the poorer countries and 4.7 billion people whom it calls its 'clients' as of 1998. Its ability to impact on world investment, trade flows, poverty, and social progress makes it one of the key players in the global economy.

During the 1980s LDC debt crisis, many previous World Bank loans to the LDCs found their way out of the LDCs as both legal and illegal capital flight. High interest rates and safe havens in the developed countries attracted funds from the developing countries and corruption and the deregulation of effective capital controls in the LDCs allowed the money out. Only about half of the 1972–79 LDC borrowings remained in productive investments locally (Bogdanowicz-Bindert, 1985–86, p. 261). Thus, in its 1989 *World Development Report* (p. 19) the World Bank emphasized the need to:

> ...reduce the macroeconomic imbalances within and among the industrial countries. Such measures include a program to reduce the US budget deficit, followed by an easing in monetary policy (more so in the United States than elsewhere). Real and nominal interest rates therefore fall, as compared with the 1980–88 averages, and the dollar depreciates further against the currencies of the other big industrial countries. Structural adjustment policies of the kind discussed above enable the low- and middle-income countries to take advantage of growth; the lower interest rates ease their debt burden.

This quote recognized, finally, the degree to which the US and other rich economies had become a 'sponge' that was 'absorbing' much of the LDC's discretionary savings and investment. More generally, it was increasingly realized that prospects for growth in the LDCs, and alleviation of poverty depend more on international financial flows than on the availability of local development loans.

As elaborated in Chapter 4, between 1972 and 1979, the international indebtedness of the LDCs increased at an annual average rate of 21.7 percent. During this period the interest rates charged by banks on dollar loans were less than the price-improvements in LDC exports; therefore considerable borrowing could be justified. In contrast, after 1979, restrictive monetary policies in the US and elsewhere raised LDC borrowing rates to historic highs, led to a global recession in the early 1980s and the collapse of LDC export markets, and, ultimately, the LDC debt crisis – all of which were entirely unexpected in the late 1970s.

In fairness to the World Bank, its charter in the post-World War II Bretton Woods System with its affiliates, the International Finance Corporation and the International Development Association, was to provide long-run economic development assistance. The International Monetary Fund (IMF) was more specifically obligated to oversee international capital flows including the provision of borrowing facilities for nations with balance of payments difficulties. What the author would advocate is an even greater charter-merging and cooperation between these institutions than has already been occurring. Given the pervasive nature of financial dependency and new investment-trade linkages within the new global economy, a complete merger may even be appropriate.

The IMF has historically been in a better position to influence financial flows and oversee the macro-economic stability of member countries, but the World Bank is more able to support and oversee investment projects. This monetary policy versus fiscal policy division makes sense for nations when the fiscal policy-makers (presidents and legislators) are elected frequently upon partisan agendas, but it makes less sense for international agencies with career track employees.

The 1989 (US Treasury Secretary) Brady Plan initiated some new policies which did reflect good joint planning of the World Bank and the IMF. This Plan recognized the importance of private capital flows by formalizing and subsidizing private valuations and write-offs of debt. Debt–equity swaps and other creative ways of reducing the LDC debt burden were encouraged with the provision of insurance and subsidies for the new arrangements out of taxpayer and international development bank funds.

For example, a debt-relief agreement for Mexico on 23 July 1989 provided the Mexican government with new loans and debt relief worth $12 billion over four years, an amount designed to allow the economy to grow and minimize further capital flight. International commercial banks would be able to swap some of their existing loans not directly for Mexican assets, but instead for securities whose interest payments would be guaranteed (via the Brady Plan) by the International Monetary Fund or the World Bank. Mexico's new agreement helped to reduce their total debt burden which was then $107 billion, of which $54 billion was owed to commercial banks from the US, Europe and Japan. In addition, the interest rate that Mexico then began paying for new loans was brought down to 6.25 percent, as compared to more than 10 percent less than a year before. Such subsidies were not available when Mexico completed its first debt-equity swaps of approximately $1 billion in the second half of 1986.

Debt–equity swaps and most other ways of writing off LDC debt, by replacing the LDC's foreign debt with domestically-denominated investment, generally increase the money supply within the LDC. The IMF as per its charter to oversee monetary policy within member countries has therefore to coordinate the timing of these arrangements with the World Bank. To 'mop up' extra domestic money supplies, domestic government bonds may be issued; thus the foreign debt would simply be replaced by domestic debt.

However, even before the 1989 Brady Plan, many developing countries saw the opportunity to reduce their foreign debt with their own 'soft' devaluing currency as a tremendous benefit. By the end of 1987, Chile had reduced its $20 billion foreign debt by 15 percent through swaps. In early 1988, Bolivia bought back nearly half of its $670 million total foreign debt for 11 cents on the dollar.[7] A total developing country debt of $2 billion was swapped in 1986, $5 billion in 1987 and with the help of Brady-Plan-like arrangements these market volumes continued into the 1990s.

The developed countries are thus cooperating in the new, global financial markets to reduce the risk of further money-liquidity crises. Banks that would suffer if developing country loans were not repaid have already reduced much of their exposure via swaps and they will increasingly have the option of recouping more of their risky loans. Lending is increasingly done by those most willing and able to bear the risk, regardless of who the original lender was. The risk that any one creditor will lose enough money from bad loans to pose a systemic threat to the financial markets is thus reduced.

Just as the author argued earlier that the G7 should encourage the development of forward-looking financial markets, he would argue that the IMF and World Bank should encourage the development of forward-looking financial markets for its affiliated countries. Compared to the current system of massive and risky intervention and refinancing by these agencies, it would seem much more efficient for the IMF and World Bank to remove some of the exchange rate and interest rate risk from LDC loans, investment and balance of payments arrangements by subsidizing forward market contracts between the LDCs and private financial intermediaries.

As financial liaisons between the LDCs and international capital markets, the IMF and World Bank are in a position to set up interest rate and currency hedging operations for the LDCs. The LDCs and their foreign partners would thus increasingly be able to know with certainly what the long-term rates of return on LDC development will be. Much of the 1980s LDC debt crisis was due to unexpected, unhedged swings in interest-rates and exchange rates, and therefore much of the LDC debt burden could have been avoided if appropriate forward contracts had been built into the original loans. The same observation is true of the recent Asian crisis. The fee paid to the private risk-holder of the forward contracts would in most cases be less than the negative consequences of periodic money-liquidity crises.

Covered interest-rate parity as per Chapter 1 should be made available within the LDCs as well as within the developed countries. Various LDC investment projects would thus be able to assume only what level of interest rate and exchange rate risk is deemed appropriate. The excessive risk of underwriting forward contracts would be shouldered only by private financial institutions that are in the business of handling such risk, and the official institutions could subsidize these arrangements until a mature market has developed.

Significantly, recent LDC financial arrangements are effectively discounting and writing-off substantial portions of LDC debt, and encouraging the developed countries to take more active interests in the types of investment which are occurring in the LDCs. Instead of the famous pre-LDC-debt crisis quote from Citicorp Chairman Walter Wriston that 'countries do not go broke', which encourages bad management and the moral hazard problem, the post-debt-crisis perspective seems to be 'how do I gain greater management control over the use of international loans and subsidies?'

Developing country debt-for-nature swaps provide one example of how management rights to global resources can be made more enforceable and even transferable. In 1989, Costa Rica and the Nature Conservancy concluded the largest debt-for-nature swap to date. The Nature Conservancy, a Washington-based international land conservation group, purchased $5.6 million of discounted Costa Rican debt with $784,000 of donated funds. The Nature Conservancy received $3 million in interest payments from these bonds over five years which was used for conservation projects in Costa Rica.[8] The Nature Conservancy, as the international group with the highest willingness to pay for management rights to this ecologically sensitive region, was thus allowed to be the caretaker. Ecuador, Costa Rica, and Bolivia had concluded five debt-for-nature swaps with international organizations by 1989.

With debt-for-equity swaps, debt-for-nature swaps, and other market-based arrangements, the international community gains management rights to undeveloped water and land resources, business assets, developed real estate, and other economic assets within the LDCs. Typically, developed-country governments provide insurance, subsidies, and general guidance for these arrangements as per the Brady Plan.

Economists have been devising many other market-based international management solutions to deal with environmental-economic crises. Dan Dudek, an economist for the Environmental Defense Fund who served on the

US delegation at the successful 1987 Montreal conference to reduce world production of ozone-depleting CFCs, has suggested that Brazil and other developing nations could earn credits against their international debts by preserving forest land. But instead of debt-for-nature swaps, permits to burn fossil fuels would be issued according to a formula based upon GDP, population, and the preservation of forest land. The formula would initially give developing countries more permits than they needed. Developed countries such as the US would be issued fewer permits than they needed, thus initially requiring them to reduce their fossil fuel burning. A global market for these permits would allow corporations, environmental groups, and other interested international parties to buy them from the developing countries. The market could thus redistribute income in a rational way, while at the same time the burning of fossil fuels could be reduced, and the preservation of forest land could be encouraged.

These market-driven responses to the world debt crisis and LDC development problems are favored by the author, up to a point, not because of any fervent belief in free-market capitalism, but because of the virtually irreversible fact that private capital flows increasingly dominate the ability of official institutions to influence events. It is therefore important that official institutions use their scarce resources to influence marginally the private markets rather than wasting their resources implementing policies that fail because of contrary private market forces. In globalizing economies governments will increasingly lose their ability to provide public goods when they waste resources fighting the private markets.

Just as it makes little sense for central banks to take huge currency trading losses trying unsuccessfully to support a currency, it also makes little sense for the World Bank to lend money to a capital flight country, especially if the Bank does not have enough management influence to keep funds invested in specified projects. It would seem better for the Bank to increase the efficiency and fairness by which private markets transfer both capital and management. For example, the World Bank might expand its program of matching funds for environmental projects such as the protection of resource rich regions in Brazil close to the Bolivian border and in the mountain ranges on the South Atlantic coast.

The most desirable international techniques could be developed and propagated as the World Bank subsidizes and oversees designated land and water use areas. As an example, representatives of the World Bank and other international agencies that have increasingly gained management influence over South America's rain forests may not be sufficiently trained in tropical agriculture methods. Many are unaware of how slash and burn tropical agricultural practices in Southeast Asia were gradually replaced by the paddy rice culture, which utilizes the energy of the sun more effectively, controls weeds, and maintains the nutrient contents of the soil. Various social and economic changes are required by this ecological transformation, such as increased property ownership, regional water management, and regional labor exchange.[9] Slash and burn agriculture in many regions of South America might be replaced with the more beneficial paddy-rice culture if government officials and land developers had the appropriate training derived from human experiences on the other side of the globe. The World Bank did emphasize the environment in its 1992 *World Development Report*, but much work still needs to be done on the design of environmental-economic policy initiatives.

Much of Latin America had largely stabilized by the late 1980s, but the situation in Africa continued to deteriorate. As stated in the Foreward of the 1988 *World Development Report*: 'For the poorest countries, especially those in Sub-Saharan Africa, concessional debt relief and increased aid are necessary to facilitate resumed growth'. In 1988, the World Bank loaned sub-Saharan Africa $5 billion. By June 1988 the sub-Saharan African nations owed a total foreign debt of approximately $110 billion, not quite 10 percent of the LDC's total foreign debt of $1.2 trillion.[10] This excessive debt, which required the total export revenues of some African nations to service in 1988, began to be partially forgiven: in June 1988 France indicated that it would cancel outright one-third of its loans to 20 of the poorest nations; also in June 1988 West Germany decided to forgive $50.3 million of its loans to the poorest countries.[11] The US opened the door to these concessions when it decided at the beginning of June 1988 no longer to oppose interest-rate relief or debt forgiveness by other governments in the case of sub-Saharan Africa and other 'poorest of the poor'. Unfortunately, this debt forgiveness in the late 1980s was too little too late, as sub-Saharan Africa continued to fall farther behind other developing countries. According to the IMF, the total external debt as a percentage of GDP for sub-Saharan Africa rose from 180 percent in 1981 to 330 percent in 1990. For all developing countries, this ratio rose from 100 percent to 130 percent.

Whereas the 1980s was the 'lost decade' for Latin America, the 1980s and 1990s have been lost decades for sub-Saharan Africa. In addition, with new economic crises beginning in 1997 and 1998, parts of Asia and Eastern Europe now risk entering lost decades. Meanwhile, Latin America and other poorer regions continue to struggle.

Clearly, more is at stake here than 'financial crises and recession'. Addressing the joint meetings of the World Bank and IMF on 6 October 1998, President of the World Bank James Wolfensohn stated:

Twelve months ago, we were reporting global output that grew by 5.6 percent – the highest rate in twenty years. Twelve months ago, East Asia was stumbling, but no one was predicting the degree of the fall…there was optimism about Russia with its strong reformist team. And then came a year of turmoil and travail. East Asia, where estimates suggest that more than 20 million people fell back into poverty last year, and where, at best, growth is likely to be halting and hesitant for several years to come…17 million Indonesians have fallen back into poverty, and across the region a million children will now not return to school...an estimated 40 percent of the Russian population now lives in poverty...across the world, 1.3 billion people live on less than $1 a day; 3 billion have no access to sanitation; 2 billion have no access to power...

We talk of financial crisis while in Jakarta, in Moscow, in Sub-Saharan Africa, in the slums of India, and the barrios of Latin America, the human pain of poverty is all around us... We must go beyond financial stabilization. We must address the issues of long-term equitable growth, on which prosperity and human progress depend. We must focus on the institutional and structural changes needed for recovery and sustainable development. We must focus on the social issues...we cannot pretend that all is well...neither can we afford a lost decade like the one that afflicted Latin America in the aftermath of its crisis in the early 1980s. Too much is at stake, too many people's lives...

This 'human crisis', which Wolfensohn distinguishes as 'the other crisis' as opposed to 'the financial crisis', is more within the historic jurisdiction of the World Bank than the IMF. For example, the World Bank can be an emergency lender for social assistance, and the IMF cannot; whereas the IMF can be an emergency lender for money-liquidity and balance of payments problems, and the World Bank cannot. This institutional distinction seems appropriate, because different processes and expertise are involved. However, clearly both types of assistance affect the success of the other, and coordination between the two is essential. 'Money is wealth' as discussed earlier in this chapter, in that it represents the power to produce, consume, as well as direct a wide variety of social processes.

The author would like the reader to know that he views economic crises, such as those discussed in Chapter 4, as social crises as well. Thus, in evaluating World Bank and IMF crisis management, he tends to take the side of those who criticize the IMF (and now to a lesser extent the World Bank, at least since the four-year-to-date regime under Wolfensohn) for emphasizing macroeconomic financial criteria in its policy directives more than social criteria. For example, when the recent Asian crisis hit, the IMF provided loans under its usual 'austerity requirements' that imposed severe social hardships on local populations. Local subsidies for food, utilities, fuel, etc. were reduced, taxes were raised, interest rates were raised, etc., so that government budget deficits and balance of payments deficits could be reduced, and so that foreign loans could be better serviced. Yes, these macroeconomic stabilities are important, but the author's view is that social criteria were under-emphasized. Income distribution became more unequal and contributed to abject poverty and political instability, and in some cases recessions were suddenly deepened into socially-devastating depressions by the austerity requirements.

In recent crises, the author would have preferred less emphasis on stability of exchange rates and balance of payments; and, he would have preferred quicker discounting of foreign debt despite the moral hazard problem which continues anyway to be a major problem.

In the author's view the IMF should assist the G7 with Proposals 1, 2, and 3 listed in the previous section, especially maintaining money-liquidity in a crisis-ridden country. IMF loans of hard currency help if they can truly be maintained in the monetary base (unlike in the recent Russian crisis), but lower-interest rate monetary re-inflation strategies should be favored more than the current high interest rate austerity policies which risk monetary wealth destruction as debtors suddenly forfeit. These changes in IMF policy emphasis, in the author's view, could allow just as much macroeconomic stabilization and performance without such adverse social consequences.

For further discussion of the complicated linkages between economic, social, and environmental systems in the global economy, and the type of policy-making which the author would recommend based upon non-economic as well as economic criteria, the reader is referred to *Encyclopedia of Human Ecology* (2000), especially the 'Economic Systems' section which the author edited.

IV. NATIONAL STRATEGIES IN THE GLOBAL ECONOMY

A. Monetary Policies

As discussed in Chapter 3, deregulation, internationalization, and technological change increased the profitability of financial markets in the 1980s and 1990s relative to non-financial markets, and thus reduced the income velocity of money, *ceteris paribus*. Income velocity has also declined during chaotic economic episodes such as German reunification as people hold onto money and figure out the new economic environment – an 'options demand' for money. Also, when financial institutions are in severe distress, as in Japan after the mid-1990s, income velocity declines when money supplies are used to re-capitalize weak institutions rather than induce GDP.

Despite the failure of economists to anticipate the 1982 recession because they 'missed the collapse of velocity almost entirely' (Gordon, 1984, p. 406), and despite subsequent investigations of the velocity debacle, economists have not yet identified the new structure for monetary policy. Decades of historical data have been allowed to obscure the recent changes, and there has not been sufficient recognition that expanded money supplies have been necessary since the 1980s to support both the natural growth of the new financial markets and the natural growth of nominal GDP. As documented in

Chapter 3, the decline in income velocity is still treated as a temporary anomaly rather than a continuing structural shift.

The possibility of regaining a viable link between monetary aggregates and GDP is usually dismissed. In economic literature as per Benjamin Friedman and Kenneth Kuttner (1992), one finds the conclusion that:

> extending the [econometric] analysis to include data from the 1980s sharply weakens the time-series evidence from prior periods showing that such [defensible] relationships existed between money and nominal income or between money and either real income or prices considered separately...the deterioration of the evidence supporting a relationship to either real or nominal income, or to prices, appears not just for M1 but for other monetary aggregates and for credit as well. These changes over time in observable empirical relationships bear strongly negative implications for many familiar monetary-policy frameworks...there is no evidence to show that fluctuations in money contain any information about subsequent movements in income or prices.

Reflecting this new environment for monetary policy in which income velocity is no longer predictable, even Milton Friedman in his recent book *Money Mischief* begins to change his historic emphasis on the importance of fixed money growth rules: 'Friedman now hesitates to legislate the means of monetary policy, seeming instead to suggest that we permit discretion in the use of those means to pursue low and stable inflation' (Laidler, 1993, p. 206).

What policy-makers should be doing is monitoring financial market profitability and trading volumes more closely as new, dominant factors in the determination of the income velocity of money, and therefore inflation, economic growth, and other macroeconomic aggregates. The structural coefficients of the author's equations in the Appendix of Chapter 3 are likely to change significantly over time, and they should only be viewed as a starting point for this research. Nevertheless, they quantify what is meant by the appropriate money supply levels for central bank targeting of both financial and non-financial market expansion.

Accurate forecasts of the volume of financial transactions is not yet possible. Technological change, deregulation, and internationalization continue to allow for a more dynamic, evolving marketplace – one for which there is no historical precedent. But it seems better to continue with the research of the author and others, such as Richard Werner (1993) and Robert Laurent (1994) who seem to have regained the link between money and GDP for Japan, than to abandon money as an important policy tool.

In his testimony before the US Senate Banking Committee in mid-July 1993, Federal Reserve (Fed) Chairman Alan Greenspan said that the Fed would no longer use growth in the money supply to guide the economy. The Fed would instead emphasize movements in interest rates and especially the difference between nominal interest rates and inflation. But as argued previously, one can increasingly be pessimistic that the Fed can significantly control important longer-term US interest rates unless there is highly directed G7 cooperation. In contrast, the Fed can control the US money supply, at least with the possible exception in the short run of foreign holdings of dollars that wash in and out of the US economy.

What can be concluded here is that dramatic declines in the income velocity of money have not been expected because insufficient attention has been paid to the way in which deregulation, internationalization, and technological advance have caused financial markets to expand and absorb money away from other uses. Consequently, during important episodes, overly restrictive monetary policies have been used. Overly restrictive monetary policies were a primary cause of recent financial crises and recessions as elaborated in Chapter 4. Money-liquidity crisis episodes were more severe if the monetary contractions occurred suddenly on the heels of a financial liberalization phase. It is also important that money supplies should not be increased faster than deregulation, internationalization, and technological change allows new-found profitability and wealth-formation in financial markets

Boom and bust cycles remain a problem, but as a longer-term trend there has been too much worry of GDP inflation within world-reserve-currency developed countries. Inflation in GDP, rather than deflation and recession, has been seen as more threatening – just the opposite of what the author has tried so hard to argue since his first publication on the topic (Allen, 1989). For example, the risk of economic crisis in the post-1980 international economy is elaborated in a series of interrelated studies initiated by the National Bureau of Economic Research (NBER) and edited by Feldstein (1991). In Feldstein's introduction (p. 17) one finds the following:

> In the decade of the 1980s the United States faced four major shocks to its financial sector and to the economy more generally. Each of these threatened to precipitate a financial crisis and a major economic downturn... A primary culprit identified in each of the four cases has been the rising [GDP] inflation rate that resulted from the monetary and fiscal policies of the late 1960s and the second half of the 1970s... [and the risk of economic crisis was reduced when] the Federal Reserve brought down the high rate of inflation inherited from the 1970s...

The 1970s certainly was a period of worrisome GDP inflation. But since the early 1980s, excessive worry about GDP inflation and, consequently, overly restrictive monetary policies have increased the risk of financial crises and recession as per the case studies of Chapter 4, and have reduced the sustainable gains that could appropriately be realized from asset price inflation and globalization – the 'golden eggs' of Chapter 3.

It is difficult to pick up the golden egg once it has been dropped. Lost confidence in financial markets is regained very slowly. The options demand for money liquidity increases, money supply may fall even farther behind money demand, and the risk of liquidity crises may remain high. For example, as financial institutions in Japan experienced increasing stress in the mid-1990s from these processes, broad money supplies continued to drop, and then the institutional crisis deepened further.

Japan has been the biggest saver country and the US has been the biggest dissaver country for natural economic development and demographic reasons as elaborated in Chapter 2. Yet new-found gains in the global economy from expansionary monetary policies are for the most part unrelated to a country's saver versus dissaver status. Instead, the gains depend upon the degree to which the country has been able to participate in the profitable new opportunities in globalizing financial markets and is therefore able to enjoy the golden eggs allowed by globalization and asset price inflation without over-stimulating GDP markets.

Japan and other monetarily-expanding saver countries can increase their monetary wealth while gaining claims on foreign assets, while the US and other monetarily-expanding dissavers can increase their monetary wealth while increasing foreign debts and divesting abroad. However, as argued in Chapter 2, countries should be much less concerned with their overall financial balance than with the quality of their debts and investments. Presumably the reason that financial transactions occur is that both parties to the agreement perceive a net benefit. And technological advances, deregulation, and internationalization continue to increase the potential net benefits for both parties by reducing costs and increasing efficiencies.

B. Fiscal Policies

Structural changes in the global economy create a new environment for national fiscal policies. Those policymakers who manipulate government tax and spending levels to regulate economic growth and inflation may, to quote John Maynard Keynes, make us 'slaves to defunct theories' if these structural changes are not appropriately considered. Especially important to consider are the increased international transfers of investment based on interest rate and financial strategy parity conditions, and the increased dominance of private financial markets over central banks and other official institutions.

As elaborated throughout this book, the new hegemony of private capital has been a mostly irreversible trend that policy-makers must accept as a 'given' over the long term. In the short run when the private markets are quiet the G7, the IMF and others can redirect net capital flows, currency exchange rates and interest rates, but in the long run these official institutions should not be expected to maintain narrow target ranges for these variables.

In the economics literature, when a country finds that its interest rates and related variables are fixed by international conditions beyond its control, then the country is called 'small'. Relative to international financial markets, many countries including even the US are thus becoming small or are small in some case studies.

Fiscal policymakers, when they attempt strategically to manipulate the domestic economy, should therefore pay attention to the economics literature regarding small countries. For example, a small country is able to borrow global funds to cover rising government budget deficits at a fixed interest rate, but a large country would have to pay rising interest rates. Due to the size of government borrowings relative to the global market for loanable funds, rising government budget deficits in a large country increase the borrowings significantly enough to raise global interest rates. By contrast, increased government borrowings in a small country do not draw on international financial markets enough to affect global interest rates significantly.

The interest rate impact of government borrowing is crucial to fiscal policy. If fiscal deficits raise interest rates, interest-rate-sensitive business and household purchases are discouraged or 'crowded out' to support fiscal policy goals. Fiscal policy-makers in large countries thus have a crowded-out constituency to consider, whereas no such constituency exists in small countries. Symmetrically, reduced government deficits in large countries would lower interest rates and 'crowd in' this same constituency, but reduced deficits in small countries would not provide any spillover benefits to the private sector via the reduced interest rate effect.

The constituencies that are crowded out and crowded in by the fiscal policies of large countries are global constituencies. For example, the rising federal budget deficit of the US in the early and mid-1980s increased the net US capital inflow by at least $50 billion per year, *ceteris paribus*, and raised world interest rates. In the early 1990s, German government financing for reunification, and the Japanese fiscal stimulus package each independently attracted net capital inflows of perhaps $20–30 billion per year, *ceteris paribus*.

The combined yearly demand on international capital of German and Japanese expansionary fiscal policies during the early 1990s was probably similar to that of the larger US budget deficits during the early 1980s. However, in the early 1980s international capital was less available and therefore the US deficits put significant upward pressure on global interest rates. In contrast, during the early 1990s international capital was more readily available and therefore the early 1990s German and Japanese fiscal expansion did not increase global interest rates so noticeably – although temporarily in the early 1990s Germany's EMS partners chose to increase interest rates with monetary policy to maintain EMS parities with Germany and thus they experienced some crowding-out.

The early 1990s German and Japanese fiscal expansion did compete successfully with the early 1990s US federal budget deficit for international funds and the reduced US capital inflow contributed to the early 1990s US recession. However, not being concerned about maintaining its exchange rate, the US policy response was to increase money supplies to prevent continuing recession and there was recovery in 1992–94.

US government debt increased from 1993 to 1997. The debt-limit was raised in 1996 to $5.5 trillion so that the government could pay its bills, and the annual deficits remained high. Then in 1997 the deficit began dropping quickly and became a surplus early in 1998, thus peaking the debt. However, during this period, the US was so well supplied with a net inflow of foreign investment – $194.6 billion in 1996, $254.9 billion 1997, and $43.1 billion in the first quarter of 1998 – that changes in the government deficit appeared to have no effect on credit availability, crowding out, or crowding in of private consumption and investment in the US – instead, there was crowding out in the countries of Asia and elsewhere that were sending monetary wealth to the US. As of late 1998, the US net international investment inflow remains high; therefore the effect of reduced US government borrowing has mostly translated into an increase in private borrowing. The US household savings rate dropped to zero in late 1998.

As discussed earlier in this chapter, the US is in a unique position to avoid credit crunches because of its 'money mercantilism' that allows it the use of foreign savings and investment. Various countries thus need to maintain money liquidity and take other steps discussed in this chapter to avoid US money-mercantilism and global crowding-out that might result from US economic expansion.

If appropriate global monetary policies are used, then the author would argue that fiscal policy everywhere should be conducted more on a project-by-project basis with cost-benefit analysis as if it were more of a microeconomic affair. Currently, fiscal policy is more of a macroeconomic affair in which government spending and taxation levels are expected to have complicated impacts on economic growth, inflation, and other economy-wide aggregates via the interest rate effect. The interest rate impact is usually assumed to be significant because of the large-country assumption. Emphasizing the interest rate effect, and focusing on aggregate government spending and taxation levels has, in the author's opinion, directed the economics profession and policy-makers away from the more important business of fiscal cost-benefit accountability with regard to the various public goods that are being handled.

C. Trade Policies

The trade-weighted exchange value of the dollar peaked in 1985, and then fell approximately 40 percent from 1985 to 1988. The dollar fluctuated moderately around its 1988 levels until 1997, when it began rising significantly. From the beginning of 1997 to the middle of 1998 the dollar appreciated 20 percent against the currencies of its trading partners.

Those who expected the devaluation of the dollar from 1985 to 1988 to eventually reduce the large US current account deficit – which reached a record -$163 billion in 1987 – were finally heartened when the deficit dropped to -$90 billion in 1990 and -$4 billion in 1991 (Figure 2.2). However, in the first two quarters of 1991 the US received net 'official unrequited transfers' of $17 and $8 billion respectively – a current account line item reflecting payments in this period from allies due to the US Persian Gulf actions, which was unrelated to exchange rates. The official unrequited transfers balance of the US is generally negative. Its annual balance over 1987–1992 was -$12, -$13, -$13, -$20, $20 (in 1991), and -$18 billion, respectively.

The 1991 improvement in the US current account balance can be explained both by the temporary $35–$40 billion improvement in this one category, and by a temporary $100 billion/yr collapse in US net capital inflows from 1989 levels which led to a weak US economy, weak US import demand, and a slightly more competitive dollar. Chapter 4 argues that this temporary collapse of capital inflow, due to interest rate parity conditions initiated by Germany (reunification) and Japan (money-liquidity crisis) was the major cause of the 1990–91 US recession.

The US official unrequited transfers balance returned to its deficit position in 1992, and the capital inflow resumed, increasing $50 billion from its low level of 1991. The return of the capital inflow restored growth to a weak US economy, improved US import demand, and to a modest degree strengthened the dollar. The US current account deficit, which had dropped close to zero in 1991, thus deteriorated again in 1992 to -$62 billion. Since 1992, the net capital inflow and current account deficit have consistently increased, and as of 1998 they balance each other at approximately $200 billion and -$200 billion, respectively.

It is debatable, therefore, whether a major US dollar depreciation, as per 1985–1988, can eliminate the US current account deficit. As shown in Table 1.1, the dollar remained consistently and significantly undervalued relative to purchasing power parity (PPP) levels during the 1990s, yet the current account deficit worsened to new record levels. PPP levels would presumably balance trade price-competitiveness, and the undervalued dollar would presumably give US firms a price advantage and improve the US current account balance. Why has just the opposite happened? As argued in Chapters 1 and 2, structurally high US capital inflows are required by global financial conditions (interest rate and financial strategy parities) which are mostly independent of trade price competitiveness. The strong US economy and wealth enhancement caused by capital inflows increases US imports by households and businesses. With the US high-tech business sector booming and becoming more global, many of these imports are critical components and sub-assemblies that would be 'imported' at almost any exchange-rate-adjusted cost as intra-firm 'trade' (and thus price is mostly irrelevant) or from foreign affiliates.

Whether a real depreciation of the dollar (adjusted for inflation by PPP calculations) is an effective tool for balancing the US current account, or whether a fundamental reversal of the US net capital-importer dissaver status is required, is actually one version of an historic debate. David Ricardo, Bertil Ohlin and others have argued that real depreciation is necessary to correct a trade deficit, and John Stuart Mill, John Maynard Keynes and others have denied that international price mechanisms are an essential ingredient in the adjustment process. A summary of this historic literature is contained in Mundell (1991).

More recently, supporting the Mill-Keynes side, Mundell (1987) and others have claimed that national savings-investment imbalances can translate themselves directly into trade imbalances with currency alignments playing no useful role. In addition, if misguided currency realignments do take place, it can lead to undesirable consequences such as an international 'fire sale' of business assets and real estate. This doctrine of Mundell and others has been called by John Williamson 'immaculate transfer', and it is flatly denied by Paul Krugman on both empirical and theoretical grounds:

> The argument that devaluation leads to excessive selling off of assets to foreigners must be made consistent with the accounting identity that capital inflows have as their counterpart current deficits. If depreciation leads to capital inflows, it must lead to a widened trade deficit – as Mundell recognizes. However, we have seen that there is no direct channel by which the savings-investment balance somehow gets translated into the trade balance without affecting the real exchange rate (Krugman, 1992, p. 23–4).

The author's position is essentially in support of the 'immaculate transfer' side of the debate taken by Mill, Keynes, and Mundell (as usual, Keynes turns out to be right). In contradistinction to the quote by Krugman, the author would point out that foreign savings increasingly move between US dollar-denominated merchandise, services (current account), and assets (capital account) indiscriminately. For example, corporate equity, particularly equipment and 'intellectual property' used in the production of advanced technologies in the Pacific Basin, is not only being physically moved as a final-product export, but may account for more than half of the US official trade deficit with Asia. Furthermore, due to the rise of offshore finance (Chapter 3) and the 60 percent global reserve-currency role played by the dollar, it is not necessary that foreign currency transactions are required in these processes – immaculate transfer can be facilitated by the $250–$300 billion of non-US savings in dollars which are made available each year for new uses in the global economy (Table 3.1).

Immaculate transfer whereby savings-investment balances get translated into trade balances without affecting the real exchange rate can also be facilitated by changes in the stock market and other asset revaluations. For example, the appreciation of US stock markets from a combined valuation of $6 trillion in 1996 to $12 trillion in 1998 raised foreign-owned wealth as well as US-owned wealth held within the US. As discussed in 'Money, Wealth, and Social Consensus' earlier in this chapter, a significant portion of this appreciation reflects invisible 'social agreements' or 'belief systems' rather than measurable income and expenditure flows – perhaps this new-found monetary wealth held in the US can be called 'immaculate conception' as well as the author's earlier term 'a golden egg'. New monetary wealth can be immaculately conceived in any currency in the hands of both residents and non-residents (with a little help from banking-system money creation and globalization opportunities), and it can therefore be used for new exporting or importing without any initial need for foreign-currency operations.

The US Commerce Department increasingly uses international investment and foreign debt calculations which are based on appreciated or depreciated 'replacement cost' of assets rather than 'initial purchase cost'; although technically speaking appreciation and depreciation are not changes in 'investment' or 'savings' (GDP flow variables) but rather changes in wealth (non-GDP stock variable). As discussed in Chapter 3 under 'Monetary-Wealth Creation', wealth creation or 'wealth-productivity' can occur independently of GDP creation or GDP-productivity. 'Immaculate conception' of wealth and 'immaculate transfer' of wealth can then in turn be a driving force for changes in international trade and other GDP flows. In this case, it is not the changes in exchange rates which drive trade balances, but rather the (independent of foreign currency) changes in wealth or appreciation-adjusted savings which drive international trade and other GDP flows. Exchange rates would then also be driven by the more autonomous financial changes, and they need not move toward PPP levels.

To elaborate some of these processes, a majority of the most controversial trade-imbalance in the new global economy, between the US and Asia, may be accounted for by shipments of corporate equity that has yet to (fully) generate income for its owners. Simply recording the value of products moving between the US and Asia is not very helpful in identifying US economic interests; it is more constructive for policy-makers also to monitor the changing ownership rights and equity content of this trade flow. To the considerable extent that the US trade deficit with Japan and others is accounted for by US-owned-equity-products coming in, the deficit adds to the productive base of US-owned industry and reflects a potential for future US income and wealth. Those who consider US trade with Japan to be unbalanced in favor of Japan may be less inclined to think so after these considerations.

What should be considered is the extent to which a true economic difference exists between current and capital account transactions. For example, when imports of Japanese semiconductor products to the US were slapped with 100 percent tariffs in March 1987, Toshiba increased its US direct investment for a fabrication and sales facility in Irvine, California. Toshiba products thus remained competitive with US rivals such as Zenith. Yet when the author purchased his laptop computer from Toshiba-Irvine in 1988, it was associated with Japanese direct investment in the US (capital account inflow) and increased economic activity in California rather than US imports.

And during the same year US Steel's Pittsburg, California, facility received $200 million of foreign direct investment for a joint venture with Korea's Pohang Iron & Steel Company Ltd. This joint venture firm, Posco, became the largest steel processor on the western coast of the US. Much of the original investment was used to buy international equipment for a state-of-the-art fabrication facility that could be run by seven operators rather that the 100 or so needed for the old US Steel plant a stone's throw away. The author was told that favorable financing was obtained from international lenders due to their affiliation with Pohang.

Is this joint venture US foreign debt or the foreign buying of American, is it foreign direct investment or US imports, and should whatever balance of payments debits or credits that show up be cause for concern and regulation? Similar examples are increasingly found, such as the Toyota purchase of a General Motors plant in Fremont, California – appropriately called 'New United Motors'.

Distinctions become ever more fuzzy between debt and equity, equity versus intermediate and final products, and national versus international activities. Therefore, it becomes ever more troublesome to interpret current account and capital account entries. Gerrit Jeelof of Holland's Philips group jokes about buying a ship, equipping it with computer assisted design and manufacturing, and dropping anchor on the shore of whatever country at the moment offers the best currency-exchange opportunity.

In the US–Korean Posco joint venture, Korean savings could be used to: (a) buy an existing facility from US Steel for production as is; or (b) construct a new US facility that uses some existing US assets, some US merchandise and services, and some foreign-imported merchandise and services. Option (a) would involve only a US capital inflow. Option (b) would involve a US capital inflow to the extent that US assets are used, and a US current account deficit to the extent that foreign merchandise and services are used. The US merchandise and services that are used would not directly affect the balance of payments.

In this example, US assets thus substitute directly for US merchandise and services, for the Koreans, and the rate of substitution would probably not be affected by changes in the value of the dollar. For example, if a decline in the real dollar exchange rate increases the attractiveness of option (a) to the Koreans, then it would also increase the attractiveness of option (b). Under option (b) US assets, and non-traded US merchandise and services would be substituted for foreign imports when the dollar declines. The main import of Posco is approximately one million tons annually of hot rolled steel that it purchases from Pohang. At some point a falling dollar could lead to some substitution of US hot rolled steel for Pohang steel. Perhaps Pohang would even buy or build a US hot rolled steel facility, and options (a) and (b) would repeat themselves in a second round.

Therefore, unlike Krugman's quote, a fall in the dollar could in this case lead to an increased US capital inflow and a *narrowed* US trade deficit as more of both US assets and non-traded US merchandise and services are purchased instead of foreign imports. All US assets, merchandise and services have become more attractive to the international firm relative to non-US goods, and money flows to the US. The international savings–investment imbalance which attracted the Koreans to the US in the first place was directly channeled into a narrower US trade deficit via the joint venture's substitution of US for foreign capital goods. To maintain the accounting identity that capital inflows have as their counterpart current deficits, of course the statistical discrepancy account could be used, but the author fails to see the logic of such artificial accounting.

The above scenario has also taken place in the US automobile industry. Encouraged by the 50 percent fall of the dollar against the yen from 1985 to 1992, Japanese direct investment in US vehicle production rose rapidly. Japanese production in the US rose from 400 thousand vehicles in 1985 to 1.7 million in 1992. The falling dollar also helped to increase the US-parts content of Japanese automobiles made in the US. When Japanese car makers began building cars in the US in the 1980s, they relied heavily on Japanese parts. But, the US part purchases by these firms increased from $2 billion in 1986 to $12 billion in 1992.[12] The official US auto-parts trade deficit with Japan hovered around $10 billion during the early 1990s, but the official deficit does not include this increased US auto-parts sales to 'Japanese' companies. Through the 1990s, US automobile companies have done well. However, especially now that Daimler Benz has purchased Chrysler, and the new company began trading on the New York Stock Exchange in November 1998, what is a 'US' auto company?

Assuming that favorable price/earnings ratios are arranged as discussed in Chapter 2, international joint venture activity in the US and other foreign buying of America which is encouraged by dollar devaluation provides a net benefit for the US economy and possibly allows the US trade deficit to shrink as a share of the economy. The author thus does not take issue only with Krugman – he also takes exception to Mundell's doctrine that an *undesirable* international 'fire sale' of US business assets and real estate will occur as 'the American dog eats its own tail'.

As the Korean manager of the Posco venture told the author, the goal of the venture is to create a world-class specialty steel factory that can generate local economic growth and even export successfully. Such an example is also provided by Honda. The 30 percent fall in the foreign exchange value of the dollar from 1985 to 1988 encouraged Honda to ship cars produced from its US plants across the Pacific for sale in Japan (an official US export). Honda's first such shipment arrived in Japan on 8 April 1988, the same day that its one-millionth US-produced car rolled off its assembly line in Ohio.

More complete scenarios of international trade-investment linkages would require an explanation of why the dollar would decline in the first place. For example, in this chapter's discussion of G7 policy, the Triffin dilemma was presented as a cause of the dollar's depreciation from 1985 to 1994; but in the spirit of the literature an important issue is what happens to an economy assuming an arbitrary policy-imposed devaluation of its currency. In contrast to much of the literature, the above discussion concludes that an arbitrary devaluation could be quite beneficial to the devaluing country's economic growth and balance of payments.

The likelihood of new, misunderstood trade patterns increases as multinationals account for larger shares of international commerce, and as 'latch-key', internationalized facilities are increasingly able to substitute domestic for foreign assets, materials, and services in construction and operation.

In the growing high-technology and intellectual properties industries, domestic and foreign assets, services and materials are especially substitutable. Also, it is less clear how a change in exchange rates affects international balances in these industries. For example, if the dollar depreciates, more international telephone calls are initiated from the US rather than the foreign side, which leads to an increased US current account deficit as the US side pays for foreign servicing. Because of (not in spite of) unmatched telecommunications capabilities and low costs, the US has run a telecommunications service deficit (approximately $2 billion per year) due to this structural condition. In trying to sort out the effect of dollar devaluation on the US trade deficit, William Cline (1991) has had some success except that 'the main culprit is computers' and related industries and the way that they are priced.

Chapter 2 discusses trade protectionism in light of these new trade patterns, and concludes that protectionism is increasingly impractical due to the following: (A) trade deficits are now required by countries which, due to interest rate and financial strategy parity conditions, receive a net capital inflow; (B) rising imports as a share of national purchases is increasing the national welfare cost of using trade protectionism; (C) the increase in international joint ventures and overseas production is making it less likely that trade protectionism will achieve the desired income transfers; and (D) the increase in international ownership of once national corporations is making it less likely that trade protectionism will achieve the desired income transfers.

These (A)–(D) structural changes, each of which was encouraged by the rapid globalization of financial markets in the 1980s, have allowed for the inevitable flows of funds and wealth-revaluations between saver and dissaver countries and the inevitable trade imbalances despite all forms of trade protectionism.   Recent trade protectionism has even encouraged the integration of investment and production processes across national boundaries as 'a way around' the protectionism, and the flow of merchandise and services between nations is increasingly likely to be for intra-firm and intra-industry purposes.

Given the escalating national costs and inefficiencies of trade protectionism, other non-trade-related policy instruments are beginning to look more attractive. Alternative domestic policies exist which could transfer the same amount of income to politically favored firms and industries, and yet impose a much smaller cost on the nation.

For example, direct government subsidies to agriculture have been used successfully in the US for decades as a means of preserving desired production levels and profits. These 'deficiency payments' are currently used in combination with government loans and government purchases to transfer money to US wheat, rice, and corn farmers, as well as to the producers of many smaller crops. The same programs could be used in place of the costly trade quotas which have recently transferred income to auto, steel, sugar, textile, beef, and other industries. In fact, before the US Sugar Act expired in 1974, the US sugar industry was protected by these domestic policies rather than by trade restrictions.

Careful studies have shown that the net US welfare costs of US trade restrictions could be reduced by more than 90 percent in some cases if producers were instead given the same level of income protection with domestic payment schemes. Table 5.1 shows the economic effects of trade quotas established in the 1980s to protect US auto, steel and sugar industries, broken down by US producer benefits, US consumer costs, and net US welfare costs. The annual net welfare cost to the US economy of using trade quotas to protect its auto, steel and sugar industries in the years shortly after quotas were put into place was $1.06 billion, $770 million, and $1.36 billion, respectively. These are the annual amounts by which the costs to US consumers from the protectionism exceeded the benefits to US producers. Also, given that approximately the same level of benefit to producers has been maintained by subsequent revisions to these quota levels, these costs have increased by indeterminate amounts since those years due to structural changes (A)–(D) mentioned above.

Table 5.1 *The economic costs of US trade quota protection in cars, steel, and sugar ($billion/year)*

	Cars 1984–	Steel 1985–	Sugar 1983–
US producer benefit from quotas	3.13	2.61	1.35
US consumer cost from quotas	4.19	3.38	2.70
Net US welfare cost from quotas	1.06	0.77	1.36

Sources: Babcock et al. (1985), Leu et al. (1985).

Table 5.2 shows the US Treasury expense and net US welfare costs if instead the same amount of income had been transferred to these US industries with domestic payment schemes of the type currently used in agriculture. The net US welfare costs could have been reduced by 95 percent, 94 percent, and 76 percent in autos, steel, and sugar, respectively.

Why aren't domestic payment schemes used instead of trade protectionism, then, if most of the national welfare cost of US protectionism could thus be avoided? First, it is because of the large Treasury expenses that would have been incurred at times when the US government was receiving considerable criticism for its large budget deficit. Although these Treasury expenses would only reflect an income transfer from taxpayers to select industries, and therefore have little effect on the overall US economy including savings and investment, they are widely and incorrectly felt to be a net cost to the US economy. Actually, as shown in Table 5.2, the net welfare cost to the US economy of using domestic payment schemes to replace the trade quotas in cars, steel, and sugar would equal only 2, 2, and 24 percent, respectively of the actual US Treasury outlay. Now that the US federal budget is in a surplus position as of 1998, maybe we should choose these lower-cost domestic policies rather than the high-cost trade barriers.

Secondly, domestic payment schemes are not used instead of US trade protectionism because they make the public very aware of the exact, discriminatory benefits that are provided to the protected industries. If GM or Ford are to receive X dollars from taxpayers because they are facing hard times, why shouldn't companies P and Q receive Y dollars? These debates would go on forever, as industry lobbyists would pit their skills against Congressmen, and taxpayers would protest the well-publicized subsidies and bureaucratic costs.

Politicians find it easier to use trade quotas because the income transfers are difficult to measure and thus difficult to call discriminatory; because the costs are spread over countless consumers who have little political clout; and because foreign exporters are widely and incorrectly perceived to suffer a majority of the costs anyway. Tampering with trade flows to transfer income instead of directly transferring income has thus allowed policy-makers to escape from considerable accountability and criticism. The responsibility of dealing with firms on a case-by-case basis is avoided even though in most protected industries (for example autos, steel, sugar refining) only a few firms account for most of US domestic production.

Table 5.2 The economic costs if a deficiency payment scheme replaced quotas in cars, steel, and sugar ($billion/year)

	Cars 1984–	Steel 1985–	Sugar 1983–
Actual Treasury expense	3.13	2.61	1.35
Net US welfare cost of deficiency payments	0.05	0.05	0.32
Reduction in US welfare costs if deficiency payments replace trade quotas	95%	94%	76%
Net US welfare cost as a percent of Treasury expense	2%	2%	24%

Source: Babcock et al. (1985).

Protectionism that attempts to cover all imports, such as US Congressmen Gephardt's bill (first proposed unsuccessfully in 1988) to systematically reduce the trade deficit, is undesirable because, as discussed in Chapter 2, the net capital inflow into the US would have to decline along with a decline in the US trade deficit. At current international interest rates and price-earnings ratios, US economic interests would be severely hurt by a decline in foreign investment inflow, including the US government which relies upon the capital inflow to finance much of its borrowing. This lesson should have been learned by the US in 1990–91 when the reduced foreign capital inflow led to recessionary conditions. The recessionary conditions in turn contributed to the ouster of the Bush administration in 1992.

Policy-makers will therefore have to accept the inevitability of a continued large US trade deficit as long as global financial markets continue to channel funds into the US. Protectionism designed to reduce the US trade deficit will be ineffective unless it is a very costly financial-market-protectionism designed to stop the inflow of foreign investment. Such protectionism would in effect have to reverse the almost complete integration of the global money centers that has occurred since the 1980s – an almost impossible task.

Several half-hearted attempts were made to 'protect' the US financial market before the simultaneous crash in world stock markets in October 1987 showed policy-makers just how irreversibly integrated the money centers had become. For example, in 1986 and early 1987, Representative Charles E. Schumer (Democrat–New York) was leading various attempts to limit the activities of Japanese financial firms on Wall Street, including their ability to buy US government bonds directly from the New York Federal Reserve Bank. Schumer 'freely admits that he knows more about shaking hands in front of the Sheepshead Bay subway station in Brooklyn than about international finance'.[13] After the crash in world stock markets, Schumer's bills for financial market 'reciprocity' lost support.

Also, in early 1987 the New York Stock Exchange threatened to ban its members from trading on the London Stock Exchange in shares listed on both markets during the two and one-half hours that both markets were open. Denounced by many analysts and Wall Street firms as 'a crudely protectionist effort by the NYSE to handicap London as a competitor exchange',[14] which additionally would handicap Wall Street firms who had been completing many block trades through London, the ban lost support. As *The Economist* stated about the proposed ban even before the crash in world stock markets, 'national pettiness ill-fits global financial markets'.[15]

The author would thus agree with John Williamson (in Milner and Snowden, 1992) that inter-country differences in economic structures could quite appropriately require unbalanced trade and investment flows for decades. Williamson calculates that appropriate capital inflows and current account deficits for the US and Canada would be 1 percent and 1.5 percent of GDP, respectively, while Japan and Germany would have surpluses of 1.5 percent, and Italy, France and the UK would have balanced trade. Over time these percentages would change as the global economic structures change, and Williamson provides various forecasts.

V. CONCLUSIONS

Many lessons should have been learned by economists from their experiences since the 1980s. First, there has clearly been a failure to understand how pervasively integrated the new global economy has become. This failure has resulted from the widespread belief that the national economy should be the basic frame of reference, and international influences should be viewed as external 'shocks' to the system. Historically, macroeconomic forecasting models have been based upon this assumption, especially the more popular computer models such as the one owned by Data Resources Inc. which add on the international effects almost as an after thought. Instead, economists should have learned from their experiences in the 1980s to view international effects as extremely important, internal parts of national systems. For example, in many countries there is now no identifiable national market for most types of financial assets – the market is global as per the interest rate and financial strategy parities of Chapter 1.

Secondly, economists should have learned from the monetary velocity debacles and other case studies of the 1980s that they have difficulty modeling economies when irreversible, structural changes are taking place. Change is typically thought of as an out-of-equilibrium situation which will eventually adjust back to equilibrium based upon traditional models. Instead, in the new global economy, economists should think of change as something more evolutionary, and even revolutionary. For example, the decline in the income velocity of money, when it was finally noticed, was felt to be a temporary disequilibrium, rather than a more permanent consequence of the deregulation, expansion, and globalization of financial markets (Chapter 3). In addition, as discussed in Chapter 4, the failure to recognize, explain, and react to the decline in income velocity could very well be the single most important cause of the global recession of the early 1980s, the world stock market crash of 1987, the 1980s and continuing world debt crisis, and to a lesser degree the slumps of the 1990s.

Other recognition and policy response failures relate to the increased transfers of international investment and new trade patterns. For example, new profit-seeking flows of foreign investment into the US in the 1980s were not predicted, and therefore the large US trade deficit was not predicted. Trade protectionism has proven ineffective in reducing this deficit because of worldwide increases in trade shares of domestic economies, increased overseas production and international joint ventures, and increased international ownership of once-national corporations (Chapter 2).

Even before the structural changes examined in this book began to make their impacts, economic forecasts were frequently unreliable due to the complexity of economic systems. In 1985 TV host Louis Rukeyser stated:

> The late Otto Eckstein, who built Data Resources into the model for all econometric models, once confessed to me that he figured his organization's results were only about 5 percent better than the scribbles on the back of an envelope.

Since the early 1980s, because of the structural changes discussed in this book, the popular econometric models cannot be relied on to forecast even 5 percent better than the scribbles on the back of an envelope. Therefore, it is time to admit that a significant change in theory is needed. This change should formally recognize the globalization processes as per the author's monetary velocity equations and the interest rate and financial strategy parity equilibria. Rethinking of 'international investment' definitions is necessary to understand better 'debt' versus 'equity' now that, increasingly, 'everything is for sale' as a security. Also, rethinking of 'trade' definitions is necessary to account for intermediate vs. final products and the increased activities of multinational corporations.

Regarding the complexity of economic systems, the interest-rate-parity 'equilibrium' is a 'tendential equilibrium' or a pattern that emerges out of a dynamic evolving system. That is, the absolute magnitudes of interest rates and exchange rates have not been successfully predicted; only the pattern which relates them has been predicted. Where there seems to be new hope for better modeling and prediction of the magnitude of variables such as interest rates and exchange rates, the hope seems to rest in 'the new science of complexity', which increasingly makes its way into economics as an alternative to mainstream thinking [Waldrop, (1992); Arthur et al., (1997)].

Slowly, the literature is realizing that financial processes have become a more autonomous and complex driver of the global economy – and a somewhat reckless and unpredictable driver. Philip Cerny calls finance the new 'infrastructure of the infrastructure' and possibly 'in the ascendancy over the real economy', and some of his collaborators (including this author) 'go so far as to suggest that the transnationalization of finance is at the heart of the booms, slumps and austerity policies of the 1980s and 1990s' (Cerny, 1993, p. 10). As discussed at the beginning of this chapter, 'a new political economy of money' is therefore necessary. In this regard, definitions of money and wealth need to be rethought and related to notions of social consensus and differential power, and a revisiting of mercantilist theory seems desirable, especially as recast by the author in the form of 'money-mercantilism'.

Perhaps during the ongoing globalization period many of the structural changes are so difficult to model with formal methods that economists should yield to a more globalized intuition (and scribbling on envelopes) for forecasting purposes. From the 1993 American Economic Association meetings is this assessment from John Helliwell of Harvard:

> International linkages are increasing in strength and pervasiveness, yet most theories and applied models still tend to represent growing trade shares (which doubled between 1960 and 1985, on average, for all industrial countries) as being the consequence of some combination of high income elasticities of demand for imported goods combined with trends of uncertain duration. It will not be easy to explain either the determinants or the full consequences of increasing openness...[There are] large and persistent departures from purchasing-power parity, and...failure of forward [currency exchange] rates to be predictors of future spot rates...The determinants of longer-term international capital movements and the split between direct and portfolio investment also remain poorly understood (Helliwell, 1993, p. 294–99).

Where Helliwell and others find some prospect of salvaging macro-economic modeling:

will be increasing attention paid to the determination of the longer-term growth rates of technical progress, and analysis of the links between technology, investment and trade...[especially as these affect] the utilization rates of both capital and labor (ibid.).

Gene Grossman and Elhanan Helpman (1991) are even going so far as to emphasize that the international transfer of ideas might explain international income and growth levels. In Chapter 1 new information technologies were presented as a reason for the rapid expansion and integration of international financial markets, but the impacts of the global information revolution on non-financial markets are also important.

Regarding the recent difficulties of his profession, the author believes that globalism provides a new orientation or 'camp' for economists in contrast to the dominant monetarist and Keynesian schools of thought.

Monetarists believe that erratic national government economic policy is the major cause of undesirable national unemployment and inflation, and therefore moderate fixed policy rules are necessary. For example, monetarists have presumed a fairly constant long-run relationship between the money supply and nominal GDP, i.e. a stable velocity of money, and have thus argued for a 'constant growth target' for the money supply in order to achieve stable, non-inflationary economic growth. The velocity debacles of the 1980s proved otherwise and led to a significant decline in the popularity of monetarism. The author's velocity equations help regain some of the correlation between money supply and economic growth, and to that degree the author would advocate activist monetary policy, especially to maintain money-liquidity across the global system. But, that does not make the author a monetarist or a Keynesian – he simply and pragmatically accepts the quantity equation ($m \times v = p \times q$) as true by definition and a good starting point for solving problems.

In contrast to monetarists, Keynesians believe that undesirable national unemployment and inflation are caused by instability of household and business private sector spending, and therefore activist national government monetary and fiscal policies should be used to regulate the economy. Keynesians are more optimistic about the usefulness of economic forecasts for policy-makers, and they are generally more pro-government. After reading in this book that activist, Keynesian, nationally-oriented monetary and fiscal policies were a primary cause of the economic crises discussed in this book, the reader can understand why the author is skeptical of Keynesian schools of thought. In addition, the author argued earlier in this chapter that fiscal policy should be more of a micro-economic cost-benefit affair rather than a Keynesian attempt to regulate macro-economic aggregates. The increased likelihood that the US and others are 'small' countries with respect to international financial flows trivializes much of the traditional Keynesian analysis and leads to this recommendation (Crotty, 1993).

Also, both Keynesianism and monetarism typically view change as an out-of-equilibrium situation which will eventually adjust back to equilibrium based upon static mathematical models. In addition, both schools of thought devote considerable attention to national business cycles. In contrast, the author views recent change in the global economy as something more evolutionary and even revolutionary. A whole series of structural changes presented in this book have no historical precedent, and they continue to provoke other structural changes. It is within this context of an evolving global economy that one should attempt to understand recent economic crises and other economic phenomenon. Compared to recent structural changes in the evolving global economy, national business cycles are likely to be trivial affairs. As discussed earlier in 'A New Political Economy of Money', the author does not take the common position that economic crises are generated by 'outside shocks' to the otherwise stable market capitalist system, but rather he finds these crises to be endemic within the system, especially now that financial markets have become more important 'drivers'.

In contrast to existing orientations which prescribe national economic policies to prevent undesirable national inflation, unemployment, financial crises and recession, globalism prescribes international economic policies as the best prevention. Globalism recognizes that international factors are the primary sources of instability in national economies, whether or not they are government-related. The monetarist-Keynesian debate over whether it is national governments that cause undesirable instability in national economies misses the point. Are OPEC oil price changes and the recycling of petro-dollars through the LDCs government or private sector sources of instability in national economies? Likewise, are technological change, deregulation, and internationalization of the type that led to the velocity debacles of the 1980s government or private-sector phenomena?

Shifting the focus of economic policy-makers toward a more global perspective is indeed a change. International economic policy-making is quite different from national economic policy-making. Managing the globalized economy will require greater cooperation between national governments than ever before, especially given the increasing hegemony of private capital. Yet without such cooperation, inflation and unemployment problems will persist, and national economies will be disrupted by the kinds of instability and mismanagement which led to recent financial crises and recession.

For example, the US Federal Reserve is responsible for 60 percent of world money reserves, and is in effect more of a central bank for non-US citizens than US citizens. Yet the Fed acts primarily in the interest of US citizens and the performance of the US economy. Therefore, as discussed in Chapter 4's 'Asia's Crisis, 1997–', this nationalism (instead of international policy coordination) allowed the Fed unilaterally to stabilize the US economy in 1997–98 with restrictive monetary policies. Unfortunately, these restrictive monetary policies were just the opposite of what Asia's increasingly dollar-based economies needed during 1997–98, and the policies contributed to Asia's crisis.

Earlier in this chapter, the author thus calls for the development of regional currencies and supporting regional central banks (like the euro and the European Central Bank) which would slowly replace the global role of the dollar and the Fed. In terms of explaining wealth creation, destruction, and transfer across the global economy, perhaps the most important error of mainstream economics is the failure to recognize the 'money-mercantilism' advantages enjoyed by the US and others in the 'dollar core'.

The author's policy proposals regarding 'The Role of the G7', 'The Role of the World Bank and the IMF', and 'National Strategies in the Global Economy' are neither monetarist nor Keynesian nor Marxist nor predominantly from any other established 'camps', but rather they use elements of these camps including institutional and evolutionary economics and political theories of value, wealth, and power.

Recent financial crises and recession should have taught economists that the political realities of international relations must be directly included in current theory if current theory is to be useful to policy-makers. Economics should become more interdisciplinary in this sense. When models of the overall economy are too rigid to be 'softened' and 'enriched' with an interdisciplinary approach, then they should be used with caution. Where possible, the models should allow for with-international-cooperation and without-international-cooperation scenarios, and they should allow for the importance of institutional regimes and currency blocs.

In the 1980s, the major industrial countries increasingly discovered that cooperation was in their mutual interest. The Plaza accord agreement on 22 September 1985 is one notable example. Another example is the Venice Presidential summit in June 1986 when statements were made about achieving common economic growth and inflation levels. Yet, the destructive lack of international monetary cooperation in 1987, which precipitated the crash in world stock markets, indicated that the global perspective was not yet the dominant one.

The simultaneous crash of world stock markets made it almost impossible to ignore the growing economic interdependence of nations and the need for greater international policy coordination. Another significant event was the perceived failure of the all-mighty US Federal Reserve Bank in late 1989 to determine independently the direction of US interest rates.

By 1990 many prominent economists, especially those who were well-connected to the financial markets, had adopted a more global perspective. As stated in 1990 by Lyle Gramley, chief economic forecaster for the US Federal Reserve Bank in the 1970s:

[In the 1970s] I considered the international division more of a nuisance. The direct link from interest rates abroad to interest rates in the US to the outlook from the US economy – I never had to deal with that intellectually before. Who ever thought that developments in West Germany were going to be a very important influence on interest rates in the US? Maybe somebody did. It wasn't me.[16]

And as echoed in 1990 by David Jones, the widely quoted chief economist at Aubrey G. Lanston & Co.:

When I started 17 years ago, I'd spend 80 percent of my time worrying about the Federal Reserve Bank, worrying about domestic inflation, domestic capacity; now I spend 80 percent of my time worrying about the foreign side – or at least how the foreign side affects the domestic side.[17]

The global perspective that is increasingly adopted out of necessity by economists such as these emphasizes recent structural changes more than traditional equilibrium processes. It must be somewhat 'reactive' rather than theoretically 'active' in the sense that current events must be followed carefully in order to understand the newly evolving economic structures. For example, the case studies of this book emphasized the new, unexpected effects that high US interest rates in the early and mid-1980s had upon global economic welfare. The power of US policy-makers to affect world economic welfare via US interest rates was unprecedented during these early boom years for globalizing financial markets.

However, as the 1990s were reached, the more fully globalized financial markets were instead occasionally treating the US as a 'small country' with respect to finance. The increased role of private unregulated markets now makes it more difficult at times for US economic policy-makers significantly to affect interest rates anywhere, even in the US. Also, how can one evaluate the degree to which the US is losing control over its own interest rates, and therefore its own financial system – if true, certainly a profound new development? Not from economic theory, only from a careful analysis of current events.

Much empirical research needs to be done by economists before the most useful models of the evolving global economy can be derived. During this transitionary period for national economies, it is likely that many economists will be too conditioned by out-of-date and overly theoretical nation-based monetarist and Keynesian theories. The author's suggestion is that a more global perspective is needed. Global economic trends must be understood before national economic trends can be identified.

NOTES

1. *Choice*, January 1995, Vol. 32, No. 5.
2. 'The Globalization of the Industrialized Economies', *Barron's*, 4 May 1987, p. 45.
3. 'The International Euro,' *The Economist*, 14 November 1998, p. 89.
4. 'Making the Tokyo Summit Serve Up More Than Rhetoric', *Business Week*, 7 April 1986.
5. Obstfeld and Rogoff (1995), p. 73, 77 and 80. See also the Bank for International Settlements, *Settlement Risk in Foreign Exchange Transactions*, 'Report prepared by the Committee on Payment and Settlement Systems of the Group of Ten', Basle, March 1996.
6. 'Business Bulletin', *The Wall Street Journal*, 14 January 1988, p. 1.
7. 'Bolivia Buys Back Nearly Half of Its Debt To Banks at a Fraction of the Face Value', *The Wall Street Journal*, 18 March 1988, p. 15.
8. 'A Debt-for-Nature Swap In Costa Rica Biggest Yet', *The Wall Street Journal*, 13 January 1989, p. A8.
9. The processes whereby paddy rice cultures are developed, and the ecological and economic benefits are discussed in: E. Boserup (1965), *The Conditions of Agricultural Growth: The Economics of Agrarian Change Under Population Pressure*, Aldine, Chicago; and, C. Geertz (1963), *Agricultural Involution: The Processes of Ecological Change in Indonesia*, University of California Press, Berkeley.
10. 'France, West Germany Plan to Forgive Some Loans to World's Poorest Nations', *The Wall Street Journal*, 9 June 1988, p. 25.
11. Ibid.
12. 'Japan Auto Makers Buy More US Parts', *The Wall Street Journal*, 24 August 1993, p. A2.
13. 'Will the Trade Wars Spread to Wall Street?', *Business Week*, 22 December 1986, p. 58.
14. 'Stonewall Street', *The Economist*, 14 March 1987, p.14.
15. Ibid.
16. 'Fed. Has Lost Much Of Its Power to Sway US Interest Rates', *The Wall Street Journal*, 12 March 1990, p. 1.
17. Ibid.

References

Allen, Roy E. (1989), 'Globalisation of the US Financial Markets: The New Structure for Monetary Policy', *International Economics and Financial Markets*, Chapter 16, Oxford: Oxford University Press.

Arthur, Durlauf, and Lane, (eds) (1997), 'The Economy as a Complex Evolving System II', *SFI Studies in the Sciences of Complexity, Vol. XXVII*, New York: Addison-Wesley.

Artis, M. and M. Taylor (1989), 'International Financial Stability and the Regulation of Capital Flows', Conference Paper (University of Surrey), September.

Axelrod, Robert (1984), *The Evolution of Cooperation*, New York: Basic Books.

Babcock, Bruce, Roy E. Allen, and Andrew Schmitz, (1985), 'US Agriculture and Manufacturing: The Net Cost of Government Intervention', University of California, Department of Agricultural and Resource Economics, Working Paper No. 380, Berkeley.

Baker, George P. and George David Smith (1998), *The New Financial Capitalists: Kohlberg Kravis Roberts and the Creation of Corporate Value*, Cambridge: Cambridge University Press.

Batten, Dallas S., and Daniel L. Thornton (1985), 'Are Weighted Monetary Aggregates Better Than Simple-Sum M1?', *Federal Reserve Bank of St. Louis Journal*, June/July.

Bergsten, C. Fred, editor (1991), *International Adjustment and Financing: The Lessons of 1985–1991*, Washington, DC: Institute For International Economics.

Bhagwati, (1998), 'The Capital Myth: The Difference Between Trade in Widgets and Dollars', *Foreign Affairs*, Vol. 77, Number 3 (May/June), p. 7–12.

Black, Fisher (1985), 'Noise', *The Journal of Finance*, Vol. XLI, No. 3, July, p. 529–43.

Blanchard, Olivier (1993), 'Consumption and the Recession of 1990–1991', *American Economic Review*, Vol. 83, No. 2.

Blumenthal, W. Michael (1988), 'The World Economy and Technological Change', *Foreign Affairs*, Vol. 66, No. 3.

Bogdanowicz-Bindert, Christine (1985–86), 'World Debt, the US Reconsiders', *Foreign Affairs*, Winter.

Brown, Brendan (1996), *Economists and the Financial Markets*, London and New York: Routledge.

Carchedi, G. (1996), 'Review Essay: Financial Crisis, Recessions and Value Theory', *Review of International Political Economy*, 3:3, Autumn: 528–37.

Cerny, Philip G. (ed.) (1993), *Finance and World Politics: Markets, Regimes and States in the Post-hegemonic Era*, Aldershot, Hants (UK) and Brookfield, Vermont (US): Edward Elgar Publishing.

Chote, Robert (1997), 'Thai Crisis Highlights Lessons of Mexico', *Financial Times*, 19 September.

Clark, Gregory (1998), 'Too Much Revolution: Agriculture and the Industrial Revolution, 1700–1860', paper presented at the 38th Annual Cliometrics Conference, Washington University in St. Louis, May 8–10.

Clarke, Simon (1994), *Marx's Theory of Crisis*, New York: St. Martin's Press.

Cline, William R. (1991), 'US External Adjustment: Progress, Prognosis, and Interpretation', in: Bergsten (1991).

Crotty, James (1993), 'The Rise and Fall of the Keynesian Revolution in the Age of the Global Marketplace', in Epstein, Gerald (ed.), *Creating a New World Economy: Forces of Change and Plans for Action*: Philadelphia: Temple University Press.

Daudin, Guillaume (2000), 'A Mercantilist Model of Growth and Trade in 18th Century France', in *Encyclopedia of Human Ecology*.

Davis, P. (1990), *International Investment of Life Insurance Companies*, European Affairs.

Department of Commerce, *Survey of Current Business*, February 1997.

Dotsey, Michael (1985), 'The Use of Electronic Funds Transfers to Capture the Effect of Cash Management Practices on the Demand for Demand Deposits', *Journal of Finance*, December.

Drucker, Peter F. (1985–86), 'The Changed World Economy', *Foreign Affairs*, Winter.

Encyclopedia of Human Ecology (2000), San Diego, CA: Academic Press.

Federal Reserve Bank of Kansas City (1997), *Maintaining Financial Stability in a Global Economy: A Symposium Sponsored by the Federal Reserve Bank of Kansas City*.

Federal Reserve Bank of St. Louis (1998), *International Economic Trends*, August.

Fehrenbach, R.R. (1966), *The Gnomes of Zurich*, London: Leslie Frewin.

Feldstein, Martin (1998), 'Refocusing the IMF', *Foreign Affairs*, March/April.

Feldstein, Martin, (ed.) (1991), *The Risk of Economic Crisis*, Chicago: The University of Chicago Press.

Fisher, Irving (1933), 'The Debt-Deflation Theory of Great Depressions', *Econometrica*, vol. I, pp. 337–57.

Frankel, J. (1989), 'Quantifying International Capital Mobility in the 1980s', National Bureau of Economic Research, Working Paper No. 2856, February.

Frankel, J. and K.A. Froot (1989), 'Forward Discount Bias: Is it an Exchange Risk Premium?', *Quarterly Journal of Economics*, February.

Friedman, Benjamin M., and Kenneth N. Kuttner (1992), 'Money, Income, Prices, and Interest Rates', *The American Economic Review*, Vol. 82, No. 3.

Friedman, Milton (1970), 'A Theoretical Framework for Monetary Analysis', *Journal of Political Economy*, vol. 78 (March/April), pp. 193–238.

Friedman, Milton (1988), 'Money and the Stock Market', *Journal of Political Economy*, vol. 96, April, pp. 221–245.

Friedman, Milton (1992), *Money Mischief*, New York: Harcourt Brace Jovanovich.

Gates, Bill, with Nathan Myhrvold and Peter Rinearson (1995), *The Road Ahead*, New York: Viking Press.

Goldfeld, Steven M. (1973), 'The Demand for Money Revisited', *Brookings Papers on Economic Activity*, 3.

Goldfeld, Steven M. (1976), 'The Case of the Missing Money', *Brookings Papers on Economic Activity*, 3.

Gordon, Robert J. (1984), *Macroeconomics*, 3rd edn, Glenview, Illinois: Little, Brown and Co.

Greenspan, Alan (1998), 'The Globalization of Finance', *The Cato Journal*, Vol. 17, No. 3, Winter.

Grossman, Gene, and Elhanan Helpman (1991), *Innovation and Growth in the Global Economy*, Cambridge, MA: MIT Press.

Grundfest, Joseph A. (1991), 'When Markets Crash: The Consequences of Information Failure in the Market for Liquidity', in Feldstein (ed.) (1991).

Haberler, G. (1937), *Prosperity and Depression*, Geneva: League of Nations.

Haggard, Stephen and Sylvia Maxfield (1996), 'The Political Economy of Financial Internationalization in the Developing World', *International Organization* 50: pp. 35–68.

Hall, Robert E. (1993), 'Macro Theory and the Recession of 1990–1991', *American Economic Review*, Vol. 83, No. 2.

Hanzawa, Masamitsu (1991), 'The Tokyo Offshore Market,' in *Japan's Financial Markets*, Foundation for Advanced Information and Research, Japan (Fair).

Hawkes, David (1996), *Ideology*, London and New York: Routledge.

Helliwell, John F. (1993), 'Macroeconometrics in a Global Economy', *American Economic Review*, Vol. 83, No. 2.

HG Asia (1996), 'Philippine Figures Hide a Thing of Two', communiqué, Philippines, Hong Kong.

Hopkins, Terry, and Immanuel Wallerstein, eds. (1982), *World-Systems Analysis: Theory and Methodology*, Beverly Hills, Calif.: Sage.

IMF (1989), *World Economic Outlook, Supplementary Note Number 5, Capital Account Developments in Japan and the Federal Republic of Germany: Institutional Influences and Structural Changes*, Washington, D.C.: IMF, April.

Inoue, Kengo (1995), '...But Monetary Policy is Not the Villain', *The Wall Street Journal*, 1 July, p. A16.

Joffe, Josef (1992–93), 'The New Europe: Yesterday's Ghosts', *Foreign Affairs*, Vol. 72, No. 1.

Judd, John P. (1983), 'The Recent Decline in Velocity: Instability in the Demand for Money or Inflation?', *Federal Reserve Bank of San Francisco Economic Review* Summer, p. 12.

Judd, John P. and John L. Scadding (1982), 'The Search for a Stable Money Demand Function', *Journal of Economic Literature*, September.

Keohane, Robert (1984), *After Hegemony*, Princeton: Princeton University Press.

Kindleberger, Charles P. (1989), *Manias, Panics, and Crashes: A History of Financial Crises*, New York: Basic Books.

Kochen, A. (1991), 'Cleaning Up by Cleaning Up', *Euromoney*, April, pp. 73–7.

Krugman, Paul R. (1992), *Currencies and Crises*, Cambridge, MA: The MIT Press.

Laidler, David (1985), *The Demand for Money: Theories and Evidence*, 3rd edn., New York: Harper & Row, Chapter IV.

Laidler, David (1993), Book Review in *Journal of Political Economy*, vol. 101, no. 1, p. 206.

Laurent, Robert D. (1994), 'Monetary Policies in the Early 1990s – Reflections of the Early 1930s', Working Paper Series, Macroeconomic Issues, Research Department, Federal Reserve Bank of Chicago, December (WP-94-26).

Laurent, Robert D. (1995), 'Bank of Japan: The Saga Continues', *Asian Wall Street Journal*, 28 July 1995, p. 6.

Leu, Gwo-Jiun, Andrew Schmitz, Ronald D. Knutson (1985), 'Gains and Losses of Sugar Program Policy Options', Berkeley: University of California, Department of Agricultural and Resource Economics, Working Paper No. 380.

Lindgren, Carl-Johan, Gillian Garcia, and Matthew Seal (1995), 'Bank Soundness and Macro-economic Policy', Washington D.C.: International Monetary Fund.

Milner, Chris, and Nick Snowden (1992), *External Imbalances and Policy Constraints in the 1990s*, New York: St. Martin's Press.

Mishkin, F. S. (1991), 'Asymmetric Information and Financial Crises: A Historical Perspective', in Hubbard, R. G. (ed.), *Financial Markets and Financial Crises*, Chicago: University of Chicago Press, pp. 69–108.

Modelski, George, and William R. Thompson (1996), *Leading Sectors and World Powers: The Coevolution of Global Politics and Economics*, South Carolina: University of South Carolina Press.

Mundell, R. (1987), 'A New Deal on Exchange Rates', presented at the MITI symposium 'The Search for a New Cooperation', Tokyo, January.

Mundell, Robert, (1991), 'The Great Exchange Rate Controversy: Trade Balances and the International Monetary System', in: Bergsten (ed.) (1991).

The New York Times (1999), 'Global Contagion, A Narrative', February 15-18, p. 1.

Nitzan, Jonathan (1998), Differential Accumulation: Towards a New Political Economy of Capital, *Review of International Political Economy*, 5:2 Summer.

Norton, Robert (1993), 'Offshore funds maximise reward and minimise risk', *The European*, December 3.

O'Brien, Richard, (1992) *Global Financial Integration: The End of Geography*, London: Royal Institute of International Affairs.

Obstfeld, M., and K. Rogoff, 'The Mirage of Fixed Exchange Rates,' *The Journal of Economic Perspectives 9*, Fall 1995.

Oye, Kenneth A., (ed.) (1986), *Cooperation Under Anarchy*, Princeton: Princeton University Press

Palan, Ronen (1994), 'Tax Havens and the Market for Sovereignty', paper presented at the International Studies Association Convention, Washington D.C.

Porter, Richard D., Thomas D. Simpson, and Eileen Mauskopf, (1979), 'Financial Innovation and the Monetary Aggregates', *Brookings Papers on Economic Activity*, vol. 10, no. 1, p. 213.

Quijano, Alicia M. (1989), 'Capital Expenditures By Majority-Owned Foreign Affiliates Of US Companies, 1989', *Survey of Current Business*, March.

Rasche, Robert H. (1986), 'M1-Velocity and Money Demand Functions: Do Stable Relationships Exist?', *Carnegie-Rochester Conference on Public Policy*, 21 November.

Rees-Mogg, William (1993), 'Down and out on trillionaire's row', *Financial Times*, 11 October, p. 14.

Sachs, Jeffrey (1998), 'Global Capitalism: Making it Work', *The Economist*, 12 September, p. 23–5.

Schumpeter, Joseph (1934), *Theory of Economic Development*, Cambridge, MA: Harvard University Press.

Soddy, Frederick (1933), *Wealth, Virtual Wealth, and Debt*, New York: E. P. Dutton & Co.

Soesastro, M. Hadi (1998), 'Survey of Recent Developments', *Bulletin of Indonesian Economic Studies*, April, 34(1): pp. 3–54.

Solomon, Elinor Harris (1997), *Virtual Money*, New York and Oxford: Oxford University Press.

Spindt, Paul A. (1985), 'Money is What Money Does: Monetary Aggregation and the Equation of Exchange', *Journal of Political Economy*, February, vol 93, no. 1.

Stone, Courtenay C., and Daniel L. Thornton (1987), 'Solving the 1980s' Velocity Puzzle: A Progress Report', *Federal Reserve Bank of St. Louis Economic Review*, August/September, p. 5.

Taylor, M. (1988), 'Coveraged Interest Arbitrage and Market Turbulence: An Empirical Analysis', Centre for Economic Policy Research, Discussion Paper No. 236, May.

Taylor, M. and I. Tonks (1989), 'The Internationalisation of Stock Markets and the Abolition of United Kingdom Exchange Control', *The Review of Economics and Statistics*, No. 2, May.

Triffin, Robert (1961), *Gold and the Dollar Crisis: The Future of Convertibility*, revised edn, New Haven: Yale University Press.

Veblen, Thorstein (1923), (reproduced 1967), *Absentee Ownership and Business Enterprise in Recent Times. The Case of America,* Introduction by Robert Leckachman, Boston, MA: Beacon Press.

Volcker, Paul, and Toyoo Gyohten (1992), *Changing Fortunes: The World's Money and the Threat to American Leadership*, New York: Times Books.

Wade, Robert (1998-99), 'The Coming Fight Over Capital Flows', *Foreign Policy*, Winter, p. 41-54.

Waldrop, K. (1992), *Complexity*, New York: Touchstone Books.

Wenninger, John, and Lawrence J. Radecki (1986), 'Financial Transactions and the Demand for M1', *Federal Reserve Bank of New York Quarterly Review*, Summer, p. 24.

Werner, Richard (1993), 'Towards a Quantity Theorem of Disaggregated Credit and International Capital Flows With Evidence From Japan,' paper presented at the annual conference of the Royal Economic Society in April 1993.

World Bank (annual), *World Development Report*, Oxford: Oxford University Press.

Index